Who I Am

A Memoir of an American-Korean in Search of Identity

JOE EUN-SEUK PARK

ISBN: 979-8-9993505-0-3
Published by Joeun Publishing

First edition: 2025

For inquires or more information, contact: joe.eun.park@gmail.com

Contents

Dedication

First and foremost, I thank God, who gives me my ultimate identity — one that is secure, eternal, and rooted in His love.

I also want to thank my parents, Yong Woo Park and Sook Jung Park, who gave me my first identity in this world. From them I learned the meaning of love, sacrifice, and perseverance. To my brothers, Albert and Daniel, thank you for walking this journey of life with me — you've shaped more of who I am than you probably realize.

To my beloved wife, Juri — you are God's greatest gift to me on this earth. Thank you for letting me share an identity that is forever intertwined with yours. Your strength, patience, and quiet faith have been a constant anchor.

And finally, to Joanna, Juel, and Juno — you've given me the sacred identity of "appa." Thank you for being my greatest joy, and for teaching me every day what it means to love deeply and live meaningfully.

Preface

I did not start off with the intention of writing a book. This was meant to be a personal introspection, something productive to do during a six-month sabbatical from my pastoral ministry in 2023.

Before going on sabbatical, I was very tired. It's not that I wasn't enjoying ministry — I was. I enjoyed it a lot, and I still do. But somewhere along the way, it had become too routine. I had lost some of my initial passion and started to struggle with my own personal identity as a pastor. I wondered, *Who am I, and what am I doing?*

As I kept questioning that part of my identity, I started asking more questions about myself. I know it may sound a little silly, but I would question even some of the most basic existential facts about who I was, such as my cultural identity, my hometown, and even my name.

For the longest time, people told me I was very American. Yet I was never truly American — I was Korean. I was born in the city of Daegu and grew up there for most of my adolescent life. Yet I have very little affinity for that city — if anything, more of a disdain — because I always felt out of place there and never truly at home.

I have more affection for Seattle, a place I'd only lived in for three years and hadn't visited in nearly thirty. Even now, the only thing I have in common with that city is that I graduated from university there and love their professional football team. And yet, when people ask me where I'm from, oftentimes, Seattle is my default response, although I know it's not my hometown.

When it comes to my name, for nearly 45 of my 49 years I have been known as either Joseph or Joe Park, but there is no legal document anywhere that states that that is my name. Officially, it is Park Eun-Seuk, but hardly any of my close friends know me by that name.

And this is just the tip of the iceberg. I'm not sure how it happened, but somewhere along the way, I found myself in the middle of an identity crisis.

Actually, I think I've lived with somewhat of an identity crisis all throughout my life. I remember that, as a kid, when we lived in New Jersey for a couple of years, there were not many Koreans living in my neighborhood. All my friends were Caucasian, and for the longest time I thought I was too. When I found out one day that I did not look like everyone else, it caused me to start questioning who I was.

Later in life, after graduating from the University of Washington, I wanted desperately to remain in the United States and start a career and a life there. It's where I felt I belonged. However, I was a Korean citizen and had no choice but to leave. I recently found out that some of my close friends felt terrible for me, and they even had discussions among themselves about which of my female friends would marry me so I could get a green card. When I heard this, I appreciated my friends' care for me, but it proved that I was always a little different.

Although I have lived in Korea for many years now, most of my adult friends are not culturally Korean, but either ethnically American or Korean-American. Usually, I don't feel very different from them, but occasionally, there are moments that remind me that I am, in fact, different.

For example, one day, we went to play golf on a U.S. military base. Everyone else had an American passport and were eligible for a discount on the green fee, which made it affordable. I was Korean, however, and I had to pay double. I didn't mention anything at the time, especially since all my friends were raving so much about how cheap the golf was. Perhaps those who didn't know just assumed I got the same deal. But it glaringly showed me that no matter how much I wanted to deny it, my identity was different from theirs.

This was a subtle reminder that the greatest identity struggle that I've had throughout my life has been about nationality, culture, and even to a certain degree, ethnicity. Am I American or am I Korean?

In the world we live in today, many people struggle to know who they are. Similar to me, their identity struggles can be about culture, ethnicity, and nationality, but it can also be in various other areas such as religion, vocation, and even gender, just to name a few. Despite the differences in the areas where we may struggle with identity, one thing we have in common is that we're all searching for answers — and quite often, we're not even sure where to begin. That was my dilemma, too.

As a pastor, I strongly believe that all of our identities should start with knowing who we are in Christ. If you don't know Christ, then the first step is to get to know Him. Indeed, the search for all our answers in life should begin with Jesus.

From my own experience, though, I also know that as Christians, we have a tendency to over-simplify our struggles with that answer and fail to take into account that life is complicated, and that even when we know that answer in our heads and hearts, it's hard to live it out in real life.

I've preached many sermons and taught many lessons about the importance of knowing our identity in Christ, yet, when it came to the reality of life, I still found myself facing an identity crisis. It was not because I was ignorant of this, but rather because I wasn't sure how it practically applied alongside culture, society and the context I went through in my own life. So I decided to use this time during my sabbatical and try to figure it out through this personal writing project. I hoped it would allow me to reflect on my life experiences to discover who I am because of it all.

When I first began to look back on my life, I quickly realized that much of the way I saw myself in the world came from the narrow perspective of my own bubble. The questions I asked were often uneducated and self-absorbed. I would wonder things like:

Why was I born in Korea?
Why did we have to move to the United States when I was so young?
And after we moved to America, why couldn't we just have stayed?
Why did we have to move back to Korea after I had already become so Americanized?
Why did I feel so different from everyone else around me?
Why couldn't I just fit in and be like everyone else?

The only answers I could find weren't really answers at all — just excuses to place blame, on others and on myself. It was my parents' fault for moving us back and forth between two worlds. And it was my fault for never being able to properly adapt. I was content pointing fingers at the confusion and dismay I thought defined my life, without ever making the effort to ask the right questions — or seek the right answers.

Until now, I had never truly tried to find the right answers by understanding myself through the lens of the historical and cultural contexts I've lived through. No one is an island unto himself, and no one is a product of isolation. If I wanted to know who I was, I needed to see myself again in light of the world around me.

Before I began writing, I took time to read about topics I wasn't very familiar with — or even if I was, I knew I needed to go deeper if I truly wanted to understand myself. I read books on Korean history and culture. I studied the Korean diaspora. I explored the history of the Korean church, knowing how deeply the church has shaped the lives of many Koreans overseas. I read memoirs and reflections by writers who were ethnically Korean but didn't fully identify as such.

One book that especially stood out was *East Goes West* by Younghill Kang — one of the first novels written by a Korean-American. It was published in the early 20th century and tells the story of a young immigrant man struggling to find his identity and place in a foreign and often unforgiving American society.

As I read these books, I began to reflect more deeply on my own life. I realized that who I am today is shaped by many of the very things I had been reading about — things I had never seriously considered until now.

When I began writing down my thoughts, I decided to start with my earliest memories — though, as you'll soon see, many of these memories aren't mine, but my mother's. I started to worry that this might turn into an impossible, never-ending task. There were so many years to cover, so many moments to sift through. How was I supposed to recall the small details from the earliest parts of my life? And how would I know what was relevant and what wasn't?

To my surprise, it turned out to be much easier than I expected. I didn't have to try very hard. The relevant stories seemed to already be lined up in my mind, as if I had been preparing for this moment for years. It felt like the outline had always been there — I just needed to put pen to paper (or more accurately, fingers to keyboard) and fill in the details.

It all flowed so naturally because this wasn't a story I had to invent. It was already written on my heart. The real author isn't me — it's God. This is His story. He is the true storyteller, and I'm simply the subject. That's why my history is, in the truest sense, *His story.*

When I reached page 100, it dawned on me that these weren't just random thoughts I was jotting down on my computer. I stopped calling it my "writing project" and began to recognize that this was turning into a book.

That's when the question arose: *Who am I writing this for? Who is my audience — and what is the purpose?*

I've heard how some people write their memoirs as a legacy for their children. I suppose I hope for that, too. One day, I hope my three children will be curious enough to read this book and learn a little more about their dad — about the life I've lived, and how God has been with me every step of the way. I hope they'll find both lessons and encouragement in my story — in the good and even in the bad. I hope they'll see pieces of themselves in me, and maybe even be inspired to become better people. I hope, more than anything, that these writings will help them grow deeper in their love for God and their relationship with Him.

And yet—this book isn't really for them.

Before going on sabbatical, I told my congregation that I planned to spend some time reading and doing personal writing. I shared that it would be an exercise in rediscovering myself and, hopefully, something that could help others as they searched for their identity in Christ. I still believe that, and I do hope this memoir can encourage some of them in their own journeys. But I've come to realize — it's not really for them either.

You might say this book is for Korean-Americans, Korean-Canadians, Korean-Aussies, or other ethnic Koreans living around the world — people navigating between cultures, trying to make sense of their roots and identity. Maybe there are shared experiences here, and if they resonate, I'll be grateful.

But frankly speaking, I don't consider myself to be a true "Korean-American" since I am not an American. I think "American-Korean" might be a better fit — though I'm not sure that's an official term. Still, I know there are others who understand what I'm trying to say about myself by that, and can relate. I hope they find encouragement in these pages. But ultimately, this book isn't for them either.

Could I say this book is for God? In my younger years, I dreamed of someday winning an Academy Award or a Pulitzer Prize. I imagined reporters thrusting microphones in my face, and I'd begin by declaring, "First and foremost, I'd like to give all glory to my Lord and Savior, Jesus Christ." And I still believe this is His story. My life is for His glory.

But God doesn't need a book to be more glorified. He's already glorious beyond measure. So this book — ultimately — isn't for Him.

When all is said and done, I've realized: this book is for me.

If I never sell a single copy, receive no commission, no press, no glowing review in *The New York Times* — I can still say that I did this. I wrote this. And honestly? I'm proud of that.

More than anything, this process allowed me to relive some of the most important moments of my life. Whether I wrote them down or not, I began to see them differently — with new perspective. A more godly perspective. I started to make sense of things I had long questioned. And I came to understand myself more clearly than ever before.

As I was writing, I also realized that there were many things in my past that I was not able to reconcile completely and was still hurt by. As I revisited them, through prayer and reflection, I was finally able to be healed in many areas that I didn't even know were still hurting me. This process of writing was a remedy for my soul.

I also discovered that I love to write. I don't know if I'm good at it, but I know I enjoy it and will continue to do it. Writing not only helps me to process things by putting my thoughts down in a tangible way, but I also believe it will help me be a better pastor and preacher going forward, and so just my love of writing has become an extraordinary discovery.

Of course, many people have played different roles in my life. I have tried my best to be as accurate in my recollections as possible, without being biased or offensive to any of them. If I have been inaccurate in any way, I apologize in advance, but that's how I remember it from my side of the story. I realize that others may have their side and that it may be different, but I stand by what I say.

At times, I've also done my best to portray the cultural and historical background — at least where it feels relevant. Some of it may come across as a bit lengthy, but I felt it was necessary to include because it reflects important discoveries that have influenced me, whether directly or indirectly. And if any of it feels irrelevant to you, I hope you'll at least enjoy a bit of a history lesson — or find yourself reveling in some nostalgia.

The main purpose of this book isn't to teach a specific lesson about how to discover your identity in the various areas you might struggle with.

While I may touch on topics like ethnicity, culture, vocation, relationships, and faith, my goal isn't to offer guidance or prescribe steps. I'm simply sharing how I've been learning to reconcile these areas in my own life.

That said, even though this isn't a self-help book, I still hope that, in reading it, others might come to understand a little more about themselves too.

I'm currently a pastor — but I haven't always been one, and some of the stories I share will certainly reflect that. I don't feel any shame in sharing the things I've done, because they've all played a part in shaping who I am today.

But also as a pastor, it's almost an occupational hazard to always want to point out how God is present — even in the smallest details of our lives. So in many of these chapters, I've included brief reflections on the identity and character of God as they relate to the stories I tell. At times, I wrestled with whether certain mentions of God were relevant or appropriate. But I've come to believe that God is always relevant, so how could I *not* speak of Him when I talk about my life?

Finally, this is not meant to be an autobiography, not that I know much of a difference between a memoir and an autobiography. I am still only 49, so this story only covers the first half of my life, assuming I have another 50 years to live.

Perhaps one day I'll find the energy and the will to reflect further on my life, and maybe I'll write a sequel. But until then, I hope I can take the lessons I've learned up till now and live a truly abundant life in Christ – living with love, joy, and peace all the days of my life on earth, and until the day I get to see Jesus face-to-face in heaven for all eternity. And I hope that all those who read this book will one day join me there.

Praise God the Father, and may you be blessed in the name of our Lord Jesus Christ, and strengthened daily in the power of the Holy Spirit!

Joe Eun-Seuk Park

Chapter 1

Korea, JFK, Immigration Bags and Other Things I Can't Remember

My earliest memories aren't really my own — they're stories my mom used to tell my brothers and me when she got nostalgic. She still shares them now and then at family gatherings, sometimes with me, and sometimes with my kids.

She tells me I was born on a freezing and snowy day. It was November 23, 1974. According to her, it was the coldest day of the year, and there was a full-on blizzard outside. It's the kind of detail you don't forget when it's the birth of your firstborn. Or maybe, it's just one of those things parents love to exaggerate for dramatic effect.

I was born in Daegu, Korea's third-largest city, about 240 kilometers (150 miles) southeast of Seoul. For some reason, my parents don't ever mention my infancy there, even though Daegu shows up later in several chapters of my story.

My legal *bonjeok*, or address of origin, was Gyeongju, the capital of the ancient Shilla Dynasty, about an hour south of Daegu. I don't know much about my brief time there, either. It's all sort of a blank.

The only thing I know of my toddler years, before we moved to the United States, is that we lived for a brief time in tiny, cramped quarters on the grounds of the Busanjin Church in the southern port city of Busan. And even with that, I've only been told a couple of things.

One is that my grandmother, my father's mother, who I sadly have no other memory of, really adored me. She was the one who gave me the name Eun-Seuk, which means "rock of grace." I would race around on my tricycle and she would chase after me, trying to feed me.

The other is that after my brother Eun-Wook (later known as Albert after we moved to America) was born, I would apparently take empty bottles and help him pee into them because he didn't know how to use the outhouse by himself. I'm unsure why that one made such an impression on our mom. Maybe it was just a cute memory that reminds her that her now grown-up, hairy and somewhat slobby forty-something year-old sons were once her little baby boys.

Again, these are not my recollections, but stories Mom would tell me. They're all I've got from my toddlerhood. Anything else is a foggy mist. I wouldn't even have known that I breathed my first breath in poverty-stricken 1970s Korea if Mom had never told me about it.

The next story my mom told me was about our arrival in America through John F. Kennedy Airport. I don't know the exact date and year, but I'm assuming it was sometime in 1977, since this was before our youngest brother, Eun-Sung (Daniel) was born. I've been told that even at age three, I was brave and smart, a take-charge kid. I suppose mom needed me to step up, because she brought me and one-year-old Eun-Wook by herself from Gimpo Airport in Seoul to JFK. My father had gone ahead of us a few months earlier to get things set up, so he wasn't there when we boarded that plane or when we first touched down on American soil — right before passing through immigration.

In my mind's eye, I can see my mom with a toddler and an infant, struggling to keep her boys quiet and still throughout the restless 15-hour flight, doing her best not to disturb the other passengers. Then, after enduring a long, slow immigration line at JFK, she's finally confronted by an unfriendly immigration officer, who fires off sharp, intimidating questions like: "Why have you come to the U.S.?" "When do you plan to leave?"

Mom had been a middle school English teacher before she got married, but I'm sure her English proficiency at the time was barely enough for survival in New York — let alone at JFK immigration. And yet, somehow she managed to get us through.

Then we had to collect our very large Korean immigrant suitcases. These were not really suitcases but huge duffle bags on wheels that filled up vertically in three or four layers. We had everything in there necessary for survival: dried anchovies, chili pepper paste, dried seaweed, and heavy *damyo* blankets for the cold winter nights. The wheels on those bags were very fragile. You had to take extreme caution pushing them around, in case they broke under the weight.

Mom would tell me how she carried my little brother in her arms, while three-year-old me did my best to push those heavy bags — twice my size — on their raggedy wheels, trying to help her out. This was the scene at the start of our quest for the American Dream.

The 1970s was a very difficult period in Korea. It had already been a couple of decades since the cease-fire of the Korean War, but the country was still suffering through great poverty. Because of this, President Park Chung-Hee started to initiate plans for rapid industrial development, which continued well into the '80s and '90s. Long after his assassination in 1979, this time was recognized in history books as the "Miracle on the Han River", due to Korea's unprecedented economic growth.

However, a significant underlying foundation of his plan involved favoritism and corruption. As a result, the rich got much richer, while the average workers were not only poverty-stricken, but many lived in slums without running water and shared outdoor toilets, which were disgusting and unsanitary. Working conditions for many laborers were downright inhumane. They worked in cramped, dark factories for more than 14 hours a day, with no days off, and were incredibly underpaid.

Even for those willing to work their fingers to the bone, making a living in Korea was incredibly difficult, and there was no guarantee that life would get any better. It's no wonder that so many people sought escape to places like America, Canada, or Brazil, despite not speaking the language, facing harsh racism, and enduring long hours of grueling physical labor.

We often hear that immigrant parents made those sacrifices *for* their children. And in part, that's true. But the reality is, many chose to move overseas regardless of what challenges awaited them, because anything felt better than the conditions they were leaving behind. This was the emigration story for so many families at that time.

With that said, what I find interesting about *our* story is that when my parents first moved us to the U.S., they did not go to work at a dry cleaner or a convenience store, like many other Korean immigrants did (though sometimes my mom had to work in some of those places to help put food on the table). It was also not because my dad dreamed of starting his own business, such as a restaurant or a Taekwondo studio. For us, the American Dream was not about building our own business and becoming wealthy. My dad chose a different path.

Of all the ways he could have chosen to escape poverty in Korea, he chose ministry and seminary studies. Today, no one chooses to become a pastor to escape being poor, but for my dad, perhaps there was no other path.

He came from an impoverished upbringing, raised by a single mother in the southeastern port city of Pohang. My dad never knew his father. Before he was born, my grandfather was killed in an accident involving a bull.

Dad grew up in a pre- and post-war society that was not only extremely poor, but was especially harsh towards single mothers and their children. Many kids were abandoned and left to die during this time because they could not be provided for.

But my grandmother was a fighter and a survivor. She did this through the church. She studied at a small Bible college and became a Bible teacher and female evangelist at a church in Gyeongju. Through her faith and determination, she was able to rise above the stigma, provide for her son, and send him to school. And so, perhaps it was only fitting that my dad would one day follow in her footsteps — turning to the church not only for faith, but as a way to provide for his own family.

Dad went to the U.S. looking for scholarships to advance his education, but his deeper intention was to find any opportunity to make a better life for himself and his family. Not long after arriving in the U.S., he was able to join the Presbyterian Church USA. Through this organization he was able to attain a religious visa for himself, and then legal status for his wife and boys to join him in America.

By the time we arrived, my dad was enrolled in a Master of Theology program at Union Theological Seminary in New York City, which allowed him to secure student family housing. And so, we began our lives in America on the grandest stage of them all — New York City, the Big Apple.

I don't remember much from those early days, but I've seen a few photos of little me and baby Albert in our small apartment. By today's standards, it probably wasn't much. But it was home. And it was there — in that modest space in Manhattan — where my American journey began.

Looking back on my life, even from the very start, I can see that God has provided for everything. He provided for my grandmother, my father, and me, and now, because I am a pastor, He provides for my wife and kids, too, through my compensation from the church (although my kids were shocked to first hear that my paycheck came from people's offering money).

One of God's names in the Bible is *Jehovah-Jireh*, meaning "The Lord will provide." Many people associate this with material provision — jobs, food, shelter. And while that's true, the name goes much deeper.

It first appears in Genesis 22, when God tells Abraham to sacrifice his beloved son Isaac — the very child through whom God's promises were to be fulfilled. Abraham obeys, trusting that somehow God will provide. As he raises the knife to strike down his son, God intervenes and provides a ram in Isaac's place. Abraham names that place *Jehovah-Jireh*, testifying that God truly provides.

That mountain — Mount Moriah — would later become the site of Solomon's temple. Centuries after Abraham, Jesus Himself would walk, teach, and eventually be crucified near that very place — Jesus became the ultimate sacrifice for all humankind. So when we call God *Jehovah-Jireh*, it's not just about our daily needs — it's about the life offered to us through the sacrifice of Christ.

In my own family — from my grandmother to my children — we've experienced God's provision not only in material ways, but through the church, calling, and grace. We may not be rich by the standards of the American Dream, but we've always had more than enough, and I also feel that, so far, we've all lived a pretty abundant life.

I still find it remarkable that my dad chose the path of ministry back in the 1970s. It was a tremendous step of faith — one I never imagined, in a million years, I'd one day take myself. But I'm getting ahead of the story, and I'll share more details on this later. In 1977, however, becoming a pastor was the furthest thing from my mind. And I wouldn't come to seriously consider it for another 37 years.

Looking back now, I realize that even from the very beginning of my life, the *Jehovah-Jireh* of Abraham — and of my grandmother, my father, and my mother — was always going to become my *Jehovah-Jireh*, too. And one day, I pray that my children will also come to know that their provider is not me, or their mom — but the Lord Jesus Christ. He is the one who provides everything they will ever need in this world. And my family's story is living proof that this is true.

Chapter 2

What's in a Name?

My name is Joseph Eun-Seuk Park. Or is it? Sometimes I get confused. I'd like to figure it out, but I don't know if I ever will.

I know it sounds strange that I'm confused about my name. I mean, it is what people call me every day, right? So, you may ask, what's there to be confused about? But I've realized there's a lot in a name, and I'd like to focus on mine in this chapter.

Of the various things that help determine our identity, such as race, ethnicity, nationality, occupation, friend groups, hobbies, and so on, perhaps one of the more powerful identity markers that we don't often think about is our name.

Most names mean something. When parents find out that they are with a child, it's one of the first things they contemplate. To the parents, it's *that* important.

When it came time to name our children — Jueun Joanna, Juel, and Juno — my wife Juri and I spent a lot of time in discussion. With each child, it took the full nine months of pregnancy to find the name that felt right. It wasn't just about choosing something that sounded nice or started with the letter "J." Each name we gave our children was carefully chosen to be a blessing — something that would speak hope, identity, and meaning into their lives.

Jueun takes the first syllables of my wife Juri's and my Korean name, Eun-Seuk, as she is the perfect melt of us both. The "Ju" in her name means "master" or "lord," and the "Eun" in mine means "grace." Combined, it means "the grace of the Lord." We figured, of all the blessings we could provide to our daughter, the greatest would be for her to know the grace of our Lord Jesus Christ throughout her life. What better than to hear it every time someone calls her name?

Her English name, Joanna, sounds very similar to how people would call out to her in Korean: *"Jueun-ah!"* (Hey Jueun!).

Joanna means "the grace of Jehovah (the Lord)". So in both sound and meaning, Jueun and Joanna are pretty much alike. To me, this seemed like the perfect name for our child, so it would be a tough act to follow if we had another. We did. In fact, we had two more.

Our second daughter came as a surprise during my second year of seminary. Juri was working a temporary marketing job at an international insurance company in Seoul and was in the middle of negotiations to get hired full-time. This would have been huge for us, because I had no income and was bleeding away our money in tuition fees and books. Once Juri became pregnant, all offers quickly got taken off the table.

During this time, I had to come up with a name for our new baby girl. One thing I knew was that I wanted to name her with a "J" name like her dad, her mom, and her sister. I also figured that I would start her name with "Ju."

Most Korean names have two syllables and it's common for siblings to share one. This is called a *dollim*. For example, the *dollim* for my brothers and myself is "Eun". My brothers are Eun-Wook and Eun-Sung. So, we decided she would share the *dollim* "Ju" with her older sister.

At that time, I was struggling through Hebrew exegesis classes, and had to write a paper based on the original Hebrew writings of Joel 2:28-30. One day, as I was banging my head against a wall, it occurred to me what tremendous encouragement and blessing this passage was for me during that season:

> *And afterward, I will pour out my Spirit on all people. Your sons and daughters will prophesy, your old men will dream dreams, your young men will see visions. Even on my servants, both men and women, I will pour out my Spirit in those days. I will show wonders in the heavens and on earth...*

A simple summary of this verse goes like this: In a time when locusts, famine, and disasters had struck the nation of Israel, if God's people were to humble themselves and turn back to Him, then His Spirit would fall upon them, and they would all be made whole in Him again. This is the passage Peter used on Pentecost, when the Holy Spirit came down upon all the disciples in Jerusalem, and 3,000 people came to believe in the Lord Jesus and were baptized that day.

It was a reminder that no matter how difficult our lives seemed at the time – with no job, no money, my wife let go of her job, and a baby on the way – the only thing we needed in our lives was God. God would somehow make a way for us if we trusted in Him. Therefore, when it came time to name our baby girl, the perfect name was inspired by the prophet Joel.

I chose the name Juel — pronounced *Ju-Elle*, with the accent on the second syllable. "Ju" means "the Lord," and "El" is the Hebrew word for "God." Together, her name declares: *The Lord is our God*.

It was a blessing I wanted to speak over her life — that no matter what may come, the Lord would always be her God, watching over her and dwelling within her through His Holy Spirit. That's the promise I wanted Juel to carry with her all the days of her life. It's a very unique name, and I have yet to meet anyone else with the same name.

If Juel came as a surprise, Juno was an even bigger one, as he came immediately after she was born, in my third year of seminary. I didn't even know this was biologically possible. Juno was born about a month earlier than expected, and because of that, Juel and Juno are only 12 months and 16 days apart from each other.

Just like his sisters, we decided to give him the "Ju" *dollim* as well. Since he came just as I was about to finish my final year of seminary and transition into vocational ministry, we thought it would be fitting to name him Juno – "Ju," meaning the Lord, and "No," meaning "worker". After graduating from seminary, I was to become a laborer for the Lord for the rest of my days, and frankly, I couldn't think of a greater blessing than for my son to work hard for the Lord one day, as well. It doesn't mean that he needs to become a pastor like me, but I do hope that he learns to labor with love for Jesus in whatever calling God places on his life.

Getting back to my Korean name, Eun-Seuk, it was given to me by my paternal grandmother. "Eun" means grace, and "Seuk" means rock — together, "rock of grace". Perhaps she had Peter, the disciple of Jesus, in mind when she gave it to me. Or maybe she was thinking of Jesus Himself — the true Rock, the foundation of faith in our lives.

Truth be told, though, I always hated that name. It's not the easiest to pronounce, even for some Koreans, and there have been plenty of times I've struggled to say it properly myself, despite it being my own name. There's no perfectly accurate English transliteration for it, so I can't even explain it to you clearly.

So how would non-Koreans pronounce it? *Ee-oon See-ook*? Maybe *Yoon-Sook*? Or even *Yee-un Suck*? Probably the easiest way to say it is something like *UnSuck*, but even that is not entirely correct, and let's be honest, written out like that it kind of looks weird.

For someone growing up among non-Koreans, a name like mine made me an easy target for childhood teasing.

What's in a Name?

I once knew a guy named Yoo-Suk. He was actually a solid athlete — he even represented Korea on the national track and field team. But because of his name, his biggest claim to fame may have been becoming an online meme: *"You suck!"*

As for me, Eun-Seuk may not have been quite as bad — I didn't "suck"... instead, I *unsucked*.

Still, that was the name I had to start kindergarten with. And let me tell you — it wasn't the easiest way to begin.

This was around 1980. Jimmy Carter had just lost the presidency to Ronald Reagan, the U.S. and Soviet Union were in the midst of the Cold War, *The Empire Strikes Back* was the top movie in the theaters, and in Korea, Chun Doo-Hwan had staged a military coup and was the new dictator.

We were now living in Chattanooga, Tennessee. We had left New York a couple of years earlier, and lived briefly near Madison, Wisconsin. I was too young to remember any of this. The only thing I know about our time in Wisconsin is that my youngest brother, Daniel, was born there.

Dad had been commissioned by the Presbyterian Church USA to start a couple of Korean immigrant churches — one in Knoxville and the other in Chattanooga. I don't remember much about those churches, except for Sundays spent sitting in the car all day as my parents shuttled back and forth between the two sites, nearly 180 kilometers (about 112 miles) apart.

I honestly don't know how we did it every week back then. My kids complain whenever they have to sit in the car for more than 30 minutes, even though they have smartphones and video games to keep them company. As for us, a lot of times we'd just lower the backseat of our station wagon to make it a flatbed, and my brothers and I would just knock out and sleep until we got home.

I remember we lived in two neighborhoods in Tennessee. In the first, a couple of Korean families lived on the same street as us. One had this big white Cadillac convertible with huge bull's horns mounted on the hood that seemed to signify they had succeeded in the American Dream.

I must have been five or six at the time, but I remember playing with firecrackers there. In Tennessee, it seemed anyone could buy them. There were large billboards for them everywhere. We played with them as if they were just any other toy. Some of the bigger kids in the neighborhood were the instigators, and would bring out sparklers or fake TNT or exploding tanks. Young as I was, I remember setting them on fire and watching things blow up. I'm amazed I didn't lose any fingers. That's just how things were back in the 1980s in Tennessee.

We also spent a lot of time playing in the backwoods. We would often go exploring and sometimes stumble across some old abandoned furniture, set up as a makeshift living room in nature. There were often half-empty beer bottles lying around, so I assume some teenagers used that spot at nights for getting drunk or making out. But during the daytime, the other kids in the neighborhood and I would make it our secret fort. Looking back now, I should be very thankful I never ended up on the back of a milk carton or on a "Missing Child" poster.

And then, there was this one day when I had this conversation with this girl who lived on our block that stayed with me for years. She came up to me and asked if I was Chinese or Japanese. I said I was Korean. Then, she asked me a question I had never considered before: "Are you from North Korea or South Korea?"

I didn't know there were two Koreas. I can't remember which one I said, but I hope I answered correctly.

Another memory of that first neighborhood is the day our neighbors next door threw out a bunch of socks. The next thing I knew, my mom had sneaked them into our house. She washed them up really good, and after that, I started wearing them. That's why whenever I look back on old photos from that first house, I always seemed to be wearing mismatched tube socks. I think that's also why whenever anyone asks me what I want for Christmas, I always say, "Fresh, warm socks."

What's in a Name?

It was after we moved to our second neighborhood in Tennessee that I started kindergarten. I can't remember much about kindergarten, except that I didn't like nap time. I'd always pretend to nap, but just closed my eyes and waited till it was done. I can't remember the name of the kindergarten, but I do remember that the following year I started grade one at McBrian Elementary School.

It was at McBrian that I had my first crush on a girl. Her name was Nina. She was a tall, white girl with short black hair and freckles, and she dressed exactly like you would imagine a cool girl in the 1980s would dress like, with tapered Jordache jeans, a Care Bears t-shirt with a jean jacket over that, and Esprit shoes. I liked Nina, but she was too cool for me, so I just admired her from afar through the monkey bars.

I also remember my first Valentine. Karen was a rather plain-looking girl with sandy blonde hair and thick glasses. She kind of reminds me of Peppermint Patty from the Peanuts comics. We were good friends, but there were no puppy-love crushes or anything like that. Honestly, I had no idea what Valentine's Day was, but when the teacher told us we had to choose a Valentine, I chose her, simply because she was my friend. I ended up giving her a pack of Wrigley's chewing gum.

I believe it was right around when I started at McBrian Elementary when my teacher called my dad one day to tell him, "Mr. Park, you have a really smart son, but I think he may need an American name."

As I remember it, one night we sat around the living room trying to come up with new American names for all of us. It wasn't just the kids who tried to get into the action; my parents also tried. My mom wanted to call herself Mary, and I think my dad leaned towards John, as in the Presbyterian church leaders of old like John Calvin and John Knox. Eventually, however, none of them stuck, and they just remained Mr. and Mrs. Park.

As for the boys, Daniel was the easiest. When they filled in his birth certificate in Wisconsin, my parents had to give him an American name, so his legal name has always been Daniel Eun-Sung Park. It was Eun-Wook and I who were the ones in need of new western names, and since we were in America, the land of freedom, we decided we'd do it freely and choose our own.

Eun-Wook decided on Albert. I'm not sure why he liked that name so much. It was either because of Albert Einstein or Albert Schweitzer, the great theologian, philosopher, and physician. I believe it was the latter, although I'm not sure why he was so fascinated with Schweitzer at the time. Maybe he had read about him in *The Young Children's Britannica Encyclopedia* we had on our bookshelf. Kids have YouTube today, but we had encyclopedias to keep us entertained.

As for me, I resisted at first. As mentioned above, the closest pronunciation for my name was *UnSuck*. That meant I didn't suck, right? Nothing wrong with that. Besides, Eun-Seuk was my name. Why did I have to change it? But eventually, I started playing along. I listened to a few of my parents' suggestions and began to consider other options.

Since my grandmother had named me "rock of grace," it was only natural for them to consider Peter. I guess it's better than being called Jesus. But I refused. It was because it made me sound way too much like Peter Parker. I didn't want to be called Spiderman at school. I thought the idea of an American name was so that I didn't get teased. So, no Peter for me.

After some thought, and also trying on some other options, I finally settled on the name Joseph. You might think it was because of Joseph, the boy with the coat of many colors — the one who was betrayed by his brothers, sold into slavery, and eventually became the prime minister of Egypt. But actually, it was another Joseph, the earthly father of Jesus, who inspired me. I wasn't much of a theologian back then, but I told my parents that I liked Joseph because he was the closest guy to Jesus, and I wanted to be close to Jesus. And just like that, in a small duplex in Chattanooga, Tennessee, my life as Joseph Park began.

I went by Joseph for most of my elementary school years in Tennessee and later when we moved to New Jersey. If I ever ran into someone from those days, they'd still call me Joseph. Somewhere along the line, though,

I started to prefer Joe. I'm not exactly sure when it happened, but *Joseph* began to feel too formal, while *Joe* just sounded cooler.

There were cool Joes like Namath, Montana, G.I. Joe, and Joe Cool. But when I thought about famous Josephs... the only one that came to mind was Stalin, and he definitely wasn't cool.

Every now and then, I'd let a girl call me Joey, but that was rare, and only if she was cute. If she didn't make the cut, she had to stick with Joe. And for the most part, that's the name that's stuck with me ever since.

Although Joe and Eun-Seuk are the same person, they've always felt like two very different identities.

Joe was the American — the one I embraced quickly once I took on the name. He became the confident one, the version of myself that was successful, outgoing, and sure of his place in the world.

The night I became Joseph, Eun-Seuk quietly took a back seat. Eun-Seuk was the Korean me — the part I tried to bury the moment I became Joseph. He remained the shy one — unsure of who he was, timid, and hesitant. He's the part of me I've often been embarrassed by... the one I've denied for most of my adult life up till now.

I'll share more on this later, but there was a time when Eun-Seuk became the dominant persona in my life again. This was during the mid-1980s to early 1990s, when we moved back to Korea and I began attending Korean schools. By then, I had already been Joe for so long that Eun-Seuk no longer felt natural. In fact, there were many times I resented being Eun-Seuk. Being Eun-Seuk was hard. Maybe the hardest thing I've ever done.

Later, I returned to the United States for college, and with that, I got to be Joe again. It felt good. Comfortable. Like coming home.

But after graduation, when I moved back to Korea, I found myself in a new kind of confusion. I knew I had to be Eun-Seuk again... but Joe wouldn't let him come out. Since then, there's been a constant struggle inside of me — between those two names, and the two identities they carry.

In recent years, I've been learning to embrace both Joe and Eun-Seuk. I don't hate Eun-Seuk the way I used to. After all, it's the name my grandmother gave me — a name meant to reflect Peter, or even more so, Jesus. Since entering ministry ten years ago, I've come to appreciate the name Eun-Seuk more deeply for what it represents.

Even so, it still doesn't feel entirely natural. There was a time when I even considered changing my English name to Peter to embrace it more. But I've come to accept that I'm just not a Peter. Along with Eun-Seuk, I'm still Joe — and I'll always be Joe. That's just who I am.

I've been through a lot over the years with the name Joe. I've made some good friends who call me Joe, and it would be weird for me to suddenly switch that up on them. I had an entire career in sports marketing in my 20s and 30s as Joe Park, and even now, I serve at a church where people affectionately call me Pastor Joe. And although my kids usually call me Daddy, sometimes when my youngest son messes with me, even he calls me Joe.

I've sometimes thought about going back to Joseph because that's what the full name is. As I rapidly approach 50 (I'm 49 as I write this), Joseph sometimes seems more age-appropriate. But then, I think about it some more, and I reckon it would just be strange for people to suddenly start calling me Joseph. Maybe one day I will, but not yet. Not today.

Your name carries a lot of weight when it comes to your identity. I still struggle sometimes with mine, but as I do so, it occurs to me that the issue isn't the name, but rather it's all about who I'm comfortable being. Socrates said, "To know thyself is the beginning of wisdom", but knowing yourself is easier said than done.

In Revelation 2:17, Jesus says that one day He will give us a new name — one that only He and we will know. That alone speaks volumes about the importance of our names.

Jesus is the one who created us, loves us, and gave His life to save us. Through faith in Him, He promises to give us a new name and a new identity — one that will be perfectly fitting, deeply personal, and known fully only by Him. He alone has the authority to name us, because He alone can define us. He alone gives us our true worth and value. And He proved how much we are worth to Him — by dying for us on the cross.

With that said, I guess I'm good with both Joe and Eun-Seuk for now. After all, those names are temporary on this earth, and one day I'll be given a new name; a perfect name just for me. And when I receive it, I will also be given my perfect identity in Christ. I look forward to that day, and so should everyone else who has faith in Jesus.

But until that day comes, I know a part of me will continue to struggle.

Chapter 3

The Never-ending Search for that One BFF

I lived in 15 different homes in my first 21 years, so it's no wonder I had trouble finding lasting friendships — not that I haven't had any.

It's been nearly 30 years since I graduated from college and some of my best friends, even today, are from that time in my life. Whenever I visit Seattle or Portland, someone always meets me at the airport, and I always have a place to stay. It's really good to know people still care after all these years. Still, they are way over there and I am way over here in Korea, so we'll probably only talk once a year, if that.

I once had a group of friends in Seoul during my younger professional years. That was before everyone had smartphones, and we'd just agree to meet up every Friday evening in front of the McDonald's in the city's prominent Apgujeong party area. Whoever showed up, we'd go out for barbecue, get drunk on *soju*, and then head to the trendiest bars and karaoke spots. This would take us into the wee hours. We continued this tradition religiously for many years. We even had a Facebook group, when that became a thing. After I started my seminary studies to become a pastor, though, we drifted apart. Nobody calls me to come out anymore. Maybe they think a pastor can't be much fun.

Going back a little earlier, I had best friends I played basketball with in high school. I'd just go to the courts, and I knew that someone would show up, and we'd just play ball all day. To us, basketball was life, and we were crazy about it.

Then my basketball buddies started getting into girls and drinking and smoking. They were the ones who influenced me to have my first drink and cigarette, and we wasted a lot of time and money chasing after some of those things, but I was never into it as much as they were. Today, we never keep in touch, except for the occasional "like" we may give each other on a photo someone may post on social media.

If I were to go back even further, I still remember my best friend from the fourth grade in New Jersey, right before we moved back to Korea. He was a kid of Polish descent named Matt Yeasky. We hung out after school all the time. We both liked football and Cabbage Pail Kid stickers, which were crude and silly parody stickers of the famous Cabbage Patch Kids dolls of the 1980s. Both our mothers and fathers worked, so we had all the time in the world to hang out after school without anyone forcing us to do our homework. We played schoolyard football in the fall, baseball in the spring, and in the summer, we'd play in the pool his dad would set up in their backyard. We even snuck into his dad's secret stash of Playboy magazines a couple of times.

But we had a bad fallout one day, and it still makes me sad to think about. It was over something quite silly. We didn't come from wealthy families and didn't have the coolest toys or video games, so we would often make up our own games. One was "sock-boxing". We would take off our smelly shoes and our even smellier socks, and loosely holding one in each hand, we'd swing at each other. For jabs we'd sharply snap a sock in the other's face, and for haymakers we'd make huge brush strokes in the air, hoping one of our socks would land on the cheek or the lips of our friendly foe. Imagine getting swatted in the face repeatedly with your friend's socks and thinking that was entertaining. Well, that's what we did.

At first, it was innocent fun, but then Albert wanted to play, too. I didn't want to lose to him, so I got a little extra aggressive and made him cry. Matt thought I was a jerk for doing that. I thought Matt should mind his own business, and well, that was it. We stopped being friends. Before we could make up, my family moved back to Korea.

I don't have many regrets in life, but that's one. If I could go back and repair that friendship, I would.

Years later, after graduating from college, I had a chance to visit our old neighborhood in New Jersey. I knocked on his door, hoping he might still be at the same home. Nobody answered. I saw the mailbox had the name "Yeasky" on it, so I left a note. But I never heard back.

Perhaps some of these stories will show why I don't believe in BFF-ship. None of my BFFs ended up being a Best Friend Forever, so forgive my cynicism.

That doesn't mean I'm cynical about ordinary friendship, though. The first friends I remember were these kids from my old neighborhood in Chattanooga, Tennessee. This was not the earlier neighborhood I mentioned, where I played with firecrackers as a preschooler and wore other people's thrown-out socks. I'm talking about the second neighborhood. We lived in a small duplex unit at the far end of the street. From what I can remember, it wasn't much of a place.

Next to us, in this old beat-up house, with an even older and more beat-up looking rusted pick-up truck in front, was this girl named Ginger. Ginger had the reddest hair of anyone I can remember and the reddest freckles on her face too. I know some people think redheads are cute, but not Ginger! She had dirt all over her face and clothes all the time, and I swear, she stank really bad. She ate bell peppers raw like they were apples. I mean, she would stand in front of us, and bite into a pepper, and she'd enjoy it and say it was sweet. Who does that?

Ginger was a strange little girl and I didn't like her. If cooties were a real thing, she would have had it. I teased her constantly, but she still wanted to play with us.

She would follow me and my friends everywhere. When we went to the store, she'd tag along, even though she didn't have any money (well, neither did we). When we played freeze tag, she would play too, but we would never tag her. When we played hide-and-seek, she would force herself into the game, but she would always have to be the seeker. She was like our shadow. We didn't ask her to tag along, but she was always there, and we couldn't get rid of her. And yet, she never complained and was just happy to be with us. When I think about it now, we probably should have been nicer.

One day, though, we must have really hurt her feelings. I'm not sure exactly who said, or did, what. Maybe she finally got fed up being teased about her unkempt curly red hair. It looked more like a bird's nest than a little girl's hairdo. Or maybe she had enough being told to her face that she smelled like sweaty underwear. Or perhaps it finally got to her when one of us said, as we always did, "Ginger, we don't like you. Go away."

I wish I could remember, because then I might think we deserved what came next, which was unfathomable and unforgettable for a 7-year-old boy. Not that we were completely innocent.

One afternoon, my brothers and I were outside our house playing in our little yard, when I saw Ginger's dad barging out of their house like a mad bull. He made a beeline for us, fire coming out of his eyes. He towered over us in the most intimidating fashion, and with the most threatening Tennessee southern drawl you can imagine he said, "If you boys ever come past my house ever again, I'm gonna get my shotgun and shoot y'all!"

He didn't tell us what we did wrong. He didn't mention anything specific. He gave no preemptive warning. He just dropped the bombshell threat and stomped off. We ran back inside our house and locked all the doors and windows. What kind of an adult would say such a thing to little boys, even if we had been naughty? I absolutely believed he would shoot us.

For some time, we tried to avoid passing their house. But after a while, we realized this was not possible. We still wanted to play with our friends, and most of them lived on the other side of Ginger's house. We would have to risk our lives to play with them. Every time we went out to play, we would sneak along like stealth ninjas so we wouldn't get caught and have our heads blown off.

There was this one time, though, that I do remember thinking it was the end.

One day, my dad came home with an old orange and blue second-hand bicycle. He had discovered a cheap bike at a yard sale, and bought it for me so I could learn to ride. It was my first big boy two-wheeler. I often fell, scraping my arms and legs, but I didn't give up. When I was finally riding on my own, I couldn't believe how great it felt!

A few days after that breakthrough, I was outside on the bike, and then trouble happened. At the time, I could keep my balance and go straight, but I still couldn't turn or stop properly. So there I was, churning down the street, and I looked up and saw Ginger's dad's beat-up old pick-up truck parked right in front of me, and I couldn't get out of the way. Bam!

Before I knew it, I had crashed into the back of the truck, and was on the ground. My knee was all bloody, but an injury becomes secondary when you're faced with a more significant threat. My real concern was that Ginger's dad would run out of the house with his shotgun and start blasting at me. I picked myself and the bike up and rushed home. I ran into the house to hide. Luckily for me, the truck was already so battered that I don't think anyone really noticed I had crashed into it. It didn't seem like Ginger's dad had noticed anything either, because he never came out and said anything to me, so I probably got away with that one. After that, I made sure to practice and master riding my bike on *our* side of the street.

Next to Ginger lived Randy. He was a little older. I was in the first grade, and I think he was in the fifth. If our small group of friends on the street were like a little gang of rascals, Randy was our leader.

He came from a Catholic family. He always tried to get us to go to Catholic Church with him so we would get saved, although I don't think he was much of a saint himself. I think I went a few times and took mass, though I had no idea what was going on. I remember finding it very different from the church I was used to and didn't think much else about it.

One cool thing that came out of going to Catholic Church with Randy was that one day his church group invited me to see a baseball game. We took a bus to Atlanta, to Fulton County Stadium, and there I saw my first Major League Baseball game featuring the Atlanta Braves. I don't remember who they were playing, or who won the game, but it was just cool to be at my very first pro sports game. I've always been a Braves fan since then, although I don't let many people know about it.

Randy also gave us a little kitten one day. His cat had a litter, and he asked us to take one. We took home a little black-and-white kitten. I don't recall its name. I just remember it didn't like us. It wouldn't let us hold it or pet it. Instead, it tried to scratch us and get away. That kitten gave us fleas one time, and so we had to fumigate the entire house. My parents didn't really care much for it.

Then one day, it disappeared. Sometime later, we played hide-and-seek, and one of us went into the crawl space under the house and discovered some animal bones. We figured the kitten had crawled down there and died. We weren't that sad about it.

Randy also introduced me to the world of petty crime. We used to like to go to the local drugstore down the street to buy candy. My parents had a coin jar, where they'd keep all their loose change. When it got full, I'd take the whole jar to the drugstore, and we'd buy five-cent gumballs or ten-cent fireball candies with it.

One day, I was at the drugstore with Randy. He told me that his aunt worked there and that we could take anything we wanted without paying. I was in awe when he said that.

"Here, I'll prove it to you," he said. Take anything in the store you want, put it in your pocket, and just walk out. It'll be fine."

I'd never walked out of a store without paying for anything, so this was all new and exciting to me, but I didn't know what to take.

When Randy saw my hesitation he said, "Take this pack of Big League Chew!"

And so I did.

Big League Chew was a type of bubble gum that was packaged like chewing tobacco, because, back then, all the baseball players in the "Big Leagues" (MLB, that is), used to chew and spit tobacco in the dugouts. When I think about it now, it's gross, and it's even more alarming that they would sell bubble gum that looks like chewing tobacco to little kids. But back then, to have a whole pack of Big League Chew bubble gum for myself was like a dream, so I was excited he suggested it.

I took a pack of grape flavored chew bubble gum very casually and stuck it in my pocket, and then we walked out of the store. No one saw or caught us, and it was the best pack of bubble gum I'd ever had.

When I think about it now, I highly doubt Randy had an aunt who worked at that drugstore because he never took us back to do that again.

My closest friend in the neighborhood was a boy named Brian. I just thought he was the coolest kid. He was a white kid with cool blonde hair, and he wore the nicest clothes, unlike me, who always seemed to wear hand-me-downs from other people at church.

I call him my best friend from that time, but the truth is, I don't remember much of what we did together. He had a video game console, which was rare in those days, so that made him seem super cool to me. Besides that, there's not much to say. Maybe that's why we were best friends. We didn't have to do anything special, and that was good enough. I guess the only special thing I can remember is that one day his dog died, and so we had a funeral for it in his backyard, and then we dug a hole and buried it. That's about it.

I remember that when we moved from Tennessee to New Jersey, I was very sad to leave Brian. I thought it just wasn't fair that I had to go and not be able to see him again. Of course, this was well before the time of Facebook or Instagram, so when we said, "Goodbye," it wasn't a "See you later," but it was a "Goodbye" for good.

On the other hand, I was happy to no longer live next door to Ginger, and the threat of being shot by her dad. As for Randy, I don't know if I was happy or sad to leave him behind, but he sure was memorable to me.

Our friends and surroundings influence a lot of who we become. That's why I sometimes wonder how I may have turned out if I stayed in Tennessee. Would I be speaking in a thick southern drawl, listening to country music, while sipping Jack Daniels Tennessee Whiskey in my old beat-up Ford pick-up truck? I'm not sure if that would have been a good thing or a bad thing.

I used to hate that we had to move around so much, and that I could never have friends that lasted more than 2 or 3 years, if even that. I was jealous of those who seemed to have a best friend. I thought everyone had a BFF except for me. But as I grew older I realized that, except for a very limited number of people, having a BFF is a myth. Yet, so many people wish they had a best friend forever. Some people pursue it as if they are on a never-ending quest for an ever-elusive unicorn.

Maybe it's because, deep down, we all just want to belong — to have a group of friends, or even just one friend, who lets us be fully ourselves. We long to be totally and unconditionally accepted for who we are, and to feel free in that — free to laugh, cry, sing off-key, cuss, break things, or just be whoever we are in the moment. No matter how angry, sad, selfish, unreasonable, or even silly we might be, we hope that person won't be disappointed in us, and that they won't disappoint us by leaving. It's hard to find someone like that. For many people, it's nearly impossible.

Perhaps another reason is that we're all trying to discover who we are — and sometimes the best clues are found in the company we keep. We hope that when we look at our friends, we'll see a reflection of our own identity — our interests, fashion, style, language, worldview, political and social leanings, even our mannerisms.

In the same way, maybe we're still in the process of forming ourselves — our personalities, character, passions, and sense of uniqueness — and we just need a group of peers we can relate to, model after, or measure ourselves against. Whatever the case, many of us turn to our friendships to help us figure out who we are. I'm not saying that's right or wrong. It's just the way we are sometimes.

As I try to make sense of the friendships throughout my life, and also reflect on how I never found that one person I could call my BFF, I've narrowed things down to two possible reasons.

The first is that maybe God didn't want me to be influenced only by one person or a specific set of friends, but he wanted me to have a diverse perspective on the world by meeting many different people. He wanted me to be uniquely me and not just one of many.

The second reason is that He didn't want me to be overly disappointed by anyone I thought would be my BFF. People have a tendency of letting others down, after all, whether they intend to or not. I've been let down by many people in my life, some of whom I considered to be close friends. I'm sure I've also let others down, too. That's just how most people are.

After all these years, there's been one person who has always been there for me – Jesus. There were many years when I didn't see Him as my friend. I've turned my back on Him a lot. I still do sometimes. But through it all, He's never left my side, and if there is one friend who has been most influential in who I am today, it's Him.

So in my pursuit of finding that ever-elusive BFF, I guess Jesus has always been it. Not that I always knew this. I certainly didn't back in 1983, when we left Tennessee for New Jersey.

Chapter 4

American, Not American

The year was 1983. Some of the top songs that year were *Flashdance... What a Feeling* by Irene Cara, *Sweet Dreams (Are Made of This)* by Eurythmics, and Bonnie Tyler's *Total Eclipse of the Heart*. Of course, the year before, Michael Jackson's *Thriller* album came out and everyone was still moonwalking or breakdancing in black and red leather jackets and tight leather pants to *Billy Jean* and *Beat It*. However, goofballs like me preferred "Weird Al" Yankovic's *Eat It* parody even more.

This was also the year I went to see my first movie at the cinema, *Superman III*. Of all the Superman movies starring Christopher Reeve, this one, with Richard Pryor as the genius villain, is probably one of the most forgettable nowadays. But it still remains one of my childhood favorites, because it was my first. I even recorded it on a VHS player when it came out on HBO one summer when the cable company would allow one free week, and my brothers and I would watch it over and over until we had memorized the entire script.

The other big movie in 1983 was *Star Wars: Return of the Jedi*. This was the most epic movie experience of my childhood. A young Luke Skywalker had now grown up to be a full-blown Jedi master. The once whiny farm boy from Tatooine could now kick some major butt with the use of the force and his fresh new green lightsaber. And who could ever forget Princess Leia in her slave-girl bikini outfit on Jabba the Hutt's sand barge. Many little boys had fantasies about Carrie Fisher after that.

The Cold War between the U.S. and the Soviet Union was perhaps at its peak during this time. "Star Wars" was not just the name of a movie. It was also the name of President Ronald Reagan's satellite defense system. Everyone was certain World War III was right around the corner, and the entire world would come to an end because the superpowers would fire nuclear missiles at each other.

Speaking of missiles, the Soviet Union fired land-to-air missiles that year at Korean Air Lines flight 007, which had left Anchorage en route for Seoul, and accidentally drifted into Soviet airspace. The missiles may not have been nuclear, but all 269 passengers and crew were instantly killed. This sent horrifying shivers all around the world, and caused inconsolable grief all throughout the Korean peninsula.

It was also around this time that a new public health menace appeared that would terrify the world for several years. Initially, because of its name, when the first cases of AIDS were reported, many people were wondering who was helping whom. I didn't know who the actor Rock Hudson was, but in 1984, when it was reported that he was the first celebrity to die of AIDS, people were scared to use public toilets or even to shake hands out of fear of unwittingly contracting the HIV virus.

These are just some of the things I remember from around that time.

In 1983, we packed all of our belongings in Tennessee into a U-Haul moving truck, attached our station wagon to the back, and drove all the way up the Appalachian Trail and beyond to the Garden State of New Jersey. We finally stopped at our final destination, a small two-story apartment in Randolph Township in Morris County.

We lived in the top of the building's two units, and some younger single women lived on the bottom. Maybe it should have been the other way around, because we three boys running around upstairs caused a lot of noise, which led to the occasional thumping on the ceiling with a broomstick from below, and every so often, tense words exchanged between those women and my dad.

Our apartment was part of a fairly large low to middle income complex of similar two-story buildings. It probably wasn't the nicest housing arrangement, but it was home, and we had fun there.

There were several large hills in the neighborhood, so during the cold winters when it snowed a lot, we'd zip down those hills on our sleds, as if we were little daredevils, like Evel Knievel, who was very popular at the time for jumping over rows of cars and Greyhound buses. The steeper the hill, the better. Once, we found a super steep hill, and this boy named Joey McMahon, who lived a few apartments down, sledded down that hill so fast we thought he'd broken the land speed record. He didn't really, but he did break his leg, and had to be taken off to a hospital in an ambulance.

Joey was one of those kids with whom we got up to a lot of mischief. I'm not sure if they still do this, but back in the '80s, really nice cars, such as Corvettes and Mustangs, used to have chrome caps that covered the tire valves, unlike regular vehicles, which have rubber caps. And for some reason, all the kids in the neighborhood liked to steal those chrome caps, me included. Whenever we saw a fancy sports car, we'd sneak up, twist those things off, and add them to our little collection. I have no idea whatever happened to my collection.

Speaking of which, I had a huge collection of baseball cards. There was a drugstore near our apartment, similar to the one near our place in Tennessee. And so, whenever my parents' coin jar started filling up, I'd sneak it out of the house and buy baseball cards. I had some really good ones. I had a Dale Murphy rookie card, a Dwight Gooden All-Star card, and I think I also had a couple of Don Mattingly and Wade Boggs cards. Even back then, the right baseball card could get you a good price if it was rare enough and in good condition. I had all mine saved in a couple of shoeboxes, but one day my mom threw them all out. I vowed to never forgive her for that. I guess I'd forgotten all about it until now.

As you may imagine, ours wasn't the nicest of neighborhoods, and the kids weren't the nicest of kids. There was this one black kid named Larry, who lived two doors down. At first, we were friends, but after he saw a boxing match between then-heavyweight champion Larry Holmes and his white challenger, Gerry Cooney, he only wanted to fight me. He said he was Holmes and I was Cooney, and he'd try to punch me every time he saw me. I couldn't leave the house for a while, or if I did, I'd immediately try to run inside as soon as I saw Larry. A couple of times he beat me to the door, and he tried to beat me up.

Right above Larry lived a Korean kid a little older than me. His name was Young-jin, but it may as well have been Bruce, because he was obsessed with Bruce Lee. What Asian kid wasn't at that time?

Young-jin was on another level, though. He would hang upside down from a tree and do sit-ups because that's what Bruce Lee would do. He'd mail-order Chinese stars and nunchucks from martial arts magazines. They didn't check your age back then for those things, so anyone could get them. People would be horrified if that were to happen today, but that was just how things were in the '80s.

I remember Young-jin had a slightly cleft upper-lip. Although he was super-cool to me, I think some of the older kids teased him for that. Maybe that's why he tried that much harder to be like Bruce Lee.

When Larry kept trying to beat me up, I'd ask Young-jin to beat him up. He was my hero. If Young-jin were outside playing, I'd go outside too, but if Young-jin wasn't outside, I'd try to stay home as best as possible.

There was another black kid in the neighborhood also named Larry. He had an older sister named Miranda. She was my age. She was a sweet girl, a good friend to me. But Larry was nothing like Miranda. Larry was the same age as my youngest brother Daniel, who is four years my junior. And just like the other Larry liked to mess with me, so did this Larry like to mess with Daniel.

I remember one time Larry had some darts – real darts with steel tips. He would try to peg Daniel with them. He threw them as Daniel tried to run away, which was more fun for him since Daniel became a moving target. Most of them missed, but one finally got Daniel. He came crying home that day with a dart sticking out of his left calf. I guess nowadays you might call that attempted murder, or at least assault. But back then, I just pulled the dart out of Daniel's leg, told Miranda to get her brother to stop, and that was the end of it.

When Larry wasn't trying to kill Daniel, they got along well, and got into a lot of mischief together. One day they threw rocks at a beehive. The bees were not amused, and they started attacking the boys. Daniel came home complaining he got stung in the head. My parents weren't home, so I had to figure out what to do. I recalled having seen my mom put Korean *dwenjang* (soy bean paste) on our wounds whenever we got bee stings, so I grabbed the *dwenjang* jar and I started applying it all over Daniel's hair and head. I'm not sure if it worked, but he didn't die, so it's all good. Later that evening, Mom wasn't happy that we had used up her precious *dwenjang* in such a way.

In New Jersey, I attended Fernbrook Elementary School. I was there for two years — in the third and fourth grades. My third grade teacher was a very sweet woman named Mrs. McCann. Later, when I moved on to the fourth grade, she confessed that she used to call on me in class all the time just because she liked listening to my Tennessee southern drawl. She was disappointed I had lost it after a year in Jersey.

For the most part, I enjoyed school. I was only about a B student, and I wasn't great at math, like most Asian kids are. But I enjoyed English. I loved to write, and I loved being creative with my writing.

In the fourth grade, I had a really cool English teacher, Miss Rockett, and she got me into Dungeons and Dragons, the Lord of the Rings, and the Hobbit. When we had to write a short story for English class, I wrote something about dragons. I got an A-plus, which made me want to become a writer one day. Maybe after all these years, I can try to pursue that again.

I had some cool friends at school. Matt Yeasky was my best friend. I've already mentioned him, but let me just say that Matt and I hit it off immediately. We were like two peas in a pod and did everything together.

Most people who know me today know that I'm a devoted fan of the Seattle Seahawks football team. People often assume I became a fan after moving to Seattle for university. But the truth is, it started much earlier. Even though we lived in New York Giants territory, my friend Matt was a Seahawks fan, despite never having been to the Pacific Northwest. He just liked rooting for the underdog, and back then, the Seahawks were perennial underdogs. And because Matt liked the Seahawks, so did I. That's what friends do.

There was this other kid called Ryan Geary. He was pretty cool too. His parents were divorced, and he lived with his mom, while his dad lived across the country in San Diego. I didn't know what divorce was when I was little. All I knew was that he always got to go to sunny southern California during the school breaks. He would tell me all these cool stories of beautiful beaches and the San Diego Zoo. I was so jealous. I wished my dad lived somewhere cool like that, so I could visit him during my breaks, too.

I also had my first Indian friend there. Ricky Sinha was a smart kid who was really kind to me. He was the best at math. He was pretty good at sports too. This one time in gym class we were on the same soccer team, and we had this incredible run down the field, passing the ball back and forth between defenders with perfect precision. Too bad I missed the empty-netter goal.

The one thing I found interesting about Ricky was that he always smelled funny, like turmeric and curry. I'm not trying to be racist, it's just how I felt when I was nine. Of course, I never mentioned anything to him, because it didn't matter. I'm sure my clothes also reeked of *kimchi* and garlic all the time. I'm glad nobody said anything to me either.

Then, there was this kid named David. He was my first Jewish friend. I remember one day, we were in line for the cafeteria, and somehow we got into a religious debate about Jesus. He said Jesus was a bad man. I said He wasn't. We started fighting, and the teacher had to break it up. It puzzled me to think that David would think that way about Jesus. I didn't know anything about Judaism at the time. But I do remember thinking it must've been kind of cool to be Jewish — because at Christmas, we only got one present, but they got one on each of the eight days of Hanukkah.

It was at Fernbrook School that I met Clare Baverstock. I liked Clare. All the boys did. She looked pretty, she dressed pretty, and she smelled pretty. She was also very smart, and really good at sports too. One time, she joined us in playing soccer, and when she ran around the field, I think every boy there fell in love with her, including me. It was like that scene in a movie when everything went in slow motion, the sun beaming down on her blonde hair as it fluttered in the soft breeze, and Journey's *Don't Stop Believin'* playing in the background. She was every fourth grade boy's dream.

Clare was always very nice, but I was way too shy to say anything to her. I wasn't much of a ladies' man at age nine.

There was this one boy, though, who was super aggressive when it came to Clare. His name was Billy Dee Williams. Yes, that's right, the same name as the actor who played Lando Calrissian in *Star Wars: The Empire Strikes Back*. Billy would just go up to Clare and give her a big bear hug, and then start kissing her. Clare hated it, and the teachers would try to stop him, but he just didn't know when to stop.

I didn't like Billy that much. Billy was sort of my rival, especially when it came to sports.

For the most part, I was a pretty average kid, and I didn't have anything I really excelled at. I tried to pick up the viola once, but I only learned pizzicato – picking at the strings and not playing with the bow – and then I quit when I realized I wasn't very musical. When it came to art, I drew stick figures, and that was pretty much it. As I mentioned, I was good at English, but I was just okay with other subjects such as math or science. Actually, now that I think of it, I was pretty darn good at memorizing all the US state capitals. That's one thing I was the best at.

But if there was one thing I was sort of good at in the third and fourth grades, it was sports, and especially sprinting and football.

When it came to sprinting, I was pretty fast. One time, I represented Fernbrook in the district races, and I came first in both the 100 and the 200-meter dash. Those were some proud moments.

However, I must admit that it comes with a little asterisk, because Billy Dee Williams wasn't in those events. He was flunking many of his classes and wasn't allowed to race. If he had run, Billy probably would have beaten me. I was fast, but he was faster.

There was this one time, though, when we had to race each other in gym class, and I won. The teacher said I barely beat him by a nose. In that moment, I felt so superior to Billy, but that was a rare moment. Eight out of ten times, he'd win.

When it came to football – the American type – Billy was untouchable. He was not only fast, but also quick and slick, like a snake. He's like one of those guys who will run circles around the opposing team.

I never got the chance to play organized football in real pads and uniform because my parents were always working, and could never find the time to take me to football practice. I'm sad I never got to do that. When it came to playground football at school lunchtime, however, that was my time to shine. I was good, really good! I was so good that all the kids chose me to be one of the captains, which meant that I not only got to pick the players on my team, but I also got to play quarterback, which is the most important position.

However, the quarterback on the other team was always Billy Dee Williams. Every recess, it was Joe's team versus Billy's team. Frankly, he didn't need anyone else on his team because he'd never pass it to anyone else. He'd just run the ball himself and no one could catch him.

There was this one time when Billy wasn't allowed to come out to play because he had not finished his homework and our teacher held him back.

It was the first time that my team started to win. I couldn't believe it! We were playing so well, and it looked like we would finally get our first win.

Then, all of a sudden, Billy showed up. The teachers felt sorry for him and let him out. As soon as he came onto the field, he ran all over us again, and we lost miserably. I hated that.

Overall, though, those years from 1983 to 1985 in Randolph, New Jersey, were like my glory years. It's kind of funny to think about it that way, since I was so young, but it felt like I was finally living the American Dream. I was as American as I could be – all these remarkable friends, crushes on pretty blonde girls, playing football every day – those were some of the best days of my life. Then, one day, something happened that forced me to realize that perhaps I wasn't as American as I thought I was.

Every year, we took class photos. My mom still keeps all of ours, from McBrian Elementary in Chattanooga to Fernbrook in Randolph, and even our class photos later in Korea. It's always funny and embarrassing to look through them, but my fourth grade photo sort of changed my life and forced me to look at myself all over again in a different light.

When the photos came out, our teacher thought it would be fun to play a little game in which she would only show the top of our heads, and the class would have to guess who it was. It was a challenging game for a while, and for a few of the kids we just couldn't guess. We all had a good laugh whenever we guessed wrong.

Then it was my turn. As soon as the teacher started revealing the top of my head, without any doubt or hesitation, everyone yelled out my name. They knew immediately it was me. Of course, it's not too hard when you're the only kid in the class with a yellowish complexion, really dark hair, and a bowl haircut. Everyone thought it was funny how easy it was. Everyone... except me.

I went home that day thinking, *Why was it so easy for everyone to guess it was me?* And why did everyone laugh so hard when they knew they were right? It hurt my feelings a lot.

That's when it dawned on me. I was different. I was not American. I was Korean.

Everything I knew about myself at the time was American. I hardly spoke the Korean language or knew anything about Korea. I didn't know Seoul was the capital, and I didn't know there were two Koreas – one in the north and one in the south. I hated that we always had to eat rice and *kimchi* at home, and I always envied my American friends for being allowed to eat hot dogs, microwave TV dinners, or pork chops with peas. Why couldn't I ever eat anything like that at home?

At the time, I didn't even realize that I had a different citizenship from everyone else. Although I identified as American, I was legally not American. I still had a Korean passport, and only a green card allowed me to live in the U.S. A few years later, after we moved back to Korea and had lived there for a while, I found out that my parents could have applied for me to become a naturalized U.S. citizen, but they didn't. Instead, I had to give up my American green card. When I discovered this, I was furious! I had a chance to become American, and yet they kept me from doing it.

Once I realized I was Korean, I started to hate everything about Korea, even though I knew nothing about it.

At least the Chinese had kung-fu and Chinese buffets, and the Japanese were known for Sony Walkman and Godzilla. Even Vietnam had a war that put them on the map, even if it was for the wrong reasons.

But Korea? Korea had nothing! No one even knew that it was a country. There wasn't even a proper derogatory term that Americans called Koreans because nobody knew anything about it.

The biggest reason I hated being Korean, though, was because I wasn't white. Most of my cool friends seemed to be white, and they all seemed to dress in nice clean clothes and live in houses with white picket fences with swimming pools in the back.

But I was Korean. All my clothes seemed to be other Korean people's drab hand-me-downs. We lived in a beat-up old apartment complex. And we had to play in the bathtub if we got hot in the summer.

Even the other white kids who lived in our apartment complex seemed cooler than us. They all had several cool action figures, such as Star Wars toys and Transformers, whereas, on our birthdays, we were lucky to get a book or whatever was on sale at K-Mart.

Even when it came to girls, it was always the white girls who were the prettiest. I always thought to myself, *the pretty white girls would never like a slanty-eyed Korean boy like me.*

If I were granted one wish, I would have wished to become white.

I tried my best to deny my Korean-ness, and the best way that I could think of was to refuse to speak Korean at home. I wasn't good at it in the first place, but my parents didn't want us to lose our language, so it was a rule that we had to speak Korean at home.

A few times I had seen some of my other Korean-American friends from church talk to their parents in English, even though their parents spoke to them in Korean. I thought that was brilliant and decided that's what I would do too. Besides, we were living in America, so if my parents couldn't understand my speaking American, it was their fault, not mine!

Mom: *Palli waseo bab meo-geo.* (Come here and eat your food.)
Me: What's for dinner?
Mom: Bab hago dwenjang. (Rice and bean curd stew.)
Me: Oh mom! Can't we eat normal food like other people?
Mom: *Hangook saram-eun bab moeg-neun-geo-ya!* (This is what Koreans eat!)
Me: It's not real food, Mom! I want real food! You know, like spaghetti or hamburgers!
Mom: *Nee mich-yeon-na? Geo-ree-go nee eon-jae boo-teo eomma han-tae yeong-eo-ro mal het-na? Hangukmal hae! Hangukmal!* (Have you lost

your mind? And since when did you start speaking in English to your mom? Speak in Korean! In Korean!)

Me: *Umma-neun nae mah-eum molla!* (Mom! You just don't get me!)

Identity is a tough thing to come to grips with, and even at a very young age it was not easy for me. In my heart and my mind I wanted nothing more than to be American, and to be more specific, a white American. But despite my defiant efforts to deny my Korean-ness, and assert to everyone that I was American, deep down inside, I knew I wasn't American, And that would be something I would struggle with for many more years to come.

Chapter 5

It's Time for Church!

C hances are, if you have ever lived in America and are a Korean, a Korean-American, or have close Korean friends, that at least once in your life you've been to a Korean immigrant church. It didn't necessarily mean that you were a devout Christian or even a nominal one. It also didn't mean you were spiritual, or particularly good, or even interested in faith. On Sundays, in the U.S., that's just what Koreans did — they went to church. Or at least that was the case in the 1980s as I remember it to be. I'm not sure if that's still the case today.

Of course, when you got there, you went to service, worshipped God, and did all that. But frankly speaking, that wasn't the only, or even the main reason people went. People were there to get some *kimchi* and other Korean foods, meet other Korean friends, or gossip about the people who hadn't shown up that Sunday. For that last reason alone, people did their best not to miss church.

If you missed the motherland and were tired of trying to speak broken English all week, church was that one place you could let loose and speak a little Korean. If you were single, church was also probably your best shot at meeting a nice Korean boy or a nice Korean girl to marry. For some people, marriage was the ticket to staying in the country legally. So, people went to church for one of those reasons, or some of them, or all of them, or for other reasons that weren't necessarily about worshiping God. Church was just the place where the Korean community would gather, for better or for worse.

I was still in elementary school at the time, so I went to church because my dad was the pastor there, and I had no choice. Still, I liked it. I met up with all my Korean-American friends once a week there, and we had fun.

Nowadays, the church, worldwide, is in decline. Some people have even started calling our age the post-Christian era. In the 1980s, though, the church was seeing its glory days, especially in Korea and America.

I still remember watching famous televangelists like Robert Schuller and *The Hour of Power* from the Crystal Cathedral in LA. There was Jim and Tammy Faye Bakker and their *PTL Club*. And there was also Pat Robertson and *The 700 Club*. I didn't really know much about televangelism at the time. I just remember they would ask us to get on our phones and make a pledge right away before it was too late, and that their operators were always standing by. I never understood why we were supposed to give, and I also didn't understand why God needed our money so badly. Later, I realized that it wasn't God who was asking us for our money.

In Korea, the 1980s was a decade of rapid economic growth, with conglomerates such as Samsung, Hyundai, Daewoo, and Lucky-Goldstar about to take off on the global stage.

Growth was a big part of the Korean church as well. Presbyterians and Methodists were the most active denominations, with over 10,000 churches established in Korea in this decade alone. There were so many churches that the night of Seoul was illuminated by hundreds, if not thousands, of neon crosses, each on the roof of a church, or a building containing a church.

The '80s also saw the emergence of the megachurches in Korea. Twenty-three of the fifty largest churches in the world in terms of membership numbers were in Korea. As these megachurches continued to grow, they would buy up or start new media companies that gave them access to other places worldwide. Given their vast, global reach, many senior pastors would be put up on pedestals as if they were just one level below God Himself. Although not considered religious cults in the formal sense, many of these churches often functioned as cults of personality.

It was during this time that Korean churches started to send out missionaries and plant immigrant churches in other nations in mass numbers, especially in places where many Koreans resided. One driving force was the growing belief among Koreans that God had blessed them financially, and that it was now time to give back. Another reason was the practical need to provide jobs for seminary graduates, who were being churned out in large numbers, but were struggling to find work in Korea. Soon, in most countries, as far as immigrant communities were concerned, more churches were Korean than of any other nationality. This was especially true in the United States.

From my own church experiences in America, I don't recall any life-altering sermons or thought-provoking Bible studies. Honestly, I can't remember a single Bible lesson from that time. I'm sure they must've been good, though — I was pretty solid at Bible trivia by the time I was a teenager. In fact, I even cried once when I was eight, after losing to one of the elder's kids.

But really, 99% of my church memories aren't about the teachings — they're about community. Since most of my friends and classmates in my neighborhood and school were non-Korean, church was probably the one place that anchored me to my Korean identity.

I was too young to remember much about the churches we went to in Tennessee. As I mentioned earlier, my dad had been commissioned by the Presbyterian Church USA to start two small Korean immigrant churches there, so every Sunday we'd drive long distances to shuttle back and forth between the two churches — one in the morning, and the other in the afternoon.

I do vaguely remember this one church picnic we had, where my brother Daniel, who was only a toddler, fell on some rocks and got a nasty cut on his forehead. I think some men were fishing on a river, where the banks were covered in sharp rocks. Daniel teetered toward the river banks without adult supervision, and fell face first on those rocks. Thankfully, one of the church members was a doctor, so he stitched him up immediately. As a kid, Daniel had a history of falling on his face and getting scars. That was the first of many.

I have one more memory of one of the churches in Tennessee, although I can't remember which one. It had this old soda machine, which sold smaller-than-normal bottles of Sprite and Fanta. I was about six or seven, and my hands were small enough to reach up the slot and pull the bottles out. When the adults were not looking, some of the kids and I would have free soft drinks. Fanta never tasted sweeter than that.

After we moved to New Jersey, the church we were part of was called New Jersey Somang Presbyterian Church. It may have been affiliated with Somang Church in Korea, which is still one of the largest in Seoul (and home to former Korean president Lee Myung-Bak), but ours was far from a megachurch.

It rented space from another small American church. There was a small sanctuary and a separate annex building with a cafeteria for Sunday school and other activities. I loved that cafeteria, because a lot of times the tables were cleared and it was just an empty hall, and so my friends and I would play many games in there.

Among the friends I remember, there were these brothers, Chee-Young and Chee-Cheol. We jokingly called them Cheech and Chong, after the comedy duo most well-known for their counter-cultural movies about getting high. Chee-Cheol and I were the same age, so we became good friends. Chee-Young was a couple of years older, but we all played together because there weren't many kids at the church.

There was also a boy named Kelly. I thought it was weird that he had a girl's name. I didn't know what gender-neutral was at the time. His dad owned a silver Corvette with "Official Pace Car" printed on the side. That was pretty cool. Whenever we went over to his house we played lots of video games. But unlike most people, who had an Atari 2600, he owned an Activision and an Intellivision. When my dad surprised us with a video game console one day, he got us an Intellivision, and I think it was because he saw it at Kelly's house.

My best friend there was a kid named Eugene Pak. He was a couple of years older, and his dad was one of the elders at the church. I can't remember exactly what he did, but I think he had a distribution business for Samsung products in America, back when nobody knew what Samsung was. He must've done well for himself because he drove a Mercedes to church. He also owned a 4x4 Jeep Wrangler, in which they once took me and my dad off-roading in the mountains. He also owned a Porsche. That one, I never got to ride it. But Eugene told me his dad would get many speeding tickets in that Porsche.

One of my favorite things to do on the weekends was to sleep over at Eugene's. I just thought that he was super cool. Part of it was because his family lived in the fairly rich neighborhood of Livingston. He's the first kid I knew who had cable TV with HBO. He also introduced me to my first stand-up comedy cassette tape. It was Eddie Murphy's "Delirious." And it was Eddie Murphy who introduced me to some four-letter words that started with "s" and ended with "t", or started with "f" and ended with "k". Eddie Murphy helped expand my vocabulary.

Eugene had two sets of cousins in our church. First there was Jaewon and Yumi. I'm not sure what their father did, but they lived in a house that resembled a cabin in the woods. It was the creepiest place because it was literally in the mountains with no one else around them for miles.

There was another cousin named Paul, whose family had just moved to New Jersey from Korea. He didn't speak much English, which, under most circumstances, would have made him an easy target for bullying. But because he was Eugene's cousin, we automatically accepted Paul into the in-crowd.

Other kids who had recently come from Korea weren't as fortunate. And I regret to say that I was one of the worst bullies.

There was one boy in particular who had a very 1980s Korean perm — the kind parents gave their kids because most Koreans have naturally straight hair, and if you wanted any kind of style, you needed a little wave or curl. Because of that, we called him Boy George, after the metrosexual lead singer of the band Culture Club.

Another "FOB" ("fresh off the boat") boy from Korea had somewhat fat lips, so we called him "Frog Lips". He had a little brother that looked just like him, so we called him "Frog Lips Junior". We were pretty mean.

The funny thing is, though, whenever my dad did pastoral house visits, he would take us along. And whenever we went over to Boy George's house or Frog Lips's house, they were nice to us, and we got along wonderfully. But when we were back at church and the other kids were around, I acted like a jerk to them again.

The ironic part of this story is that I've been back living in Korea for nearly 25 years now, and they've remained in the U.S. since then and have become American citizens. So who's the FOB now?

Dad's pastoral house visits were always fun affairs. The adults would do their adult stuff in the living room, and the kids would play in the basement or one of the kids' rooms. We'd play Atari or other games, and then eat some great Korean beef ribs with *japchae* glass noodles and other assorted Korean side dishes. At the end of the evening, we'd always have a small, family-style worship time. Since the kids were included, we almost always sang *Jesus Loves Me* or *I Have Peace Like a River*. Of course, we'd intentionally pronounce "river" as "liver" — playfully mocking the way our parents mispronounced it with their Korean accents.

Some of the best times at church would be the picnics and barbecues. To this day, I will say that the best barbecue I've ever had was our church LA *galbi* beef short-ribs, prepared in the park over a charcoal grill. Our Oldsmobile station wagon always smelled like *kimchi* because of these church barbecues, but I didn't mind it too much because they were *that* good!

There was this one time, after church, when a group of us decided to go fishing at a nearby river. I'd never gone fishing before, but I was eager to try. The problem was, I had no idea what I was doing. As I cast the rod — without much care or skill — the hook accidentally caught my friend Jaewon... right in the face.

Needless to say, it was quite frightful for me, and even more so for Jaewon. Thankfully, his dad could unhook him, and minimal damage was done. No harm, no foul, right?

It wasn't just me who sucked at fishing — all the dads were pretty bad. But the one real catch we had that day was unforgettable... because it came from my dad.

He had stopped trying. He cast his line one more time, left it in the water, and started reading his Bible. When it was finally time to eat, he casually started reeling in his line, and to everyone's surprise, there was a large freshwater eel on the end of it. Jaewon's dad didn't hesitate. He cut it up and cooked it right there over the fire. It was one of the best eels I've ever had.

Of all the families in New Jersey, there is no way I can forget Dr. Sam Kim and his family. Their daughter Connie was a couple of years older than me. Then there was Cathy, Albert's age, and the youngest was Brian, who was the same age as Daniel. They were like family to us. When Albert broke his arm, he stayed with them for a few days, and Dr. Kim took care of him as if he were his own son.

One time, I was playing at Eugene's house, and while we were running through the woods in his backyard I got stung by a yellowjacket. I immediately started breaking out into hives. Eugene and his mom rushed me to the emergency room. The last thing I remember was Eugene telling me that I shouldn't fall asleep or else I might die. I fell asleep in the car. The next thing I knew I was in a hospital bed with tubes all up my nose.

After that, Dr. Kim and his family took me in for a few days to stay with them, so he could observe me. It was so lovely to stay with the Kim family at that time. Dr. Kim was not only our family doctor, but his whole family was a second family to me.

After I moved back to Korea as an adult, every couple of years, either Dr. Kim or Mrs. Kim would come to visit Seoul, and when they did, I was always happy to see them. When I heard that Mrs. Kim passed away from cancer a few years ago, I was heartbroken. It was like I had lost my second mother.

After we left New Jersey, I used to dream that one day, when I was grown up and had my own family, I would go back to the New Jersey Somang Church and see all my friends. Sadly, that dream will never come true, because not long after we left, the church apparently split up into different communities and no longer exists.

The building is still there, though. After I graduated from college, I had a chance to visit Dr. Kim and his family, and I went and saw the old church. I never remembered it as a particularly big church, but seeing it again as an adult, I couldn't believe how small it actually was. I guess, as a kid, everything just feels bigger.

I saw the small chapel my dad used to preach in. I saw the old cafeteria, and I couldn't believe that my friends and I used to play dodgeball in there. It was so tiny. The parking lot only had space for around 15 cars, and yet we used to play football there. It was nice to see it again, but something was missing. It was all the people.

Eugene is now married and living in San Francisco, doing well in real estate. We reconnected on Facebook and eventually met up in person. One time, I was visiting my brother Daniel in Portland, and on the way back to Korea, I had a layover in San Francisco. Eugene came to the airport to see me. He hadn't changed one bit. And even though many years had passed since we used to run around in his backyard and listen to Eddie Murphy's stand-up comedy, the moment I saw him, it felt like no time had passed at all. It felt like it was still 1984, and my feelings for my old friend were just the same.

I'm not sure where Boy George is these days, but my parents still keep in touch with Frog Lips's folks, who now live in San Diego. Frog Lips is doing well for himself. He's married, lives in a beautiful house, and has an even more beautiful family — complete with his little *tadpole* kids. My parents have visited them a couple of times, and they've even played a round at Torrey Pines Golf Course together. During the COVID pandemic, when everyone was doing church online, his dad even "liked" a couple of my sermons. Honestly, I should probably learn his actual name by now instead of still calling him Frog Lips.

As far as I know, Dr. Kim is still in New Jersey. I assume he is now retired, but I'm not sure. Mrs. Kim is buried not too far from their house in Phillipsburg. Last I heard, Connie was living in the Chicago area with her husband and kids. At the same time, Cathy had become a successful pastry chef in Manhattan, and Brian was married and living somewhere in Connecticut or Massachusetts. We don't really keep in touch anymore. I used to stay in touch with Brian on Facebook, but I think he must have unfriended me at some point.

Sometimes I wonder why I dreamed about returning to that church with my wife and kids. If you think about it, we only spent two years there, so it's not like it was a long time.

But the more I thought about it, the more I came to the simple conclusion — I wanted to show my family my home church. After all these years, New Jersey Somang Church was still my home church, and I wanted my wife and kids to see it because it mattered to me.

During my time there, I grew up a lot. Even though I was a brat and a FOB bully, my identity in Christ probably first started taking shape at that church.

When I look back now, I miss my home church. I wish I could go back. I wish I could have one more time with my friends there. But I know that there is no going back. And so, I can only think back and smile about every Sunday morning when my mom would wake us from our sleep, force us to put on our clothes, wash our faces, and shout at us, "Kids, it's time to go to church!"

Chapter 6

Coming to Korea

I n the movie *Coming to America*, Eddie Murphy plays an African prince who travels to the United States in search of a wife. His cultural misunderstandings and language slip-ups as he tries to navigate American life lead to plenty of laugh-out-loud moments for the audience.

It's hilarious on screen, but in real life, situations like that aren't always so funny. I'm sure it wasn't for Frog Lips when he suddenly had to move from Korea to America. And it certainly didn't help that a punk like me was teasing him for being a FOB.

What I didn't realize at the time is that life has a funny way of flipping the script. And for me, that moment came in the summer of 1985.

But before I get to that, I need to take you back to the summer before.

Since moving to America, I hadn't been back to Korea at all. It felt like a faraway place, and an even more distant memory. As far as I was concerned, I was an American, who mostly spoke the American language, loved American food, watched American TV, laughed at American jokes, and loved American culture.

I was part of the original MTV generation. I got emotional when Michael Jackson, Lionel Ritchie, and a host of other artists came together as *U.S.A. for Africa* and performed *We Are the World*. My favorite sport was American football, followed closely by America's favorite pastime, baseball. I thought the prettiest girls all had blonde hair and freckles. And if I'd had a vote in the 1984 election I would have voted for Walter Mondale over Ronald Reagan, not because I liked his policies or even knew anything about them, but because he was the underdog, and gosh darnit, in America you cheer for the underdog!

Because I had become so Americanized, my parents decided to send me to Korea in the summer of 1984. They thought it would be good for me to reconnect with the motherland and finally meet some of my relatives, most of whom I didn't even know. I was only nine years old and was set to fly out alone. Well, not completely alone — my friend Eugene would be on the same flight to go visit his relatives. He was about ten or eleven, a bit older than me, and he quickly became my unofficial security blanket for the trip.

You might be surprised to hear, but I wasn't really scared of traveling by myself. I kind of thought of it as an adventure. The last time I was on a flight was when I was three years old and coming to America, and I had no recollection of that, so I was excited to be on my first airplane that I could experience as an older kid.

Eugene had told me ahead of time that it would be smart to pack all my belongings into a single carry-on duffel bag so I wouldn't have to check anything in. I had no idea what he was talking about, but I figured he was smarter and knew what was best. So I crammed everything — clothes and gifts for relatives — into a single bag. It turned out to be really heavy, and as I lugged it around the airport, I second-guessed that decision with every step.

I can't remember if Korean Air Lines provided any special care or escort for minors at the time. I kind of vaguely remember that family and friends were allowed to go up to the boarding gates, so maybe such care was not needed. But whatever the case, after we boarded that plane, we were on our own.

When I got to my seat, I didn't know how to store my luggage in the overhead compartment. I was probably too short to reach it anyway. So I kept the bag under the seat in front of me for the entire flight. It took up so much space that even my small frame felt cramped in that economy seat.

For the in-flight meal, I remember choosing the beef instead of the *bibimbap*. I couldn't believe someone was actually giving me the option to have an American meal instead of rice, so of course, I took it. Sadly, they wouldn't let me have any wine… but they did let me have an entire can of Coke all to myself. That felt like a win.

This was a time before we had personal entertainment on every seat. Instead, they played in-flight movies on a single screen at the front of the cabin. I didn't get to go to the movies very often, so I was excited — until they started playing *Gorky Park*. I fell asleep not long after it started.

We had a brief layover at Anchorage, where I got off and had the best udon noodles ever. Then it was another seven hours or so before we landed at Kimpo Airport. At the time, Kimpo was Korea's main international airport — Incheon Airport wouldn't open for another 17 years. This was also before the new Romanization system that changed "Kimpo" to Gimpo, and also "Pusan" to Busan, as well as "Taegu" to Daegu.

Since Eugene and I had not checked in any luggage, we were both out of there pretty quickly. But one strange thing I still remember was that, going through immigration, we had to stand in different lines. He was in the foreigner line, while I stood in the Korean line. For the first time in my life, I was separated from one of my friends because of my nationality. It was a very new and strange feeling.

Once we came out into the terminal, Eugene's relatives were waiting for him, and my maternal grandparents and relatives, people who I barely knew, were waiting for me.

We looked at each other.

"Hey Eugene... I guess this is it. Do you think I might get to see you while we're in Korea?"

"I don't know. Maybe."

Eugene's relatives, speaking in Korean, started to shuffle him away, *"Hurry! Hurry! The car is parked outside!"*

"Eugene, I'll see you lat...," I started to say, but never got to finish.

My own relatives had surrounded me.

"So you're *Eun-Seuk!* My, you've grown so much!"

"Eugene? Eugene?" I called out. But by then, we were already going our separate ways.

Now that I was without my friend, it started to dawn on me that I was a foreigner in a foreign land. Suddenly, I had no one to speak English to, and there was no one around me I was familiar with. Everyone was Korean and they were all speaking the Korean language. I was no longer in America. I was no longer where I felt comfortable.

I was only there for a month. I spent a little time in Seoul with my mom's sisters, but most of my time was spent in Daegu, where most of my mom's brothers lived. She was the fifth child in a family of five boys and four girls, so there were a lot of uncles and aunts to visit. My grandfather also took me to Pohang, and we went to the house where my dad grew up as a kid.

I did a lot during that trip, but here are just a few of my recollections.

I remember Korea looking very gray and dirty. Even though it was the middle of summer, I could hardly see a blue sky — nothing like the bright, open skies I was used to back home in New Jersey.

I remember the heat being unbearable — thick, humid, and suffocating. And everything smelled. It was the smell of sweat — everywhere — clinging to the air and to the people around me.

There was one night at my aunt's apartment in Seoul when a loud siren suddenly went off. Everyone had to turn off all the lights. The entire city went pitch black. It's hard to imagine that today.

I wasn't quite sure what was happening at the time, but I was told it was a civil defense drill — an exercise to prepare for potential air raids from the North. I was still pretty ignorant about the divide between North and South Korea, so I had no idea what they were really talking about.

After that, I started noticing posters all over the city, urging people to report anyone they suspected of being a North Korean spy. They said it was everyone's responsibility to help root out the communist threat.

While in Daegu, I stayed at my oldest uncle's house, which was tucked away at the end of a small alley. If you've seen the TV show *Squid Game*, there's a scene where they play marbles in an old neighborhood — narrow alleys, aging houses, and metal gates. That's very much what it looked like.

What fascinated me was that three of my uncles lived right next to each other in that tiny neighborhood. It felt like the entire alley belonged to the Kang family — my mother's maiden name is Kang — like our own little village within the city.

It was here that I met most of my cousins. All the male cousins shared the same *dollim* — "Wook" — as the second part of their name. The oldest was Kiwook, the son of my oldest uncle. My mom had another older brother who was a well-known piano professor; his son, Chanwook, later became a cellist. He had two sisters — Eunsong and Hyesong — who played the flute and violin, respectively. The most memorable, though, were two brothers younger than me: Hyoungwook and Jeongwook.

Hyoungwook was the older of the two, and because of that, his parents always expected him to act more maturely and take care of his younger brother. But when he found out that *I* was older than him, he was thrilled. It meant he could finally let loose, be a little goofball, and latch onto me instead.

Jeongwook was absolutely adorable — a carbon copy of Hyoungwook. He did whatever his older brother did, so naturally, when Hyoungwook started following me around, Jeongwook did too.

"Hyoungwook. Jeongwook. This is your older cousin, Eun-Seuk," grandmother said.

"Heeya! Heeya! It's so nice to meet you!" said Hyoungwook, giving me a big hug.

"Heeya! Heeya!" Jeongwook copied him.

"Ummm.... Hi. It's nice to meet you too..."

Before I can finish, Hyoungwook is right in my face. "You look American, Heeya!" he said.

"Yeah, you look American, Heeya!" echoed Jeongwook.

"Ummmm. Okay... ummm... what's heeya?"

That's when my aunt stepped in and said, "Boys, your older cousin Eun-Seuk doesn't know what heeya is." And then she turns to me to explain, "It's just how we say *hyoung-ah* ("older brother") in Daegu."

"So, Heeya, what do you eat in America? Do you eat lots of cheese?" Hyoungwook asked.

"Uh... I guess..."

"That must be great! We don't have much cheese here. Do you all have blue eyes?"

"Uh..."

"Does everyone have a gun?"

"Uh..."

"Are you gonna stay with us? We can all sleep together in the living room!" said Hyoungwook.

"Uh... Okay..."

Back then, houses didn't have air conditioning, so they would leave the windows open and sleep on the living room floor because it had the coolest surface. The boys would strip down to their briefs to stay cool. The first time I saw this, I was a little taken aback.

"Uh... Hyoungwook, what are you doing?"

Hyoungwook replied, "Heeya, I'm gonna wear only my underwear. That's what we do. You should do it too!"

"Yeah, heeya! You should do it too!" Jeongwook added.

"Ummm... I think I'm okay."

"Come on, heeya! Take off your clothes like us! It's really cool!" Hyoungwook implored again.

Jeongwook chimed in too, "Yeah, take off your clothes, heeya!"

Even more surprising was how they dealt with the heat during the daytime. They'd drag big plastic tubs out into the alley — the kind that could probably fit about three little kids at a time. Looking back, I'd guess those tubs were originally used for laundry, or maybe for making *kimchi*. But when the weather got hot, they'd fill them with cold water, and the kids would pretty much strip down and jump right in — completely carefree.

One of the most shocking things I saw that summer was a little girl, maybe three, if that, completely naked, playing in a tub of cold water by herself. I grew up with only brothers, and during bath times, sometimes our mom would wash us together. But this was different! I had never seen the private parts of a girl before, let alone in the middle of a public alleyway.

If that wasn't alarming enough, Hyoungwook said, "Heeya! Take your clothes off. Let's play in the water."

"You mean get naked?" I asked with a hint of terror in my voice.
"Of course not! You should wear a swimsuit, silly!"

Five minutes later he and Jeongwook reappeared from the house in the tiniest and most tightly fitting swimsuits.

When I told them I didn't have anything like that, Hyoungwook happily replied, "Oh really? I think I have an extra one." He went and fetched me a pair.

To his disappointment, I did not put it on, but I did put on another pair of shorts, and allowed him and Jeongwook to splash me a few times as they joyfully played in the old *kimchi* tub.

There was one week in Daegu when I got really sick. Maybe it was the food, or maybe the water. Something definitely didn't sit right, and I had a rough case of diarrhea that lasted nearly a week.

They took me to see an oriental medicine doctor, and I got acupuncture for the first time. They also gave me some kind of herbal remedy that had such a strong funky scent that I eventually started to think I'd rather just keep the diarrhea.

At one point, it got so bad I was sitting on the toilet for half the day. But in those old homes, the bathroom also doubled as the laundry room for hand-washing clothes, since there were no washing machines back then. So while I was on the toilet, trying to survive the war in my gut, my aunts would squat in front of me with tubs of clothes, doing the laundry like it was just another normal day. It was super embarrassing for me. But for them, it was just life as usual.

One day, one of my aunts commented that my shoes were getting faded, and so she took me to buy my first pair of Korean shoes. I was hoping she might get me a pair of Nikes or Adidas, since they were too expensive for me to have in America, and Eugene had told me that they were much cheaper in Korea, since that's where many of the shoes were made.

Rather than going to a shoe store or department store, we went to a traditional outdoor market. There, we found a small stall stacked with piles and piles of Korean shoes, but no Nikes in sight. Instead, my aunt picked out a pair of bright red and yellow shoes I'd never heard of before. They were called Cavallo.

"Oh my goodness! These would look so pretty on you," she said, holding up the shoes.

Ummm... they kind of look like Ronald McDonald shoes, I thought.
Before I could object, the store owner started echoing my aunt's enthusiasm: "Yes! Your son would look great in those shoes!"
Son? I'm not her son! I thought.
My aunt laughed, "Oh Eun-Seuk! We must look alike! She thinks you're my son," my aunt said. Then she turned back to the shop owner and clarified, "Oh, he's not my son. He's our nephew, visiting from America."
"No wonder these shoes would look good on him! It's American style!" the shop owner responded.
I wouldn't be caught dead in these red and yellow shoes in America, I thought.

But before I could say anything, the shoes were already on my feet, paid for, and we were walking away. I didn't have a choice — my aunt had thrown my old shoes in the store's trash can. I was officially doomed to return to New Jersey in those red and yellow Cavallo shoes.

All in all, my one-month trip to Korea wasn't a bad experience. Although it felt like stepping into a time machine and landing 20 years in the past in a developing country, I knew it was only temporary, and I'd soon be back in the comfort and familiarity of America. And sure enough, as soon as I returned to New Jersey, life went back to normal, and everything felt good again. At least... for a while.

The following summer of 1985 turned out to be one of the most dramatic turning points in my life. Earlier that year, I had overheard some conversations about my dad possibly finding a job in Korea as a professor. It was an *adult* matter, so my brothers and I weren't included in the discussions, and we had no idea what was really going on. Then, all of a sudden, our parents told us that Dad had received an offer from a university in Korea, and once the school year was over, we'd all be moving there together.

It all came so suddenly that I don't even know if I had time to process what was happening. I just kept going as if nothing was about to change. I was enjoying school. I played football with the kids during recess. I hung out with my friends in the neighborhood. All was normal with the world.

Then, one day, the movers arrived, packed up all of our belongings, and threw them all into a big truck. The only thing we had left in the house besides some clothes to change into was a rice-cooker and a jar of *kimchi*.

Just like when we first moved to America, Dad went ahead of us to get things ready. But this time, he didn't want to go alone, so he took Daniel with him.

Mom did her best to put a positive spin on things for Albert and me. She told us that Dad had been offered a very lucrative position at a prestigious Christian university in Daegu, and that he'd be making a lot of money. That was sweet music to my ears, because deep down, I secretly hated being poor.

My parents did everything they could to make sure we didn't feel like we lacked anything. But I always wanted to wear Nike shoes instead of Pro-Keds from K-Mart. And I was always a little jealous that I couldn't have all the nice stuff and cool toys the other kids had.

Mom also told us that Dad had found a great new house for us to live in called Yongma Mansion. The name alone made me imagine a spacious, two-story luxury home in a place like Beverly Hills.

She also said we'd be attending the best private school in Daegu once we got there.

I liked the sound of all of it — so whatever Mom was trying to sell us, I was buying it.

That is... until we actually *arrived*.

In 1977, mom had brought us, Eun-Seuk and Eun-Wook, by herself through JFK. Eight years later, we were back at JFK, going the other way this time, but now as Joseph and Albert.

When we arrived at Kimpo, dad was waiting with a driver. He led us to an old Kia Bongo van. I was pretty disappointed. Now that we were rich, I was expecting some sort of luxury limousine. The Bongo wasn't even the length of our old Oldsmobile station wagon.

It was still better than what dad was driving though, which was a cheap, second-hand, brown-colored Hyundai Pony with no air conditioning, and one of its side-view mirrors hanging on by a loose wire and some tape. This Pony hatchback is now considered a vintage car and one of Hyundai's most iconic, but it wasn't back then. Everyone had them. If you had a little more money, you might drive a Pony 2 or a Stellar; if you had a lot, you might have the brand new luxury Sonata.

Dad soon realized the Pony wouldn't cut it for us, especially with no air conditioning, so he splurged on a new blue-colored Hyundai Presto. It was the same size as the Pony, but a sedan instead of a hatchback. It was the hot new ride in town and the new line of cars that Hyundai was trying to push. All Ponies and Prestos later became the Excel. I was hoping we would upgrade to a Mercedes, BMW, or even a Buick, but they didn't allow foreign cars then. Anyway, the new car at least had air conditioning, so I couldn't complain too much.

When we arrived in Daegu and got to Yongma Mansion, I discovered it wasn't a mansion at all. It was a small, rundown apartment that could barely fit all of us. Apparently, in Korea, they named all apartment buildings something with "mansion" in it — maybe to give them a sense of luxury. But let's just say, it wasn't exactly high-end living

Thankfully, we didn't have to live there long because the university soon gave us housing on campus. So for the first four years of our time in Daegu, we lived inside the back gate of the campus of Keimyung University.

At first, I thought it was great to live on campus, and indeed it was far better than Yongma Mansion. The house was far more spacious, and it was next to the campus sports field, so I'd go out there and play basketball and other kinds of sports all the time.

Living on campus certainly had its perks, but it came with its share of drawbacks, too. From 1985 to 1987, college demonstrations against the dictatorship of then-President Chun Doo-Hwan reached their peak. Campuses across the country were frequently filled with protests, and local police responded with tear gas and brute force in an effort to suppress them.

Many times, we felt the impact of the police crackdowns on these demonstrations. On our way to school, we often passed shattered windows, sidestepped broken glass from firebombs, and saw stones littering the streets — leftovers from clashes with riot police. Tear gas would frequently seep into our house, and whenever we heard the thud of the tear gas launchers, we'd grab candles and huddle in the master bedroom closet, locking ourselves in until the air cleared enough to breathe without our eyes stinging.

At the time, I didn't really understand why the students were demonstrating so often. It honestly just felt annoying. Later, I came to realize how important those protests were, and that without them, Korea might not have become the democratic nation I live in today. But back then, all I knew was that every demonstration meant it was tear gas time, and I had already shed more than enough tears and snot.

The private school we went to, Keisung Elementary School, was the best in the city, as mom had told me it would be. But being the best didn't mean it was prestigious, like I had imagined. I had pictured a private country club-like atmosphere, where we all wore sharp blue blazers and read Shakespeare all day. In reality, it felt more like an old country schoolhouse straight out of rural Mississippi, back in the days of *Tom Sawyer and Huckleberry Finn*. The desks and chairs were wooden and looked practically ancient, and each classroom was packed with nearly 60 students. It may have been 1985, but I could've sworn I had stepped into a bizarre time warp that took me back to the 1800's.

One of the first things I noticed was that there was no air conditioning for the sweltering summer months, and there was no built-in heating system for the freezing winters. Instead, in the summer there were a couple of fans in each classroom, but as they were insufficient, everyone had their hand fans to wave at themselves during class. In winter, there was a furnace in the front of the classroom, and students would take a big kettle of water and place it on top. Then, they'd fill their individual water bottles with hot water, and hold it between their legs. That's how they kept warm. It would take me a long time to get used to this new way of life.

Another thing that took some getting used to was the Korean flag hanging at the front of the classroom. Every morning, we had to stand and salute it while the national anthem played over the school P.A. system. It wasn't all that different from what we did in America — reciting the Pledge of Allegiance to the U.S. flag — so it shouldn't have felt unfamiliar. But each time I saluted the Korean flag, it felt a little strange, almost like I was betraying America in some way.

Despite the rough conditions, most of the students at Keisung Elementary came from well-off families, which meant they could bathe regularly. In contrast, students at other schools often appeared unkempt. Some even had lice or ticks in their hair. Many were noticeably short and thin — likely a reflection of poor nutrition and limited access to proper meals.

With everything going on around me, all I wanted was to go back to New Jersey. I couldn't speak Korean well, and whenever I spoke English to my brothers in public, people would stare and give us strange looks. I hated how everyone dressed. I hated how everything smelled. Everything I loved — my friends, my church, American football, even a good hamburger — was gone. It felt like I was stranded on an island I couldn't escape. All I wanted was to go home.

But Daegu was now my home. And I had to find a way to live with that.

In some of the earlier chapters, my instinct as a pastor was to weave in some kind of reflection about God. But with this chapter, it's not so easy. This was the beginning of a very difficult season in my life. Everything I had once known to be good was suddenly gone, and I was left to face a harsh new reality. When everything feels dark and uncertain, it can be hard to find any redemptive angle, let alone offer a hopeful lesson.

I guess if there's anything godly to be said, perhaps it can be found in Romans 5:3-5:

> We glory in our sufferings, because we know that suffering produces perseverance; perseverance, character; and character, hope. And hope does not put us to shame, because God's love has been poured out into our hearts through the Holy Spirit, who has been given to us.

These are words I often cling to in times of suffering. But let's be honest, it's not always easy. Who really wants to suffer? If I had the choice,

I'd much rather avoid the pain than have to search for hope in the middle of it. Still, God led me down this path of suffering in Korea at such a young age, and when things became unbearably dark, He was the only one I had to hold on to.

That said, it wasn't all bad. I eventually found my footing and even had some fun during my time in Korea. But if I could go back and do it all over again, I think I would've fought and cried with everything in me until my parents gave in — until we stayed in America and grew up there together. You have no idea how many times I've dreamt about that. Or, if that wasn't possible, maybe I could've convinced them to let me stay with someone we trusted, and I'd find a way to make it on my own. Who knows if that would've ever worked? In the end, it's all just hypothetical "what ifs," and none of it matters anymore.

As it was, I was completely stripped of the identity I once knew. I wasn't just lost in a foreign land, I had lost myself.

And yet, it's through that very suffering that I've become who I am today. Somehow, I didn't just make it through, I grew stronger and wiser because of it. I guess God always knows what He's doing, and I do praise Him for His wisdom. Though to be honest, His way isn't always the most pleasant path.

Sometimes I wonder if God allowed me to go through all of that so I could use my experiences to minister to others facing similar challenges today. Back in 1985, people were still leaving Korea, not returning. In that sense, I may have been part of the first generation of the Korean diaspora to come back. I guess you could say I was a kind of pioneer.

These days, in the early 21st century, more Koreans are returning from all over the world. Some come seeking new opportunities. Others are sent back under difficult circumstances. But when they arrive, many quickly realize that Korea doesn't feel like home. They feel like foreigners in a foreign land. The culture shock unsettles them, sometimes even shaking the foundation of their lives and sense of identity.

Maybe that's why God let me walk through all of this first — so I could share my journey, and others might find courage and hope in it. And if that's the case, then I'll gladly be used in that way.

Still, if I'm being brutally honest, there will always be a part of me that quietly wonders: *What if I had never come back to Korea? What if...?*

Chapter 7

Korean, Not Korean

A s soon as I started in fifth grade at Keisung Elementary, rumors spread that this new kid had come from America. All the kids from the other classes flocked to my classroom to try to get a glimpse of this "American Boy."

Nowadays, Korea is a popular destination for foreigners from all over the world thanks to things like Psy's *Gangnam Style*, BTS, *Crash Landing on You*, *Squid Game*, Samsung smartphones, and CJ *Bibigo bibimbap*. But back then, hardly anyone knew or cared about Korea. There were hardly any foreign tourists, and if any foreigner did show up, they were stared at like monkeys in a zoo.

Every once in a while, I remember seeing the rare westerner at one of the traditional markets, and the older Korean women (*ajummas*), who are well known for their lack of social filters, would go up to them and just start touching their skin and hair because it was so different from theirs. This American guy once told me that he hated using Korean urinals because Korean men would stand next to him to see if he was any "different" from them.

So, when kids at Keisung School heard that an American boy had started attending classes there, everyone had to come and check me out.

There used to be a saying, "There's something different in the water in America than in Korea." They would say this because Americans were so much bigger than Koreans. Maybe there was or maybe there wasn't. I will admit that I probably did look a little different from the average Korean kid.

For starters, I was already about 175 centimeters tall — around 5 feet 7 inches — so I stood noticeably taller than most of my classmates. I also had slightly lighter hair than most Korean kids. As I got older, my hair darkened, but back then, it had a more reddish tint. My eyes were bigger and rounder too, and the pigment of my pupils was a lighter shade of brown. On top of that, I guess I dressed a little differently. In America, we didn't have much, so I wore whatever my mom could find at the thrift store. But even the cheapest clothes had a distinctly American feel compared to what the other kids in Korea were wearing.

I have a funny story related to this. A few years later, when I was in high school, I bumped into a kid on the street — someone I had known back when I first arrived in Korea. He came up to say hi but gave me a strange look. Then he said, "You've changed a lot. You look way more Korean now."

I asked him what he meant, and he said, "Well... you used to have blonde hair and blue eyes. But now your hair is black, and your eyes are, too."

I couldn't help but laugh. I guess when I first came to Korea, it wasn't just him, but most of the kids probably saw me that way. Not because I actually looked like that, but because in their minds, I might as well have.

Soon after I started school, everyone called me "Ah-me-li-kan Boy!" That was my nickname all throughout the fifth and sixth grades. I didn't like it. It made me feel very different. I didn't like standing out so much and being looked at as an anomaly.

When I think about it now, it's pretty ironic. Back when we lived in New Jersey, all I ever wanted was to be seen as American. But now that people were finally acknowledging that about me, I hated it.

The fifth grade was pretty tough. I didn't understand much of what was going on. To say it was culture shock was an understatement. At times, it felt more like a cultural electric chair.

On the first day of school, for example, I arrived not knowing that everyone was supposed to pack their lunch. In America, when lunchtime came around, we'd go to the cafeteria, pay a dollar, and get a slice of pizza or a hot dog. But there was no cafeteria here. When the lunch bell rang, the kids stayed in their classroom and pushed their desks together in groups of four. They would pool their *banchan* — side dishes like *kimchi*, seaweed, sausages, and other items — while eating rice from their individual containers.

Neither my mom nor I knew about this lunch routine, so on that first day, I showed up without any lunch. Our teacher ate with us in the classroom, and that day, he had ordered *jjajangmyeon* — Chinese-style black bean noodles. It still amazes me that they delivered it right to the classroom.

When he noticed I didn't have anything to eat, he handed me his noodles and said, "You'd better bring your own lunch starting tomorrow, or you'll starve."

I was really bad at Korean, and I was often clueless in class. Most of the time, I would sit at my desk, doodling in my notebook, and stare at the clock, hoping the time would go faster. I soon learned that when you do that, time goes by the slowest.

One time in Korean class, the teacher suddenly called on me to stand up and read a paragraph in front of the whole class. I was struck with utter horror. Not only was my Korean terrible, but I also hadn't been paying attention and had no idea what page we were on. My *jjak-kung* — my deskmate — quietly turned my book to the right page and pointed to the spot. With my heart pounding, I stood up hesitantly.

Back in New Jersey, my parents had tried to teach me *Hangul*, the Korean alphabet, so I could sound out words phonetically. But I had never actually learned how to read full sentences, let alone entire paragraphs. Still, with all eyes on me, I stood up and did my best to stutter through the unfamiliar characters on the page.

I don't remember how I got through it, but somehow I did. When I finished, the teacher told the class to clap for me. It was his way of encouraging me, but honestly, I didn't feel encouraged. I felt humiliated. I never imagined getting applause just for reading a paragraph out loud, and doing it like a toddler, at that. If anything, I felt stupid.

Because I was having such a hard time at school, more than anything, I just wanted a friend. Most of the kids were friendly enough, but I always felt like it was more out of curiosity than anything else. I was a novelty to them — interesting, but not someone they truly connected with. It was hard to think of any of them as real friends.

There were a couple of rich kids who invited me over to their homes to play. Their families had chauffeurs and fancy cars, like a black Ford Mark V sedan. Back then, if you had a Ford in Daegu, you were somebody important.

One kid's parents had access to Camp Walker, the U.S. military base in the city, and they took me there once to eat American food. You'd think that might've led to a real friendship, but it didn't. It felt more like his mom just wanted me to help her son practice English.

In fact, that seemed to be the case with most of the kids who invited me over. Their moms had similar ambitions, and it became clear that their interest in me wasn't genuine. They were just hoping they could use me as an English tutor, compensating me with home-delivered Chinese noodles. They didn't really want to be my friends, and I hated the feeling of being used like that.

Birthdays were a big deal back then. If you were invited to someone's party, it meant you had made the list — and the list was usually short, so being on it actually meant something. I got invited to a few, but I always wondered if the kid actually wanted me there, or if it was just their mom's idea.

There was one time, though, when I got invited to the birthday party of a kid I really wanted to be friends with. I actually thought we were friends, so I was genuinely excited. I used my allowance to buy him a gift, wrapped it carefully, and got everything ready for the party. But a couple of days before the big day, he uninvited me. He said there were too many people coming, and I didn't make the cut.

I still remember going home that day and crying in my mother's arms.

Ever since I could remember, sports had been a big part of my life. Back in America, I played all kinds of sports with my friends, especially American football. But I quickly learned that in Korea, no one had a clue what that was. Instead, all the kids played the kind of football the rest of the world plays.

What surprised me most was how good the Korean kids were. In the U.S., soccer usually looked like a chaotic swarm of kids chasing the ball around with no real structure. But in Korea, even during casual schoolyard games, they had positions and formations. It felt organized, almost professional, at least to me.

I didn't know all the formal positions, but there was one thing I did know: I was fast. Faster than anyone else out there. And because of that, I turned out to be a pretty decent player. That's how I finally started making some friends.

Then one day something happened that made me want to give it up. Some of the kids said they would stick around after school to play against another class, and they asked me if I wanted to join. I was like, "Heck yeah!" I went out to the playground, put my backpack in a pile next to all the other kids' backpacks, and started to run around and play.

But not too long into the game, our teacher came out of the school building and told us to stop. And then he called us all over to where he was standing. He looked very angry and made us line up next to each other. I wasn't sure what was happening, but something didn't feel right because all the kids next to me were hanging their heads low as if they were in trouble for something, but I wasn't sure what. He told all the kids to put out their hands, palms facing up. And with his teacher's pointing rod, from one end of the line to the other, he started hitting the kids in their palms. I didn't know what was going on, but it didn't look good. And with each smack of the rod, I could see each kid retract their hands in pain.

When it was my turn, the teacher looked at me with an expression of disappointment and said, "Eun-Seuk, I thought you were a good boy, but now I can see that you're no different from the others." Then he hit me in the palms as well.

That was the first time I was disciplined by a teacher in Korea through some form of physical punishment. It certainly wouldn't be the last. I don't actually remember it hurting that much, though I'm sure it stung. What I remember more was the confusion. I had no idea what I'd done wrong. No matter how much I thought about it, I couldn't figure it out.

Looking back now, it was probably because we stayed at school to play instead of going straight home. But even so, it's still hard to understand why that was such a terrible offense. When I got home that day, I told my mom what had happened and asked her why I got in trouble. She didn't have a clear answer either.

After that, I didn't feel like playing soccer anymore.

As I went through all of this, I often asked God, "Why? Why, God, do I have to go through this? It just feels so unfair! Why can't I just grow up like a normal kid, back where I belong — back in America?"

But the only answer I got was silence. I didn't hear anything.

Still, I kept praying. I kept asking, "Why?"

No matter how much I prayed or hoped to return to America, deep down, I knew I couldn't. I was stuck here, and all I could do was keep praying and hope for some kind of miracle.

I used to relate a lot to the characters of Joseph and Daniel in the Bible. They were both taken away from their homes, their comforts, and what they were familiar with. Joseph was sold as a slave by his brothers into Egypt, while Daniel was captured and exiled to Babylon. They became strangers, outsiders, and victims of circumstances beyond their control. Both were given new names, new identities, and told to adjust, or face the consequences. Their stories felt eerily familiar to me.

But what stood out most was how steadfast they remained in their faith. Despite being in unfamiliar and often hostile environments, they kept trusting God and doing their best to adapt. And as they did, God was with them.

I prayed that God would be with me in the same way — that somehow, I too would be able to fit into this new life in Korea.

But in that first year in Daegu in 1985, life was tough. I know it may sound kind of funny that a 10-year-old kid would say that life sucks, but that's exactly how I felt. The life I had known for all of my short existence was gone, and I had no idea what to do anymore.

During this tough period, the only people I think who understood me were my parents. For this, I'm deeply thankful. They were always supportive, loving, and caring, and they never pressured me to be someone I wasn't.

I later learned that around the same time we returned to Korea, one of my dad's colleagues had also come back from Germany with his family. Tragically, one of his sons couldn't handle life in Korea and took his own life.

After hearing that, my parents made a quiet but firm decision: they would never pressure us — whether it came to school, or anything else in life — in ways that made us feel overwhelmed or unsafe.

My mom was my biggest cheerleader. She always told me I was a bright boy and that I should never get discouraged. Honestly, at the time, that was hard to believe. I used to argue with her, saying, "No, Mom! Don't you see how much of a failure I am?"

But she never gave up on me. She kept believing, even when I couldn't believe in myself.

Going back to Joseph and Daniel — there was a time when Joseph was thrown into a dungeon, forgotten, and left to rot. And there was a time when Daniel was cast into a den filled with starving lions.

In both of their darkest moments, when all seemed lost, there was still hope. That hope came from one thing: the presence of God with them. Even in the depths of despair, they were never truly alone.

As a kid, when I prayed to God, He felt silent. I couldn't see Him, and I couldn't feel Him. But looking back now, I know He was there. I know because I'm still here — writing this memoir, reflecting on that time not with bitterness or resentment, but with a faint grin at the corners of my mouth. I wouldn't have made it through those days if God hadn't been with me.

Back then, in fifth grade, what I longed for most was a friend. And I couldn't seem to find one. But now I realize, I *did* have a friend. Jesus was my friend. I just didn't know it yet.

The year 1985 was quite memorable for me — though not always in the best ways. Still, it was a landmark year, one I had to go through to become who I am today.

Eight years had passed since I first left Korea, and it would be another eight before I returned to America. Until then, this *Ah-me-li-kan Boy* had to learn what it meant to be Korean.

Chapter 8

The *Han* of Trying to Be *Daehanminguk* Number One

*D*aehanminguk — the Republic of Korea — is a nation obsessed with being number one. For many Koreans, being "okay" is simply not good enough. From a very young age, kids are taught that the goal isn't just to be good — it's to be the best. It's not about fitting in, but about standing out, rising above, and excelling beyond everyone else.

In the United States, if a child comes home with a 90% on an exam, the response is usually, "Great job! I'm so proud of you!" But in Korea, it's different: "Why didn't you get 100? What did you get wrong? Make sure you don't mess that up next time."

Koreans love rankings, lists, and awards. From an early age, students know exactly where they stand academically — not just within their class, but across the entire school, and even nationwide. Percentile rankings are common knowledge.

You can see this obsession with rankings in pop culture too. When a Korean K-pop artist hits number one on the U.S. Billboard charts, it becomes headline news, and they're celebrated as national heroes.

The same mindset shows up during the Olympics, where many Koreans view the medal count as a reflection of the nation's overall well-being and global standing.

Being the best is so important that there is even a popular saying, "It's better to be the head of a snake than the tail of a dragon," which sort of translates as, "It's better to be the top dog in a lesser field of competition, rather than just being an average Joe among the elite."

So you can imagine that things can get pretty intense when it comes to being number one.

Some parents spend thousands of dollars a month on private education outside the regular school system, all in the hope that their child will become number one academically in the nation. That's also why many families are content with having just one child: they simply can't afford the educational costs of raising two or more. The more they invest in that one child, the greater their hopes — that the child will get into the top university, graduate at the top of their class, land a job at a leading *chaebol* company, and earn top dollar (or *won*), becoming financially secure and socially admired as "simply the best."

For many, that is the Korean dream.

This obsessive pursuit of being number one extends far beyond education. Although Korea was once a latecomer in many global industries, it has since risen to the top in several key sectors. Today, Korea is a leading producer of ships, semiconductors, and electronic goods. Its automobiles — once the butt of jokes on the global stage — now win international awards for quality and design. Korea may have started behind, but it's caught up fast, and in many cases, surged ahead.

Korea has also become one of the top cultural influencers in the world — thanks in large part to the global success of K-pop artists who dominate YouTube, K-dramas that are widely watched on streaming platforms like

Netflix and Disney+, and internationally acclaimed films. One of the most notable examples is *Parasite*, which made history by winning the Oscar for Best Picture in 2019.

Along with the global rise of K-culture, it's no surprise that Korea is also considered one of the top countries in the world when it comes to beauty, thanks in large part to its high-quality cosmetics and skincare products. And of course, you can't talk about beauty in Korea without mentioning plastic surgery. Korea has more plastic surgery clinics than any other country in the world. Ask most Koreans how they feel about this, and chances are, as long as Korea is number one, they're proud.

There is, however, a sad and sobering side to all of this. While most Koreans take pride in their country's success on the global stage, many struggle deeply on a personal level.

Korea has the lowest birth rate in the world and one of the highest rates of depression and suicide. Much of this can be traced back to the relentless obsession with competition — the constant pressure to be number one.

I see this as the great *han* of the Korean people today. And the irony is striking — because it was the *han* of the past that drove Koreans to pursue such high standards of success in the first place, as a way of escaping their historical pain and hardship. But now, those very standards are creating a new kind of *han* — one marked by personal misery, pressure, and silent suffering.

Let me explain what I mean.

The word *han* refers to a uniquely Korean sense of collective grief. But it's more than just sadness — it's a kind of shared, soul-deep wailing that lives in the collective national psyche. *Han* is born from generations of suffering: decades of war, oppression, poverty, colonization, and injustice endured not only by individuals, but by their ancestors and the ancestors before them.

If you're Korean, whether you're aware of it or not, *han* is woven into your identity. It's part of the emotional inheritance passed down through blood, memory, and history.

One of the clearest expressions of *han* can be found in the traditional Korean song *Arirang*. It is perhaps the most beloved and iconic song in Korea — arguably even more deeply tied to the nation's identity than the national anthem itself.

Overseas, many people recognize *Arirang* as the name of their favorite Korean restaurant in K-Town, often associated with barbecue or *bibimbap*. But Arirang is far more than just a good place to eat.

In fact, most people, even in Korea, don't actually know what the word *Arirang* means. The first part, *Ari*, refers to a profound, lingering sadness — a soul-deep anguish that refuses to go away. It's the kind of sorrow that causes real pain in the heart, radiating throughout the entire body. The second part, *rang*, simply means "song." So *Arirang* literally means "a song of deep sorrow."

Its enduring popularity lies in the fact that it gives voice to the *han* of the Korean people — the collective cry of a nation shaped by suffering, yet full of resilience.

This *han* can be traced all the way back to Korea's earliest beginnings. It runs through the history of the ancient kingdoms, which were constantly under threat from foreign invasions. I'm not an expert in ancient Korean history, so I won't attempt to cover all the details, but the point is clear: *han* has always been deeply embedded in the Korean people. It's part of the national soul, passed down through centuries of struggle.

For a more recent example, we don't need to look much further than the early 1900s, when Korea was annexed by Japan and turned into a colony. During this period, every Korean, young or old, was forced to take on a Japanese name, speak only Japanese, abandon their faith traditions, and conform to Japanese customs.

Those who resisted faced brutal consequences: beatings, imprisonment, and in many cases, execution. Koreans were treated not as citizens, but as servants and slaves under foreign rule.

Even after Korea's liberation in 1945, the *han* of the Korean people did not disappear. Freedom came with a new kind of pain — division. The country was split in two: the North under Soviet influence, and the South under American control.

Just five years later, the communist North invaded the South, sparking a brutal civil war. For three years, millions of Koreans fought and killed each other in one of the bloodiest conflicts in modern history.

Although a cease-fire was eventually declared, the war never officially ended. To this day, the two Koreas remain divided. Along with that division, countless families — parents, children, brothers, and sisters — were torn apart. Many died without ever reuniting with their loved ones.

In the decades that followed — leading up to the 1980s — Koreans endured even more *han*, this time in the form of severe poverty, widespread hunger, inhumane working conditions, and unsanitary living environments. The elites who oversaw the nation's rapid development were not peacemakers or advocates for justice. Instead, they were often harsh military dictators who wouldn't hesitate to crush opposition in order to advance their agenda — even if it meant turning tanks and guns on their own people.

And I'm not just talking about North Korea. These things happened in the South as well.

Yet, in the South, those same dictators are often credited with laying the foundation for Korea's transformation into one of the world's leading economies. The rapid growth of Korea's GDP in the 1980s and '90s was unprecedented. No other nation had developed so quickly in such a short span of time.

But then, in 1997, the bottom fell out. Korea went bankrupt and had to be bailed out by the International Monetary Fund. In a moment that revealed both the strength and sorrow of the collective *han*, the people came together to persevere. In a remarkable gesture of unity and sacrifice, families across the country dug through closets and drawers, donating gold rings, wedding bands, and watches to help pay off the national debt, even if it only made a small dent.

What they didn't realize at the time, and what many were heartbroken to discover later, was that their sacrifice had mostly gone to cover the debt of the already wealthy *chaebol* conglomerates.

And all for what? So that Korea could become the powerhouse it is today — one of the most elite, advanced countries in the world. The dream was that no one would have to live in collective poverty anymore, that the *han* of the past could finally be left behind.

But somehow, the escape from the *han* of yesterday has only led to a new kind of *han* in the cutthroat pressures of today. Ironically, the success that was supposed to bring peace has instead brought more pain.

The younger generation in Korea has even coined satirical names for their homeland. Instead of *Daehanminguk* — the Republic of Korea — they call it *Manghanminguk*, "the ruined republic." Others refer to it cynically as *Hell Joseon*, a nod to the historical kingdom, but now with a bitter twist.

And so, tragically, the *han* of the Korean people continues on.

I didn't mean to go off on a tangent or deliver a history lesson. But to truly understand what it was like for me growing up in Korea during the 1980s and '90s, some of this history is essential. This was the backdrop — the emotional and cultural landscape — against which I was forming my identity as a Korean.

For the longest time, I didn't fully grasp that background. But as I began to read and learn more about Korea's recent past, my own life started to make more sense. I could finally begin to piece together why I am who I am today. And a big part of that understanding comes from recognizing that my life — my struggles, questions, and journey — was shaped by the collective *han* of the Korean people.

The year was 1987, and the world was at a dramatic turning point on the global stage. In December, American President Ronald Reagan and

Soviet leader Mikhail Gorbachev signed a monumental treaty which not only reduced nuclear-grade weapons pointed at each other, but eventually led to the end of the 45-year Cold War.

In the following summer of 1988, for the first time in 12 years, the two superpowers sent all their athletes to participate in friendly competition against each other at the '88 Seoul Olympics. Then, on November 9, 1989, the Berlin Wall, which was perhaps the greatest symbol of the Cold War, finally came crashing down. After many years, the world now seemed like it had finally come together in unity as one... that is, all of the world, except the Korean peninsula.

Despite the peace that much of the world seemed to be enjoying, the two Koreas remained deeply divided and isolated from each other. North Korea only dug its heels in further, clinging tightly to its strict communist ideology.

Meanwhile, in the South, the global winds of democracy were beginning to stir. Influenced by international movements and growing frustration at home, student-led demonstrations intensified in resistance to the dictatorship of President Chun Doo-Hwan.

In 1987, President Chun named his top military lieutenant, Roh Tae-Woo, as his chosen successor. But when news broke that police had drowned a Seoul National University student protester during an interrogation — accusing him of being a communist — the nation erupted in outrage. The brutality of the regime's tactics, and the injustice of targeting young voices for political dissent, ignited mass protests across the country.

Faced with overwhelming public opposition, Roh eventually agreed to a free and democratic presidential election to be held the following April.

Ironically, despite facing strong resistance, Roh won the election because his main opposition failed to unite behind a single candidate, splitting the vote among three contenders. And so, the handpicked heir of a military dictator became a legitimate president — serving for five years — until the country elected its first civilian leader, Kim Young-Sam, in 1993.

Although I was quite young and ignorant at the time about what was going on, I do remember one day at middle school learning that a couple of my favorite teachers had been fired because of their outspoken protests for democracy. I never heard what happened to them after that.

All of this was happening around me, and I'm sure it was influencing me in ways I didn't fully understand at the time. But as for me, I wasn't thinking about politics or democracy. All I wanted was to fit in. I just wanted to learn how to be Korean and find a way to get on with my life.

Before I continue, I want to give a quick heads-up: the next part of my story might feel like it moves a bit faster. In the earlier chapters, I focused on shorter periods, usually a year or two at most. But starting with this chapter, and in the ones that follow, I'll be covering broader stretches of time, mainly my middle school and high school years together. Because of that, some parts may feel like I'm jumping around or rushing through. But everything I share connects as part of the same journey. So if it feels a bit fast-paced at times, I hope you'll bear with me.

After graduating from Keisung Elementary School, I attended an all-boys' school called Sim-In Middle School. It was one of two middle schools within walking distance of our home, about 15 minutes away.

For those who know the Korean language you may assume that "Sim-In" means "citizen", but that word would be "si-min" (시민). "Sim-In" (심인) means a person of the mind. It's actually a Buddhist expression for someone who can control his mind and find inner peace.

As the name suggests, it was a Buddhist school. Most students were either Buddhist or atheist, and fewer than 5% were Christian. I chose to go there because I thought it would be an opportunity for me to share the gospel of Jesus with those who didn't know Him. Sometimes, I am amazed at how innocent, pure, and zealous my faith for Christ was at that time. You might even say I was naive.

I immediately saw that the kids were much different from my peers at elementary school. I was no longer with the rich and elite of Daegu, but among the common-folk and the street rats. Many of them had dirty clothes and dirty faces. Most of them didn't have a shower or a bathtub at home, so they couldn't bathe or wash their hair regularly. Many smelled funny, and you could see dandruff on their shoulders. Back then, all the boys had to cut their hair super short, like soldiers. At the time I thought it was to bring everyone into uniformity, but perhaps it was because of lice.

I'll never forget the first day of school. The first thing they did was line us up by height, shortest to tallest, and give each of us a number based on that. There were 57 kids in my first-year class, and I was the second tallest, so my number was 56.

Before the first class began, all the boys did what boys normally do without adult supervision — they joked around and got loud and obnoxious to the point that the classroom seemed like a zoo. But as soon as our homeroom teacher entered, the boys went dead silent, as if dreading what might come next, whatever that might be. What came next was indeed very unexpected and tone-setting for the rest of the school year... and very frightful for me.

"*Joobeon! Joobeon!* Who's the *joobeon*?" the teacher called out.

I had no idea what he was talking about. I'd never heard of a *joobeon* before, so I just sat there without knowing a thing.

He called out again, more angrily this time, "*Joobeon!* Where are you guys?"

Because he said "you guys" I figured it was more than one person.

Then he said something that made my heart drop, "Number 56 and 57! Where are you? Come out to the front right now!"

Wait! Number 56? That was me. One of the people our teacher had been angrily calling for was me. But I had no clue why he was calling me, what a *joobeon* was, why I was one, or, most importantly, why he was upset with me.

To explain, the *joobeon* literally means a weekly number, and it refers to the class attendants. Every week, according to their numbers, two students were to come to class earlier than everyone else, sweep and mop the floor, and fetch drinking water in the large tin water kettles provided in the classroom. In between classes, they were to wipe the chalkboard and prepare the class for the next teacher and lesson. After school, they had to stay behind to sweep and wipe the floors again, and generally clean up. The following week, two other students would become the *joobeon*.

As I said, I had no idea I was the *joobeon* for that first week. Actually, it was written in the top corner of the chalkboard: "*Joobeon*: numbers 56 and 57." But on the first day, I had no idea what that meant or that it was referring to me, so I paid no attention.

When I finally realized I was one of the people he was calling out, I shyly went out in front of everyone. This other tall boy stood beside me. I wasn't sure what was happening, but the other kid stood there with his head hung low and avoided eye contact with the teacher, as if he had done something wrong, so I followed suit. Then the teacher told the other kid to raise his head, and as soon as he did that, with all the strength in his body, he took his right hand, and slapped that kid in the face with his full force. The kid went flying half-way across the front of the classroom.

I was in shock! What the heck was going on?

Then, before I had time to brace, I felt a solid thud and smack across my left cheek, and I also found myself flying across the room. This happened a couple of more times to each of us.

The teacher said he had come into the classroom earlier in the morning and saw dust everywhere and everything in a mess. He scolded us for not doing our jobs and said we needed to get our act together. Then, he told us to go back to our seats and left the room.

Honestly, more than pain and more than embarrassment, I was just really puzzled to know what I had done so wrong. After I got home that day, I told my mom what had happened and asked her about it. She said I didn't do anything wrong, but then she also explained what a *joobeon* was so I'd know what to do the following day. I got to school really early the next day and cleaned up the classroom so well that you could have eaten your lunch off the floor.

Looking back now, here's what I think was really going on: my only "crime" was being bigger than all the other kids. That made me the perfect target — a kind of sacrificial lamb at the start of the school year. I say that because this pattern repeated itself every first day of school throughout middle and high school. It seemed like every teacher felt the need to assert authority, to make an example of someone — and the biggest kids were always the easiest to use for that purpose. Sometimes, that someone was me.

You see, back in the '80s and early '90s, teachers used two great motivators in school. The first, and perhaps stronger of the two, was fear. Teachers would hit you, slap you, force you to kneel on your desk throughout the entire class, or they'd take you outside and force you into a plank position, where they'd leave you there for the full 50 minutes of class. Occasionally they'd come around to spank you with a two-by-four piece of lumber (that they would call a pointing stick, but in reality, everyone knew it was for hitting students).

Students would be punished for anything and everything. If you were late for school, you'd be punished. If you were caught talking in class, you'd be punished. The worst was if your grades were poor, or even if they were good but you had dropped in rank, you'd be punished.

This one time our class came in near last place, compared to the other classes. So for an entire hour, our teacher took the whole class outside, and forced us to hold the plank position with our bare knuckles on the concrete floor. If anyone struggled staying up, he'd go around with his two-by-four and give them a good whooping on their butts.

In those days, people didn't bathe at home, and so I remember going to these public baths, and there I saw all these boys with black and blue bruises on their butts or their upper hamstring areas. It was just common for kids to walk around with bruises like that.

Before moving on to the second motivator, there's one more thing worth mentioning about teachers punishing students: for some, it was also a means of earning extra income. At the start of the school year, you would see the teachers punishing everyone equally harshly. But after a while, it seemed like they showed favoritism. That was because some parents would pay them a "friendly" visit, and pass along a thick envelope to "thank" them for their hard work and attention to their kid.

I'm not saying all teachers were like this, but there were enough to the point it was pretty obvious. If you had rich parents, chances are you had a more comfortable school experience. If you were poor, you got ready for more beatings.

In 2016, the Korean government passed a law forbidding teachers from receiving gifts from students or parents, and one of the reasons was to prevent things like this.

The other motivator was grades. If you got good grades, or if you ranked high in your class or your school, you were highly recognized by teachers and among your peers. Sometimes you were even given special privileges.

It was these kids who were not only the class presidents, but they were also the ones who managed to avoid getting punished. Sometimes, teachers even gave them the authority to punish other kids. You would think that the other boys would not stand for such favoritism, but it was just understood that if your grades were superior to others, you were just considered a better citizen, and you deserved such privilege. It's no wonder that privilege through merit is so deeply ingrained in my generation.

I had already had a bad experience over this back in elementary school. My sixth grade teacher pulled me aside one day after an exam. With somewhat of a disgusted look on his face, he scolded me for having bad grades. There was a kid named Maru who had come from Germany around the same time I had come from America, and the teacher said to me, "Maru seems to be able to do well in school, but what's wrong with you? Why can't you be more like him?"

I was twelve years old at the time. I had never felt so small in my life.

Because of this, I tried hard at school to get good grades. I can honestly say that I tried harder than most other kids. Every day I'd come home and review all the material from that day, and then do further reading for the following day. The first monthly exam we had, I finished in the top 10 of my class, and even ranked within the top 50 or so in the whole school.

However, that initial confidence didn't last long. My Korean was still very limited, and as the academic subjects grew more complex, I found myself falling behind. Early in the school year, there wasn't too much to grasp, so I relied heavily on memorization — even though I didn't truly understand most of what I was reading. It was all just rote learning.

But eventually, my brain couldn't keep up. I couldn't retain all the facts, and more importantly, I couldn't make sense of the *why* behind what I was studying.

To make things even harder, back in the '80s, Koreans still made heavy use of Chinese characters. They were everywhere — on signs, in books, even in newspapers. If I was already struggling to keep up with Korean, how was I supposed to learn Chinese characters on top of that?

And yet, without knowing them, I couldn't fully grasp even some of the basic lessons in school. It felt like another wall I couldn't climb.

Before long, I found myself completely lost. Forget trying to excel in the classroom — I was just scared every day that a teacher might beat me for not knowing the answers. I felt stupid, helpless, and anxious.

Still, I tried. I really did. I wanted so badly to be good at school. But no matter how hard I worked, things only seemed to get worse with each passing year. To this day, I honestly don't know how I graduated or made it into high school.

That said, not everything about my time at Sim-in Middle School was bad. I left with a few fond memories, ones I still carry with me.

For starters, I remember that during middle school, I was incredibly faithful in my devotion to God — mostly because I was terrified of what each school day might bring. I'd wake up before anyone else in the family and spend at least 30 minutes each morning reading the Bible and praying.

On the inside cover of my *Good News Bible*, I even wrote, "A chapter a day keeps the devil away." The "devil" here might have meant Satan... or maybe it was just my mean teachers. Either way, I was serious about it.

I stopped that morning routine once I got to high school, after I made some friends who started leading me in other directions. But sometimes, I miss that little middle school boy as he would pray, "Dear God, please protect me today and keep me from being hit by my teachers. Amen."

Another fond memory I have from this time is during *Shimhak* classes. This one may surprise you a little.

In the Buddhist middle school I attended, we had to participate in a class called *Shimhak* once a week. Similar to how you may have to attend chapel once a week at a Christian school, at a Buddhist school you had to take a meditation chant class, and that's what this was.

There is a Buddhist chant that most monks memorize and repeat as they rhythmically beat their wooden hand-held prayer sticks. You may have seen some monks do this at a temple or on the street. It is called *Banyashimgyeong*, roughly translated as "heart sutra". During *Shimhak* class, we had to memorize this chant.

However, this was not the easiest thing to do. It was quite long, and none of it made any sense. The teacher, who I suppose was a monk, would hit us if we could not memorize it. But of all the kids in our class, I was the first to memorize the entire *Banyashimgyeong*.

This wasn't because I wanted to be a devout Buddhist, but rather to show all the Buddhists at school that this Christian boy could be the salt and light of Jesus in that place. I would do so by excelling at the one Buddhist class in school better than everyone else. I guess missiologists might say I was taking on an incarnational mission. In other words, trying to be the message rather than preaching it. I don't know if it influenced anyone toward Jesus, but I was always proud that I could recite the *Banyashimgyeong* better than any Buddhist in my class.

After my time at Sim-in Middle School, I entered Keisung High School. This belonged to the same Christian foundation as the elementary school I had attended of the same name.

By then, we had moved to a new apartment complex called Hwangjae Mansion or "Emperor's Mansion". It was a small apartment complex, but it had a study room for residents to use, and in my first year of high school, I went there almost every night and studied until midnight. One time the apartment security guard found me there by myself, and he asked me if I was a senior preparing for my college entrance exam. When I told him I was just a first-year student, he told me that I would be someone important one day. I hoped he was right.

The whole purpose of Korean high school is to try to get into a good university, and so I tried really hard at first. But no matter how hard I tried, even in high school, the same cycle continued for me. I started off really strong, but after a few months, I couldn't keep up, and eventually started dropping in rank pretty badly. My Korean just never got good enough for me to understand everything fully, and I just continued to struggle.

After a while, I just took to daydreaming in class. It's funny what I'd daydream about, because it was about going to university in America. I watched lots of college football on TV through the American Forces Korea Network, which was the U.S. military's network, accessible on regular terrestrial TV back then. I would daydream about going to such football powerhouse schools like Notre Dame, UCLA, Oklahoma, or Florida. But really, who was I kidding? I just knew I was going to be stuck in Korea, and I would end up being a loser.

My parents would try to help me out in other ways outside of school. I tried private tutors, but it was a waste of time. They all seemed to get frustrated that I couldn't follow along their explanations. I asked my parents for money so I could go to private *hagwon* academies. Even there, I would start the first few classes trying my best, but after a while I realized that I just couldn't keep up. Later, instead of paying for classes, I would just take that money and go out and play with my friends.

During my senior year, all students were required to stay after school and study until 10 p.m. They called it "free study time," but there was no freedom in it. You just had to, and if you didn't, you'd get in trouble.

Those with high prospects of going to good universities would go after that to study even more at private academies. Then they'd go to private study rooms called *dokseosil*, which offered nothing more than a desk in a small and cramped room full of other desks, which other students would rent out. There, they'd study until 2 a.m. before going home to sleep for three hours, before going back to school the next day. The average student got three or four hours of sleep a night in their senior year, and hardly saw their parents or siblings except on weekends, and even then it was only when they came out of their rooms for bathroom breaks or meals. Although never scientifically proven, everyone believed that the less you slept, the better the university you would get into.

As for me, I soon realized that no matter how hard I tried, I just couldn't get it, and so I gave up. It seemed like a waste of time for me to stick around after school to study until 10 p.m., so I'd look for opportunities to play hooky.

There was a traditional market next to Keisung High School, so if I had money, I'd sneak out to a *pojangmacha* street food cart, and order some squid sashimi, marinated in spicy chili sauce and greens, and I'd down that with a bottle of *soju*, while chain smoking old *88 Light* cigarettes, the most popular brand at the time. Since our school didn't have uniforms, I could pass as a college student and no one asked how old I was. And besides, back then, there didn't seem to be an age limit on drinking or smoking (or at least if there was one, nobody seemed to care).

After school was out at around 10 p.m., I'd go to a *dokseosil*, not to study, but to drop off my backpack so I could go out and play. I can't remember where I went at that time of night. Sometimes I'd go to a video room where I'd watch a movie on VHS. Sometimes I'd go to a comic bookstore. Sometimes I'd go to a karaoke with friends. Sometimes I'd just hang out outside somewhere. I would go anywhere and do anything, as long as I didn't have to study.

I know that this all makes me seem like some sort of delinquent, but it wasn't all a sad story for me. There was this one time when I was nationally recognized for my excellence in academics, although I feel like I kind of cheated.

In Korean schools, the three most important academic subjects are Korean, math, and English. These are the subjects that carry the most weight on the college entrance exams.

Of course, out of the three, English was my strength, while I struggled badly with Korean and math. English was the one subject where I could actually hold my head high.

One day, in my second year of high school, my teacher approached me and asked if I wanted to enter the Daegu City English competency competition.

I took a day off school and went to a testing facility with students from other high schools in Daegu. I spent the entire day taking English assessments — reading comprehension tests, a listening section where I had to answer questions after hearing recordings of Americans reading random passages, and finally, a spoken interview with someone who seemed like an English professor.

Even though I spoke fluent English with a perfect American accent, I couldn't help but feel like I was cheating just by being there. So during the speaking portion, I actually faked a slight Korean accent — just enough so I wouldn't get caught.

When the results came out, I had placed second in the entire city. I was honestly a little surprised I didn't come in first. But still, everyone told me it was quite an accomplishment.

Later, I was invited to compete in the national English competition, which was held in Seoul. That's where I met the first-place student from Daegu, a senior from another boys' school. We ended up sharing a room during the event. He turned out to be some kind of genius. Not only had he placed first in English, but he had also ranked number one in a similar math competition.

The day of the national competition was eye-opening for me. There were high school students from all over the country, and many of them spoke English just as fluently as I did. Some even dressed very American, like they had just stepped off a plane. It turned out, they had lived in the U.S. too. It was the first time in my life that I met others like me.

I still remember one girl in particular. She was a year older than me and incredibly pretty. We had a great conversation in English, and I remember how refreshing it felt to speak so freely with someone who understood me in that way. I never saw her again, but I really wished I could have. That brief connection stayed with me.

A couple of weeks later, the results came back: I had finished second place in all of Korea.

At school, they honored me during a student-wide assembly. They said I had put the name of Keisung High School in the national spotlight. My name was even mentioned in a local newspaper.

To give you an idea of how big a deal this was — my dad and I were invited to the ballroom at the Presidential Blue House in Seoul, where I got to shake hands with President Roh Tae-Woo.

To this day, I still laugh when I think about it. All of that recognition came because of my "outstanding command of the English language" — something I had never really worked that hard at in the first place.

Despite some fond memories, I must admit that most of my time in school during my teenage years was very difficult. I was not ready for the race that I was suddenly placed in. Many days, I felt like a loser.

During some of my quiet times with God, I would cry to Him, "My God! My God! Why have you forsaken me?" This cry comes from Psalm 22, and is understood to be a prophetic statement of what Jesus called out on the cross in His final moments. This was the one moment in His life when He knew He would be completely separated from His Father.

I can't say that I knew exactly how Jesus felt, but there were many times during my youth when I felt so forsaken and alone that life felt like a cruel and excruciating crucifixion in the Korea of the 1980s.

When I look back on my life, starting from that time, I realize I carried a lot of anxiety with me. It was like I had a chip on my shoulder — a constant need to prove to the world that I wasn't a failure. I held a quiet grudge against everything. There was a lot of darkness in my heart — anger toward Korea, resentment toward my teachers and classmates, and even bitterness toward my parents for bringing me here and making me face these harsh realities.

In other words, I was living with my own personal *han*. It became rooted very deep in my soul. At times it drove me to try to be great. And at other times, it crushed my spirit.

If you were a youth in Korea during those years, chances are you know exactly what I'm talking about. You, too, may carry a similar *han*. It's the same *han* that still runs deep in the Korean people today — the *han* that drives Korea to be number one, no matter the cost. Because in this mindset, anything less simply isn't good enough.

There is a Korean saying that expresses this very well. It goes like this, "What a dirty world we live in that only recognizes those who are number one!" It's an expression that many Koreans know very well. It's an expression of disdain for this system of having to be the best. And yet, people continue to try to be the best.

A passage in Psalm 46:10 has been very helpful for me over the years: *Be still and know that I am God.*

This is not the easiest thing for me to do, because, since I was a kid, I was told not to be still, but to keep striving and accomplishing. And yet, the greatest peace that can be found can only come from being still... and knowing that He is God, and I am not; that He can do all things, and I am limited; that He is good, and because I am His precious son, I am good enough just being me. That's very hard for me, but I have to try. If I want peace in my life, I have to.

Since childhood, I have tried to be number one in most everything I did. Even though there was a time in my youth when I seemed to have given up, I know that the spirit inside me to be number one was never fully extinguished. It's not a very good spirit, because it's a spirit of being constantly dissatisfied with who you are. It's a spirit that Koreans all share. Even though Korea is doing so well right now, it's just not good enough; nothing is good enough unless you are the best, or that's what we've been told our whole lives.

Today, as a pastor serving in Korea, I have a heart for the Korean people so they can be released from their *han*. However, the only way we can truly be released is not by more competition and accomplishments and awards, but by being still and trusting in God. But it starts with me.

I've been fighting this personal *han* all my life, but lately I feel I hear God speaking to me saying, "Stop trying so hard, because you are good enough just as you are. I sent my Son for you on a cross because you are worth it."

I need to believe that. The Korean people need to believe that too.

Chapter 9

Han's Fun-Loving Brother, *Heung*

I n the previous chapter, I wrote about the communal *han* in the Korean soul. In contrast to this, there is something else all Koreans share. It is called *heung*, and it refers to the shared desire to laugh and have fun.

Although *han* and *heung* may seem like opposites, they're more like two brothers with very different personalities — inseparable, and deeply dependent on each other. Because there is so much *han* — grief, struggle, and pain — woven into the Korean soul, there must also be *heung* — joy, excitement, and celebration — to balance it out.

In real-life terms, it looks like this: because we suffer so much and work so hard to succeed, we *have* to blow off steam by finding joy in music, dance, food, and laughter. And it's only after that release that we're able to return to the daily grind of our hard lives.

Closely related to *heung* is something called *eumjoogamoo*, which means to "drink booze, sing, and dance." All Koreans love that stuff. Some consider this to be a bad trait, as if all Koreans are alcoholics and out-of-control partiers, but I don't entirely agree with that. If you want to know the Korean spirit just a bit, you can't do it without a little *eumjoogamoo*.

Of course, too much of anything can be a bad thing. I learned that the hard way when I started my first job in Korea.

One night, after a typical company dinner in Seoul's Yeouido district, I ended up having to call my brother Albert to come pick me up, literally, off the street.

These team dinners usually started with barbecue and lots of soju, followed by a stop at a beer hall, and then wrapped up at a *noraebang* karaoke room, where we'd sing until it was time to go home, or until we passed out.

That night, I had drunk so much I lost my coat and my cell phone, and ended up taking a nap on the concrete pavement in front of the KBS Annex building. It was the winter of 2000, and the temperature was below freezing. If my brother hadn't come, I'm not sure what may have happened to me. This was clearly not my finest moment.

There's more to the story, but I'll save it for later.

I once witnessed an unexpected display of *heung* at a funeral. I had always assumed funerals were supposed to be quiet, somber events. But there, at one table, people were getting drunk on *soju*, laughing, even singing. At first, it struck me as inappropriate, even rude. But then I realized: this was their way of celebrating the life of the person who had passed. It was their *heung* meeting their *han* — a release, a remembrance, and a way to carry on.

Another example takes me back to my childhood. At family gatherings, relatives would line up the kids and make us do silly dances before handing out the cash gifts traditionally given on major holidays. I was so embarrassed at the time. But I have to admit, everyone, even us kids, ended up laughing.

And here's one more: in high school, lunchtime in the classroom sometimes turned into a mini concert. Someone would play a cassette, and when a favorite song came on, kids would grab their spoons and start singing into them like microphones. Others would get up and dance, and the more ridiculous, the better. We'd all laugh until our stomachs hurt. It was a silly but much-needed break from the pressure cooker of school life.

These are all different examples of *heung* that I've experienced, and I look back on most of those times with fond memories. Anyone who has experienced Korean culture, whether in Korea or overseas, would have experienced both *han* and *heung* in one form or another. For many people, myself included, because *han* is so deep, you need *heung*. Sometimes the best thing you can do in the face of hardship is simply just to have a little fun and laugh.

From a young age, sports have always been one of my favorite ways of having fun. I don't know if I ever had real potential to make it professionally in anything, but I was good enough to be better than most others.

One of the things I was always good at was running. I was fast. I loved to run everywhere, even when I didn't have to. I mean, why walk when you can run, right? I find this funny today, because I see my son Juno do the same thing.

In the sixth grade, some teachers noticed this and put me on the school track team. I ran in my first official competition that spring. I had always run on grass or concrete pavements in America, or on the dirt-covered playgrounds of Korea, but I had never run on a real track in real spikes before, so it was all new and exciting.

In the first 100-meter heat against kids from other schools, I came first in just a little over 12 seconds, which is fast for a sixth-grader. That race put me straight into the finals, and I started to imagine winning it all. I could be the Korean Carl Lewis.

But when I saw the other kids in the line-up I was stunned. They were so big and tall. It was as if they had all grown up on steroids or some other growth hormone. I finished in fifth place, which wasn't bad, but that was clearly the end of my sprinting career. There would be no Olympics for me in the future.

One of the things that disappointed me the most when I first got to Korea was that there was no American football. I loved football and missed it. Actually, I just missed America a lot.

Then, one day, my dad bought me a basketball. We went outside on the dirt courts of Keimyung University, the college campus where we were living on at the time, and Dad started shooting around with me. I soon came to really like basketball. It wasn't football, but it kept me connected to America.

I started watching lots of NBA basketball games on TV. My middle and high school years coincided with the golden age of basketball with the likes of Magic Johnson, Larry Bird, and Shaquille O'Neal dominating the hardwood. But the king of them all was Michael "Air" Jordan. Everyone wanted to be like Mike.

As for me, though, since I was little, I have never been a fan of the favorites. I cheered for the underdog. So instead of Michael Jordan, I always preferred "The Human Highlight Film," Dominique Wilkins of the Atlanta Hawks. Dominique was another star player during that era, but he always seemed to lose to Michael Jordan, whether in basketball games or slam dunk contests. (Actually, everyone lost to Michael Jordan.) I'd watch many of Dominique's highlights and tried to play like him. Later, when I played high school basketball, I even took on the number 21 because that was Dominique's number.

I used to go outside and practice by myself all the time. I worked tirelessly on my shooting and dribbling, determined to get better. I even asked my dad to buy me a book so I could learn the proper shooting technique and different drills to improve my game.

When I was out on the playground, I'd always pretend I was in a real NBA game. And of course, I was the star player with the ball in the final seconds. My team would be down by one, ten seconds left on the clock, and it was all up to me. I'd sink the game-winning shot miraculously, every time. And if I missed? Well, then I'd pretend I got fouled, just so I could take one more shot and win it at the free-throw line.

Since I usually practiced at the courts on Keimyung University's campus, random college students would often see me shooting around alone and ask if they could join. Before long, I was playing pick-up games with guys much older than me, and more often than not, I'd beat them. Granted, a lot of them weren't very good. Some even played in dress shoes, which was risky, especially if they landed on your feet.

One time, a guy in hard-soled shoes jabbed his heel right into my toe. It hurt like crazy. When I took off my shoe to examine it, my toe was bent in a really awkward direction. I thought it was broken. But when my dad took me to the doctor, the guy just popped it back into place, and that was that.

I was by far the best player among my peers. I still remember one time in my first year of middle school, I played a pick-up game with some other kids my age — and out of 100 total points, I scored 90. These are the kinds of things legends are made of. And yes, I promise it really happened.

In the third year of middle school (ninth grade in the U.S.), our school held a basketball tournament between the third-year classes. I knew this was my one shot at glory, and I didn't want to disappoint.

Not only did we win the tournament, but I dominated the final game and was named MVP. It should have been a glorious day.

But on the bus ride home, I ran into some kids from a gang called *Ddongpari* — which literally means "dung flies." They were infamous at our school for picking fights with other students, and even with teachers. They had a terrible reputation for violence, and they were eventually expelled.

They told me to hand over all my money. I didn't have much, but I gave them whatever I had. Even after I got off the bus, they didn't leave me alone. They followed me and eventually cornered me in an alley. One of them took off his belt and started making whipping gestures with it. I was terrified. They looked like they were really going to mess me up.

A woman happened to walk by and saw what was happening. I looked at her with pleading eyes that said, *Please help me*.

She glanced at the boys and muttered, "Hey, don't bother that kid," before quickly walking away. She was probably scared herself.

So I did the only thing I could in that moment. At the top of my lungs I yelled at them in English, "F***ING LEAVE ME ALONE!"

I thought they'd undoubtedly beat me up after that. Instead, they were intrigued and asked me to teach them some cuss words in English. I obliged and taught them all the classics, along with what they meant. After that, they suggested we should be friends and hang out sometime. Who knew that cuss words could save lives and make friends?

When I got to Keisung High School, I found out the basketball team had already heard of me. They recruited me right away.

But you have to understand — there were actually two basketball teams. The *official* team was made up of kids who were hand-picked at a young age to be trained as future professionals. That's all they did — play basketball, all day. Most of them didn't even attend class.

Sadly, very few ever made it to the pros. And by the time some realized basketball wasn't going to work out, it was too late to catch up academically. A lot of them ended up drifting into street gangs.

Then there was the *unofficial* team — the hobby club for regular students like me. That's where I belonged. We had uniforms and played in a tournament in the spring and the fall each.

Sure, I had dreams of playing in the NBA one day. But the truth is, most of us were just amateurs chasing one glorious moment we could someday exaggerate and brag about to our wives and kids. (Not that mine seem to care much.)

I was a starter on that team from my first year. Of course, there were upper-classmen on the team I had to defer to, which meant I didn't get to take a lot of shots. Still, on the first play of my first game, I came out smoking with a full-court fast break dribble down the middle of the defense, finishing with an acrobatic reverse lay-up off the glass. Even though this wasn't the NBA, I gave it my all and wanted to do well and win.

In my second game, I had the most points on our team, and had a one-handed lay-up over this poor defender, who I almost jumped over. Dominique would have been proud.

By the time I reached my senior year, it was supposed to be my moment to shine. I was finally the team captain, and there was no one left to defer to. This was *my* team.

But that all changed just before our spring tournament.

The other guys recruited a new player — someone who had quit the *official* team the year before. Technically, players who were officially registered weren't allowed to compete in unofficial tournaments (it would've been like an NBA player joining a YMCA league). But since this kid had been off the official team for a year, he was eligible to play for us.

It's not like he was that much better than the rest of us, but when the tournament came around, everyone just kept passing him the ball, thinking he was our best shot at winning. So he took *all* the shots. Sure, he made a lot... but he missed a lot, too.

As for me, I spent most of the game just running around the court, getting in a solid cardio workout. I scored two points. We lost.

That was the final game of the final tournament before I graduated.

Even though I loved the game, the elite basketball teams never gave me a second look. I had only played club ball, not at their level. And just like that, any dream I had of going pro quietly fizzled out.

I still loved playing basketball with my friends, though. Even while attending Keisung High School, I'd often go back to the old Sim-in Middle School and spend all my free time playing pick-up games there. The court wasn't anything fancy — just a paved blacktop — but back then, it was the only one around that wasn't a dirt court, so it became a popular spot for kids from other schools to gather. But no matter who showed up, everyone knew that was our court. My friends and I were the kings of that blacktop.

Most of the friends I played with were from different high schools. Some were old buddies from middle school who'd gone on to other schools, while others were kids I met simply by showing up and playing ball at that court. I was actually closer to those guys than I ever was to my high school basketball team.

Sometimes, I'd spend the entire day at the court, playing over 10 games in a row. By the time I got home, I was completely wiped out.

I remember one time, I was lying on the floor watching TV after a long day of basketball when every muscle in my legs suddenly cramped up. The pain was unbearable. I had to beg my brothers to each grab a leg and stretch me out. If you can picture it, I looked like a Thanksgiving turkey on the living room floor, and my brothers were each pulling on a drumstick, trying to rip it off for themselves. I had never felt pain like that before. But sure enough, I was back on the court the very next day.

Sometime in the middle of my final year of high school, things started to change. My friends began bringing girls to the court, and then bottles of *soju* and packs of cigarettes. Before long, it wasn't unusual to see guys taking smoke breaks between games. And instead of hydrating with Gatorade, they'd down shots of liquor.

At first, I didn't understand it. But over time, with all my friends doing it, I followed suit.

There were days when I'd leave the house telling my parents I was going to play basketball, which I technically did, but by the time I got home, I'd reek of alcohol. On those nights, I'd lie and say I had dinner with friends, then head straight to my room so I wouldn't get caught. I did that more times than I'd like to admit.

Over time, my friends stopped coming to the basketball courts. They had moved on to other interests, and if I wanted to see them, I had to go where they were — usually at a *restorang* (which was how Koreans back then pronounced "restaurant").

But these places weren't what you might imagine. Sure, they served food, but it wasn't anything to write home about, because food wasn't really the point. These were hangout spots where college students, and even high schoolers, would drink beer, chain-smoke cigarettes, and sometimes meet up with girls. If you didn't have money, you could just order a soda and sit there for hours. That's what my friends often did.

I still preferred being on the basketball court, and at first, I wasn't comfortable with places like that. But if I wanted to stay connected, I had to adjust, so I did my best to go along.

One time, one of the guys I played ball with found an envelope full of cash on the street. To celebrate, he took all of us to our usual *restorang* — a place called Box Nine — and ordered *kimchi* fried rice and pork cutlets for everyone. We usually only had enough money for street *ramyun*, so this felt like a feast. We devoured the meal and enjoyed every bite

Not long after we finished eating, another friend showed up looking distraught. With a long face, he told us he had left home that day with an envelope full of cash to pay for his *hagwon* classes, but somewhere along the way, he had dropped it. He'd retraced his steps and searched everywhere, but couldn't find it.

It didn't take long for us to put two and two together. We realized, with growing horror, that we had just stuffed our faces with our friend's lost money.

The kid who'd found it fessed up. To make peace, he bought the guy an extra-large pork cutlet and a beer, and just like that, it was settled. I know that might sound silly, but that's how simple our friendships were back then.

That month, instead of going to *hagwon*, he spent most of his time hanging out with us at Box Nine.

Of course, I was a teenager back then, and as you may have noticed, teenage boys tend to have one thing on their minds: meeting girls. But in Korea at the time, most middle and high schools were either all-boys or all-girls, so opportunities to meet the opposite gender were rare.

Still, there were always one or two guys who somehow had connections with girls from other schools. They'd organize something called a *mee-ting* — a group blind date between a few guys and a few girls. Everyone would meet at a *restorang*, pair off, and try their best to impress each other.

As for me, I was never really into that Korean style of dating, so I skipped out more often than not. The few times I did participate, they ended up being pretty disappointing.

I remember this one time, there was this one girl I liked, but when I tried to show interest, she told me she didn't like me — but her *friend* did.

That "friend" wore dark glasses and had oddly pink-dyed hair tied up in a bun. She sported a Mickey Mouse t-shirt, very short red shorts with black stockings, and sparkly pink sneakers. She also smoked Marlboro Reds. She told me she liked my "American style" and had dressed like that for *me*. I wasn't feeling it.

These things just never seemed to work out for me. I still wanted to meet girls, but just not like that.

There was this one kid, though, who had some pretty solid connections with girls. One day, he invited me to join him on a *sogae-ting*. Unlike a *mee-ting*, which was done in larger groups, a *sogae-ting* was more personal — usually a one-on-one or double-date setup.

My friend, Bongjin, told me he had invited two really pretty girls and wanted me to come with him. I was flattered that he picked me. But then, right before we walked into the *restorang*, he pulled me aside and said, "Hey, can you only speak in English?"

He wanted to use me, his cool American friend, to impress the girls. I wasn't thrilled about the idea, but I went along with it anyway.

When we met the girls, I slipped into a full-on alter ego. I told them I was a 20-year-old law student at Harvard, visiting family in Korea, and that I didn't understand a word of Korean.

I'm not sure if they bought it. To be honest, I'm not sure they understood anything I said, since all I got in return were blank stares and the occasional awkward giggle.

It was funny at first, but after about an hour, I was over it. I stood up, looked at them, and in perfect Korean said, *"It was fun. I'll see you next time."* Then I turned and walked out.

You'd think Bongjin would've been upset, but apparently, the girls were still impressed, so it worked in his favor.

After that, he kept inviting me to tag along when he met new girls he wanted to impress. I never ended up with any of them myself, but at least I got to meet some, which was more than a lot of guys could say.

Bongjin was also the one who took me to my first *noraebang* back in high school. At the time, *noraebangs* — Korean karaoke rooms — were a brand-new trend, but they caught on instantly.

A typical night out with friends followed a familiar pattern: first, you'd meet at a *restorang* for some food, then head to a *hof* — a Korean-style beer hall (for some reason, borrowing the German word for "courtyard") — and finally end up at a *noraebang*. That sequence is still common today, but I like to think my generation helped pioneer it.

Every time I went to a *noraebang* with Bongjin, he'd invite a few girls and try to impress them by belting out dramatic rock ballads, even though he wasn't a particularly good singer.

I still remember the time he sang a classic called *Nae Sarang Nae Gyeotae* ("My Love, Stay Next to Me") by Kim Hyun-Sik, a beloved artist who passed away in 1990 from liver disease. Mid-song, Bongjin actually started crying. He told the girls that the lyrics reminded him of the pain he felt over the singer's death.

Now, I'm not saying Kim Hyun-Sik's passing wasn't sad, but between Bongjin's off-key singing and his overly dramatic explanation, I could hardly keep a straight face. What shocked me most, though, was that the girls *loved it*. They totally ate it up.

I wasn't much of a ladies' man in high school, and if you ask my wife Juri, she might tell you I'm still not. I was awkward around girls and never quite knew what to say.

But there was this one time when I shined, if only briefly.

During my senior year, our school hosted an open house art festival, which meant students from other schools, including girls' schools, were allowed to visit our campus. I wasn't the artsy type, so I didn't have anything on display.

But my friend Bongjin was part of the school's broadcasting club. They played music during the festival and took song requests from the DJ booth. He let me get on the mic a few times to introduce some Western pop songs, and I gave it my best shot with my smooth American accent.

While I was hanging out at the booth, a cute girl came by to request a song. I saw my chance. I asked Bongjin if I could introduce it. He gave me the nod.

So I got on the mic and said, "The next song is Bryan Adams' *Everything I Do, I Do it For You*... and this one's from me to you."

Yeah. I still throw up in my mouth a little when I think about that. But hey — high school me thought that was pretty smooth. And you know what? I walked that girl home that night. So in my book, that was a big win.

I don't remember most of the girls I met in my teenage years — their names, or even what they looked like. But I *do* remember one girl I really liked. This was back in middle school. Her name was Jenny Kim. She was a Korean-American girl I met at church.

From middle to high school, my dad used to take me and my brothers onto Camp Walker, the U.S. military base in Daegu, every Sunday to attend chapel. My parents had membership at the base golf course, which gave them access, and by extension, they could take us to church there. We went there because they wanted us to keep up our English. Eventually, the chapel granted us our own Sunday access passes, so we could go on base without an escort.

Jenny was an army brat, so I only saw her at church, and only for a couple of years, since military families usually moved around every two years or so. I never asked her out. I was way too shy. At the time, my face was covered in pimples — one of my unfortunate nicknames was "*sea cucumber*" because of all the blemishes.

But every Sunday, I looked forward to going to Camp Walker Chapel, not just because I got to be in *America* for a few hours, but because I got to see Jenny.

Nothing ever happened with her. It was just a puppy-dog crush. I used to doodle her name in my notebook. I'd work out at home to *Eye of the Tiger*, hoping that if I bulked up, maybe she'd notice me. I'd try to style my hair before church, even though my Korean school made me cut it so short I usually just looked like a monkey.

Looking back, I don't think it was just Jenny's looks that drew me to her. I think she represented something bigger — something I felt I'd lost when we moved back to Korea. To me, Jenny was the girl I always imagined I'd date in America, and being around her made me feel like maybe, just maybe, that dream wasn't completely gone.

Who I Am

It was never meant to be — not with Jenny, and maybe not with that American dream either. But every Sunday, for a little while, I got to sit in church, see her smile, and feel just a bit closer to the life I missed.

Another fond memory from Camp Walker Chapel was a kid named Tim Buck. Don't let the last name fool you. Tim was Korean-American. His last name was actually the same as mine, but his family had decided to spell it differently.

Tim's dad was a U.S. Army chaplain stationed in Daegu for a couple of years. He had an older brother named John, who was in high school and looked like the quintessential American jock — the kind of guy I always wished I could be. He also had a younger sister named Sharon, a sweet little girl who was usually glued to their mom's side.

Our dads were friends, and they wanted us to become friends too, so I'd have someone to speak English with, and Tim could pick up more Korean language and culture. We hung out a lot and stayed over at each other's homes. Tim lived on base, so every time I stayed with him, it felt like I'd stepped back into America for a day.

Tim was cool. He had that laid-back California vibe I admired so much. He wore Polo shirts and OP (Ocean Pacific) shorts, classic white Reeboks, and Aviator sunglasses. He styled his hair with mousse and combed it to the side like Tom Cruise. This was around the time *Top Gun* was all the rage, and out of all the kids I knew, Tim pulled off the "Maverick" look best.

He even told me about a couple of shops just outside the back gate of Camp Walker that sold knock-off American brands. I begged my parents to take me there, and soon I was sporting my own fake Polos and Reeboks.

Tim was the one who first introduced me to heavy metal music. I had a Samsung Mymy cassette player. He had a Sony Walkman. And in that Walkman was *Mötley Crüe*.

That was my gateway into a whole new world of rock ballads, angst-filled drum beats, and guitar riffs. Poison, Skid Row, Guns N' Roses, Bon

Jovi — you name it. Those bands helped me get through the emotional rollercoaster of puberty.

I still remember when Tim's mom found out what he was listening to. She gave him an earful for blasting what she called "the devil's music." After all, she was a pastor's wife.

One time, my dad signed both of us up for a Korean church youth retreat. Neither of us actually attended that church, so we weren't too thrilled about going. We felt totally out of place, but it was okay, because at least we had each other.

Eventually, the other kids started warming up to us. We realized this one morning when we both woke up with marker drawings all over our faces. That, apparently, was the unofficial sign of acceptance.

I was really sad when Tim and his family shipped out for their next military assignment. Saying goodbye wasn't easy.

Even now, I sometimes wonder where he is and if he still remembers me. Actually, I wonder that about a lot of my old friends, whether they ever think about me, the way I still think about them.

Despite all the hardships of my middle and high school years — what I often call my "dark ages" — I have to admit, it wasn't all bad. I did my best, the best way I knew how. And I have no regrets. Sure, there are things I'm not exactly proud of, but I'm also not ashamed to share them, because even those moments helped shape who I am today.

And you know what? I had fun. And sometimes, just having fun is enough.

Chapter 10

When the World Stood Still

H ere are a few things that happened in 1992: Bill Clinton became
president of the United States, the first McDonald's opened in
Beijing, and Jack Nicholson shouted angrily at Tom Cruise, "You
want the truth? You can't handle the truth," in *A Few Good Men*.

It was also the year of the LA riots — a moment that shook both Korean
and American communities around the world.

The unrest began after the acquittal of four white police officers who
had been caught on video brutally beating a Black man named Rodney King
during an arrest. But while the verdict sparked outrage across the country,
much of the violence ended up centered in Koreatown, where tensions
flared between African-American and Korean-American communities.

Both sides took up arms. And yes, there had been years of underlying
animosity, misunderstandings, and mistrust. But what many people don't
realize is that a big reason Koreatown became the epicenter of the chaos
was because, in anticipation of protests, the police formed a barricade —
not around Koreatown, but around nearby Beverly Hills, a predominantly

white neighborhood. As a result, much of the anger, looting, and violence was funneled into Koreatown, where Korean-Americans were left to defend themselves, often with no help from law enforcement.

In Korea, one of the biggest moments of 1992 was the debut of a new hip-hop group called *Seo Taiji and Boys*, fronted by former heavy metal bass guitarist Seo Taiji, along with Lee Juno and Yang Hyun-Suk.

While they were virtually unknown outside of Korea, they became an instant sensation at home with songs like *Nan Arayo!* ("I Know!") and *Hayeoga* ("Anyhow Song"). These three young men are now widely regarded as the pioneers of modern K-pop — a genre that would eventually spread across the globe.

Yang Hyun-Suk later founded YG Entertainment, which went on to produce internationally acclaimed artists like Big Bang, 2NE1, and Blackpink.

However, that was all secondary for me because 1992 was the year the world stood still.

The year 1992 was when I became a high school senior. And in Korea, that meant one thing: the college entrance exam. Nuclear war could have broken out. The world could have been ending. But none of that would have mattered, because for Korean seniors, everything revolved around that one test at the end of the year.

Senior year was basically a prison sentence. We weren't allowed to hang out with friends, go to the movies, play sports, or do anything remotely fun. The only thing we were supposed to do was sit at a desk from early morning to late at night, cramming as much information into our brains as humanly possible. Whether we were on the bus, on the toilet, or in the bathtub, we were expected to have flashcards in hand. It was goodbye to the rest of the world until the exam was over.

Well... that's how it usually was, and still is for most Korean students. But for me, it was a little different.

Unlike many students around me, I was fortunate — my parents weren't overly strict when it came to my study schedule. For the most part, they left it up to me and supported me in whatever way I said I needed. Honestly, I don't think they would've pressured me even if I had never studied a single day.

It wasn't that they didn't care. I think they just didn't want me to get swallowed up by the pressure. They trusted in God, and maybe even in me, that somehow, I'd figure it out. So while I didn't face the kind of academic pressure at home that some of my friends did, I still wanted to do well. I tried my best. But the truth was, Korean academics were really tough for me.

A few months into the year, I realized my grades weren't going to cut it for the top universities. Every parent in Korea dreams of sending their child to one of the "SKY" schools — Seoul National, Korea University, or Yonsei. But for me, that just wasn't going to happen.

I started looking at other schools in Seoul — Sogang University, Hankuk University of Foreign Studies, Hanyang University — but even those felt out of reach.

Eventually, I found one school that seemed like a realistic option: The Presbyterian Theological University.

Now, I'm sure some students are genuinely called to study theology from a young age. But I wasn't one of them. And if I'm being completely honest, the admission standards for that school were... let's just say, not the highest. I couldn't help but feel that at least a few of the students there were enrolled simply because they had nowhere else to go.

Well, that was exactly my situation. The Presbyterian Theological University felt like my only realistic option. So, I thought about it. Briefly.

I even caught myself wondering: *Could I sneak off campus for cigarette breaks between Intro to Old Testament and Systematic Theology? Could I survive morning Greek classes while hungover... and still find time to check out the girls?*

Still, deep down, I figured I'd probably get kicked out after one semester. So I didn't consider it for long.

My dad also had some wisdom on the matter. He told me that unless there was a specific purpose, or a clear calling from God, it was probably best that I didn't go.

I agreed.

Next, I started looking into universities in Daegu, since regional schools were generally easier to get into than those in Seoul. I was on the social sciences track, not the math, engineering, or science one, so my main options were Business or English Literature. I figured if I could get into an English Lit program somewhere, it'd be smooth sailing. English was, after all, my strong suit.

The problem was, English Lit was a very popular major. And despite my fluency, I still couldn't find a single university, even among the weaker ones in Daegu, where I measured up well against the other applicants.

These days, Korean high schoolers take the college entrance exam known as *sooneung*. You take the test first, then apply to schools and majors based on your score.

But back in 1992, the system was different. I had to choose which university and which major I wanted to apply to *before* taking any exam. Then, I would take a specific entrance test *at that school for that major*. As you can imagine, competition was intense, especially for the more popular majors at top universities. If you didn't make the cut, that was it. You were out.

You could try again later with a different school or major, if there were any openings. But if you had your heart set on that first choice, you'd have to wait and try again the following year. Some people would repeat the process two or even three times, all in pursuit of that one dream program.

For some of the most sought-after majors at the top schools, the acceptance rate could be as low as 1 in 50, or even worse. That's why it was so important to track the competition trends that the big academic *hagwons* (cram schools) published. If the odds looked too steep, you had to pivot, either to a different major or a less competitive school.

When I looked at the competition for English Literature programs across all the schools, my heart sank. The odds were steep everywhere. I knew I didn't stand a chance. Even at my dad's university, which wasn't exactly considered a top-tier school, I knew I wouldn't make the cut.

After weighing all my options, I told my parents I wanted to try a different route. I knew academics were tough for me, but I was athletic, so I suggested trying to get into college through a sports-related major.

For those majors, although there's still a written exam, the physical test carries much more weight. It includes running, jumping, push-ups, sit-ups — basic fitness drills. I figured that with a little training at a *hagwon* that specialized in athletics, I'd have a much better shot.

As always, my parents were supportive. If I had a plan and was willing to work hard for it, they were willing to stand behind me. But my senior-year teacher was completely against it. He flat-out refused to sign off on my application and insisted it was better for me to stick with an academic major.

I tried to convince him, but he wouldn't budge. To this day, I still don't know why. And because of that, I had no choice but to keep studying.

My mom saw how frustrated and discouraged I got while studying, but she never stopped believing in me. She would always tell me, "You're a smart boy."

She'd remind me how, back when we lived in Tennessee and New Jersey, my teachers used to rave about how bright I was. But every time she said that, I hated it. All I could think was, *Then why didn't we just stay in Tennessee or New Jersey?*

One time, my dad asked me how things were going. Like most teenage boys, I usually kept to myself, but he just wanted to know what I was thinking — where I hoped to apply, what my plans were.

I couldn't answer him. I had nothing to say because, truthfully, I felt like I had no hope. I had never felt so lost in my life. I looked him in the eye, and suddenly, I just couldn't hold it in anymore. I started crying like a baby.

"I'm trying," I told him. "I really am. But I just can't do it. I feel so stupid."

He hugged me and said it was all going to be okay. But all I could think was, *How? How is it going to be okay?*

Eventually, Dad encouraged me to apply for the English major at Hankuk University of Foreign Studies in Seoul. I knew I was out of my league. But he just wanted me to give it a shot and do my best — especially since English was the most heavily weighted subject in the entrance exam.

My chances were slim. But at least I had a puncher's chance.

The day before the exam, I remember taking the train to Seoul and thinking, *What am I doing? This is so stupid! There's no way I'm going to get in."*

When the exams were over, I stopped by a small restaurant, ordered a bowl of hot soup and a bottle of *soju*, and drank my sorrows away. When the results came out, wouldn't you know it, I didn't get in.

My fallback plan was to apply for the American Studies major at Keimyung University, where my dad taught. It wasn't as popular as the English Literature major, so I thought there might be a chance. But even there, I couldn't make the cut. I was so disappointed in myself and thought, *How dumb must you be to not even make it in there?*

The following year, after all my friends went off to college, I enrolled at a *jaesoo hagwon* — a private academy for students who hadn't gotten into university and were trying again. It felt just like school. We showed up early in the morning, sat through classes all day, and stayed late into the night to study.

The place was full of people from all walks of life — graduates of different high schools, people from different backgrounds and ages. Some were already in their twenties, making their third, fourth, or even fifth attempt to get into their dream university. Others had already been accepted somewhere but wanted to upgrade, so they were starting from scratch again.

As for me, I wasn't even sure why I was there. I was just following this path because that's just what people said you're supposed to do. But my heart wasn't in it. Why would it be? I didn't have much hope. And honestly, it's hard to find anything sadder than a young man without hope.

Eventually, I dropped out of that *hagwon* because I felt like it was a waste of time and money. I stayed at home and tried to prepare on my own. But when exam day came around the following year, it wasn't much different from the year before, and once again, I was left feeling foolish and hopeless.

On the other hand, my parents never gave up on me. This time, not just Mom, but even Dad, insisted I wasn't stupid. In fact, they said I was brilliant. Dad went so far as to say I was smart enough to go to Harvard. So he signed me up for the American SAT and started requesting application materials from overseas universities — Harvard, Yale, Oxford, Cambridge, and a few others.

Then he took me to my old high school to request transcripts to be printed out in English. I was sure the teachers would laugh in my face when he told them I was applying to Harvard. But to my surprise, they were excited and more than willing to help. When I saw the translated transcripts, they looked a lot better than I remembered. Go figure. I guess the school didn't mind polishing things up a bit if it meant one of their students might get into an Ivy League school. It would make for great publicity, after all.

However, Harvard said no, and so did all the others. Even my fallback, Rutgers in New Jersey, which I was almost certain I would get into, turned me down at their main campus in New Brunswick. They did offer me a spot at their Camden campus, but I wasn't interested in going there.

That was it. It was finally validated. Park Eun-Seuk was officially stupid after all! Nobody wanted me, and I had no hope for the future.

Then one day, Dad came home with an envelope — an application to the University of Canberra in Australia. Never in my wildest imagination had I considered going to Australia.

I hear that UC is a well-respected university today, but back in 1993, it was just getting started. I recently checked their website, and it says the school was founded in 1967. But I vividly remember hearing that it was only about three years old when I applied. I'm not sure which version is right.

What I do know is this: if you were an international student from Korea who had absolutely no business getting in, but were willing to pay full tuition, they were more than happy to accept you. I think the unofficial school slogan was: "If you can pay, you can stay."

And so, in the winter of 1993 (which was the start of summer in Australia), I found myself in a dorm room in the middle of nowhere in Canberra, surrounded by funny-sounding people I didn't know.

For the first time in my life, I was completely on my own. No family. Nothing familiar around me. No clue what I was doing there. It was one of the most unnerving experiences I've ever had.

To make matters worse, the airline had lost my luggage somewhere between Sydney and Canberra. I had nothing with me except whatever I'd carried onto the plane.

I felt completely lost.

Later that first day, I decided to wander around campus, hoping to make sense of where I was. Australia felt different, not just from Korea, but even from America. I didn't know if I liked it or not. I just knew I felt confused, out of place, and deeply alone.

Then suddenly, without warning, a kangaroo jumped out from the bush. A real, wild kangaroo!

It just stood there for a moment. I stared at it. It stared back. For maybe five minutes, we just looked at each other. And then, just as suddenly as it had appeared, it was gone.

It's not easy for me to look back on those days. At the start of this chapter, I said the world seemed to stand still for high school seniors in Korea, and when it did, there were many moments when I wished I could jump off and not be part of it anymore. I don't mean that I wanted to die, or anything that drastic. But I definitely didn't want to be part of the relentless cycle of how things were "supposed" to be.

I hated the system. I never felt like I belonged in it. So many times, I felt crushed by the weight of it all.

My teenage years, especially my senior year, were some of the darkest times of my life. And if I ever had the chance to go back and jump off that spinning world, I might just take it.

In Isaiah 41:10, the Lord says to His people: "So do not fear, for I am with you; do not be dismayed, for I am your God. I will strengthen you and help you; I will uphold you with my righteous right hand."

There were many days during that year — 1992, and much of 1993 — when I felt completely alone. I've already mentioned how hopeless I often felt. But I was also anxious. Afraid.

Still, the truth is: God was always with me. I didn't always know it. I rarely felt it. But He never left me.

While I was trying so hard to follow the world's script and meet its expectations, God was writing a different story for me. I wasn't stupid. I wasn't a failure. God was simply leading me on a path that didn't look like everyone else's.

Sometimes, I think back to that moment on campus when the kangaroo jumped out of the bush and stared at me. And I wonder, maybe that was God's way of saying, "I see you. I've always seen you."

No, I'm not saying God is a kangaroo — that would be silly. But in that strange and quiet moment, when I had never felt more alone, I felt seen. And somehow, I didn't feel quite so alone anymore.

Chapter 11

A Fish Back in Water

Proverbs 16:9 says, "A man may plan his own course, but the Lord makes his steps secure." In other words, we can make what we think are the best plans for our lives, but ultimately, God is the one in control.

However, when I was 19 and starting my first semester in Canberra, I had no plans, nor any clue what I was doing there. That time in my life is pretty much a blur.

During my adolescent years in Korea, I had lost a lot of self-confidence and developed a kind of loser mentality. I had already convinced myself that no matter how much effort I put in, I was bound to fail, so why even try?

It didn't help that when I got to college, I learned that attending classes was optional. More often than not, I chose not to. I also quickly discovered that the legal drinking age in Australia was 19, and that there was a bar on campus. So, I decided that beer was a better way to spend my parents' tuition money than sitting through boring lectures.

But drinking alone gets old fast. Wanting to meet people and make friends, I connected with the Korean Students Association (KSA) of Canberra. I quickly became popular, not because of any academic brilliance, but because I had a unique talent: I was the best beer chugger in town. And if there's one thing that unites Koreans no matter where you are in the world, it's our love for a good drink.

Early in the semester, the KSA hosted a sports day, and I finally had a chance to show that I could do more than just drink. I dusted off my basketball skills and even knocked a home run in a casual softball game. That day was when I made my first friends in Australia.

But not long after, the KSA started to take a more serious turn — planning community service events and drafting a new organizational constitution. As things got more official, my interest started to fade.

One thing that did come out of my brief involvement was that I met a girl. Her name was Cathy, and she was a Korean-Aussie from Sydney. I thought there might be some chemistry between us. For a brief moment, I even imagined: *What if we hit it off? What if I marry her and settle down in Australia?*

It wasn't America, but it wouldn't be the worst outcome.

But then came Mikey, her best friend since childhood. Out of nowhere, he got jealous and made a move on her. It didn't help that he was tall, muscular, and good-looking. Any thoughts I had about staying in Australia through marriage were quickly dashed.

I lived with six others in a small co-ed dormitory, which was more like a small house. In the '90s, MTV had a show called *The Real World*, where random people from all walks of life came together and lived in a loft in New York City. The dorm was kind of like that, except this was on a small college campus in Australia.

Among my dorm-mates were a couple of guys from Sydney, a girl from Adelaide, one from Perth, a Latina girl from Argentina, and a Chinese guy from Singapore, who, unbeknownst to the rest of us at first, had his

Singaporean girlfriend secretly move in with him. Those two pretty much kept to themselves, but the rest of us became fairly friendly with one another.

One bit of culture shock for me early on was to see everyone hanging out in the kitchen together in the mornings, waiting for the shower to be free — girls in nothing but bathrobes, and guys wearing only towels wrapped around their waists. And I knew they weren't wearing anything underneath because they would sit at the table with their legs spread wide, revealing evidence that no one wants to see... and once seen, cannot be unseen.

I tried to get to know my dorm-mates, and the best way to do that was to party with them. A few times, we all went together to the on-campus bar. The first time was definitely eye-opening. One of the guys met a girl at the bar, and right in front of all of us, they started making out. And when I say "making out," I mean they were going at it like they were trying to taste each other's tonsils. I had never seen anything like that in Korea. Honestly, I found it kind of disgusting, especially since everyone around them was cheering them on.

After going to the bar a few times, my Aussie dorm-mates started just bringing beer back to the dorm. Occasionally, this guy named Daniel would also bring back marijuana. One night, he invited me and the others to join him out back. Everyone else seemed to be laughing and having a great time. I tried it too, but I didn't feel anything, so I never tried it again.

Then Daniel handed me a canister of nitrous oxide. I had no idea what it was, so he explained that it was the same stuff as the laughing gas you get at the dentist's office. He was giggling like some kind of sinister wind-up clown doll and insisted I give it a shot. I must not have inhaled it properly, because again, I felt nothing. But I didn't want him to think I was ungrateful, so I forced out a giggle and pretended to join in. That was the first, and last, time I ever tried any of that stuff.

In Australia, they play three kinds of sports using a rugby ball: Rugby League, Rugby Union, and Australian Rules Football. One of the guys, Brad, was really into Aussie Rules, but to be honest, I couldn't tell the difference between any of them.

Brad would often try to get me to come out and play with him. I gave it a shot a few times, but it was just too different from what I was used to, so I didn't enjoy it much. Still, I did enjoy watching the games with him on the *telly* (that's what Aussies call a TV). For a little while, I even became a fan of the Canberra Raiders.

Besides that interaction with a kangaroo on my first day, I never saw one again. But I did have another memorable encounter with a different kind of famous Australian species.

One morning, I was taking a shower when I noticed a spider descending on a web inside the stall. I didn't think much of it, so I playfully splashed it with some water a couple of times. Then I finished up, stepped out, and headed back to my room to get dressed.

A few minutes later, there was a knock on my door. One of my dorm-mates, Donna — still in her bathrobe and looking completely hysterical — stood there, wide-eyed.

"Oh my gosh! You have to help me," she said. "The most venomous spider in Australia — the red-back — is in our shower!"

So I followed her to the bathroom, and sure enough, there it was — the same spider I had just been messing with a few minutes earlier. It suddenly dawned on me that not only could that thing have killed me, but even worse, when they found my dead body, I would've been lying there completely naked. Now *that* would've been embarrassing.

I don't actually remember what I did with the spider. I think I killed it. Whatever the case, I'm glad I didn't die in the shower that day.

Because our dorm was more like a small house, we didn't have the typical campus cafeteria to rely on for meals, so we had to fend for ourselves. Occasionally, I'd make the 20-minute trek to the main campus cafeteria to eat something, but most of the time it felt like too much effort, and the food options weren't all that great anyway. My favorite quick bite-to-go was the crispy Chinese spring rolls. Looking back, that was one of my "save me from starvation" foods, along with Snickers bars and plain white rice with *gochujang* (Korean red chili paste).

Most of the time, I'd walk about 45 minutes to the Woolworths grocery store to stock up on food I could prepare easily. I say "prepare" food, but what I really mean is heating up cup noodles, not actually cooking, because I didn't know how.

One time, I was at a friend's house and tried to microwave some chicken with barbecue sauce. I undercooked it so badly that the bones were still red. But the others took a bite and said, "Oh yum! Apricot chicken!" They had no idea there wasn't a drop of apricot in it. Since they seemed to like it so much, I just smiled and kept my mouth shut.

One food in Australia that I never understood was Vegemite. Every morning, I'd see people slather it on their toast like it was the most normal thing in the world. It looked delicious, sort of like chocolate spread. I had no idea it was actually some kind of salty, bitter yeast extract.

One day, I bought a jar and generously spread it on my toast. Big mistake. It was the most disgusting thing I had ever tasted. I spat it out immediately and grabbed a butter knife to scrape the residue off my tongue. Never again.

My go-to meal was Top Ramen. You could buy about ten for a dollar, so I'd grab an assortment of beef, chicken, and shrimp flavors. Frankly, after about the third packet, it all started to taste pretty bad, even for a college student. But on some days, it was the only food I had. So I'd cook it up and eat it with a jar of Australian-made *kimchi*, which tasted nothing like the real thing.

One day, my Singaporean dorm-mate Tim, and his girlfriend Stephanie, somehow got their hands on some actual Korean *ramyun*. Tim was cooking up a spicy *Shin Ramyun* soup — one of my all-time favorites. Stephanie was making *Chapagetti*, a black bean sauce *ramyun* that's meant to be served without soup.

I was so jealous. The smell of the spicy broth filled the house, and I wished I could have just one string of noodle or a sip of that soup. But I was too embarrassed to ask.

Then came the real tragedy. They ruined the *Chapagetti*. Instead of pouring out the water after boiling the noodles, like you're supposed to, they just dumped the sauce packet straight into the water. Total rookie move. It completely destroyed the flavor.

I was heartbroken. That poor *Chapagetti* never had a chance.

As I mentioned, most of that first semester was not spent focusing on studies. Instead, I met a couple of older Korean *hyoungs* (older brothers), who took a liking to me. They both lived together in a house a little ways from campus.

The older guy was a *Taekgyeon* instructor, who was trying to start a dojo in Canberra, so he got me to do it as well.

Taekgyeon is an ancient form of martial art from Korea, much older than Taekwondo. Its most distinct feature is the three-step dance you're supposed to do to remain in fluid rhythm while you try to strike and kick your opponent in the head and body. I wasn't very good at it, but since no one else knew what it was, there was a brief time when I could go around bragging that I knew how to do some martial arts.

Besides that, we mostly just sat around and watched Korean dramas all day. I had never really gotten into Korean dramas before then, but since all three of us weren't particularly into school, and had nothing better to do, we just hung out, ate plain rice with *kimchi* or *gochujang*, and watched the latest bootleg dramas on VHS tapes. We rented them from the only Korean grocery in town, which just happened to be operated out of the private garage of this one Korean family.

Yes, I was a slacker and very happy about it. I have no regrets about my time in Canberra. It was my first time away from home and on my own, and in many ways, I was lost. But I still enjoyed it, and I would never trade it for anything.

After that first semester, my parents had me fly back to Korea for summer break (which was winter in the northern hemisphere). It felt strange being back. The first thing I noticed was that everyone looked Korean and spoke Korean. Even though I had lived in Korea for nearly a decade before going to Canberra, the country felt unfamiliar all over again. It was unnerving, and I quickly remembered how much I didn't like it. I was eager to return to Australia.

But as it turned out, I never did.

During that semester in Canberra, I was talking with my dad over the phone one day, and he suggested I apply to the University of Oregon. He had a friend who had just returned as an exchange professor and told him that Oregon was really nice because it had lots of trees. Literally, that was the selling point — trees!

"Why don't you consider it?" he said.

I remember thinking, *Oregon? Oregon? What the heck is in Oregon? Why would I ever want to go there?*

The truth is, I was enjoying my slacker lifestyle in Canberra. I tried to make excuses to my dad, telling him I was already settled. University in Australia only takes three years, so I could finish early and start looking for a job in just a couple of years, which would be faster than most of my Korean peers.

I also told him I didn't know anything about Oregon. We had grown up on the East Coast of the U.S., and we didn't know a single person out there. It just didn't make sense. On top of that, it was already pretty late in the year, so I wasn't even sure if the University of Oregon would still accept my application.

Dad said that he understood, but what was the harm in at least applying? If accepted, I could still decline if I didn't want to go. And it turned out that Oregon was still taking late applications, so it wasn't too late.

After I returned to Daegu that winter, I received a letter from the University of Oregon congratulating me on being accepted to their prestigious academic institution. I wasn't so sure about the "prestigious" part. From what I understood, as long as you had the money and were willing to pay full international tuition, Oregon pretty much accepted anyone. That suspicion was confirmed when I arrived on campus and saw foreign students cruising around in BMWs and Benzes, but I didn't see many of them in the classrooms or the library.

I really didn't want to go. But Dad was persistent, always trying to convince me that a degree from Oregon would carry more weight than one from Canberra.

Before I knew it, I was on a Korean Air flight to San Francisco. From there, I transferred to a much smaller plane that landed at the tiny airport in Eugene, Oregon.

I didn't travel alone, though. My youngest brother Daniel came with me. Just as I had struggled in school back in Korea, Daniel had his own challenges. So my parents decided to give him a fresh start too — they sent him to Oregon with me so he could attend South Eugene High School.

Mom came along shortly afterward to help us get settled, but she had to return home not long after. So, soon it was just Daniel and me. I did my best to take care of him, almost like a dad. But the truth is, I *wasn't* his dad — I was just his older brother trying to act like one. And he didn't like that. We had a lot of differences, a lot of arguments. We were both going through our own growing pains, and living together was not a very pleasant experience for either of us.

Despite some of the unique circumstances, I'd still say my time in Eugene was one of the best periods of my life. I only spent two years there, since I transferred to one of Oregon's most hated rival schools — the University of Washington — after my second year. But out of all the places I've lived, Eugene remains the one I feel most fondly and nostalgically about.

That said, when I first arrived, it felt like one of the strangest places I'd ever been, maybe even stranger than Australia.

On my first day in Eugene, I took a walk around campus to check it out. As I walked, everyone I passed looked at me and said, "Hey, how ya doin'?" People in Eugene were surprisingly good at greeting one another, even complete strangers on the street.

Coming from a place like Korea, where no one ever says "hi" to you unless they know you, it felt strange and uncomfortable. I didn't know how to respond, so I just kept to myself.

What was even weirder was that half the people around campus had dreadlocked hair and were dressed in tie-dye and/or hemp. One random guy in dreads, who smelled strongly of incense, approached me and said, "Yo, man! You looking for a good time?"

I wasn't exactly sure what he meant, but I had a pretty good idea he was trying to sell me some pot. Honestly, I was a bit scared, so I didn't say a word. I just picked up my pace and hurried along.

Later, I found out that some people affectionately referred to the University of Oregon as the "University of California–Berkeley in Eugene." Apparently, a lot of the hippies from Berkeley in the '60s and '70s had migrated north, and Eugene had become something of a new-age hippie capital of America.

The first apartment Daniel and I lived in was on 1455 High Street. It was called The Elms, but I remember thinking it was more like Elm Street after the horror movie series from the '90s that featured Freddie Krueger. It was a nasty old cockroach-infested place that smelled like hemp and urine.

When we first moved in, there was a European couple living in the apartment above us who had sex every night. After enduring their grunting, heavy breathing, and squeaky bed, it got really awkward having to say "hello" whenever I ran into them outside.

The most embarrassing moment came when Mom came to visit. One night, she heard the strange noises from upstairs and looked at me, wide-eyed, and asked, *What is that?*

I froze. I didn't know what to say, so I think I told her they were doing aerobics or something. I'm pretty sure she didn't believe me.

A few months later, the Europeans moved out, and new neighbors moved in. They weren't sex maniacs, but instead, heavy metal-loving skinheads. They loved to blast Metallica, Pantera, and Iron Maiden until 3 a.m.

Not long after, another set of neighbors moved into the unit next to us. These guys were lowrider-driving Mexicans who blasted Latino music all day, every day.

One day, the heavy metal skinheads upstairs and the Mexicans next door even decided to throw a party together. We weren't invited, but the music was so loud it felt like we were smack dab in the middle of it.

There was never a dull — or quiet — moment at The Elms.

Sometimes we even had some unexpected guests.

One time, Daniel and I had ordered some takeout roasted chicken, but it wasn't very good. I decided to throw it away, so I went outside with the box in hand. As I approached the trash bins, I suddenly heard a strange voice from the shadows.

"Yo! Hey man! You got any food?"
I looked around, but couldn't see anyone.
Then I heard it again, "Yo! Down here!"
I looked down and saw a homeless hippie hiding underneath the staircase.
"I've got some leftover roasted chicken I was about to throw out. That's about it," I said.
"Yo! Can I have that? I'll remember you forever."

I handed it to him and watched as he started devouring it right there in the shadows. Then I quietly walked back into the apartment — and locked all the doors and windows.

However, that wasn't the most unwelcome guest we had. The worst guests were the cockroaches.

In 1996, there was a movie called *Joe's Apartment* about a guy named Joe and the thousands of cockroaches who shared his apartment. Although the movie was fictional, it could've easily been about me and my apartment at The Elms.

By day, you wouldn't see a single roach. But at night, if you walked into the kitchen and flipped on the lights to grab a glass of water, you'd see dozens of them scurrying away into the cracks.

When Dad came to visit during that first semester and saw the roaches for himself, he didn't hesitate. The very next day, he broke our lease, found us a new apartment, and we moved out. The next place we moved into was a nice two-story townhouse — free of strange people hiding under staircases, and definitely free of cockroaches.

About 30 years later, I went back to visit Eugene. I was surprised — and oddly happy — to see that The Elms was still there, pretty much just as I remembered it.

Back in middle and high school in Korea, I used to daydream about going to a university in America, mostly because I wanted to be part of the college football culture. It all seemed so exciting to me. But when I found out that Oregon wasn't exactly known for football, I was a bit disappointed.

During new student orientation, though, they handed out tickets to an Oregon Ducks football game at Autzen Stadium. I couldn't help but think it was kind of silly that the school mascot was the "Fightin' Ducks" — and even sillier that their mascot looked just like Disney's Donald Duck. They weren't highly ranked, and no one expected them to win many games that year.

Up to that point, Oregon was known more as a track and field school and had never been considered a powerhouse in the major college sports. Its biggest claim to fame, outside of athletics, was that it had served as the filming location for the 1978 college party movie *Animal House*, starring the late John Belushi.

The first game I went to was against the University of Utah Utes. I didn't know anyone there, and I had no friends, but I still found a seat by myself in the student section. It was a tight game from start to finish, but in the final minutes of the game, the Ducks defense forced a fumble, and one of the defenders scooped up the ball and took it in for what ended up being a game-winning touchdown. The entire student section went crazy, and I was high-fiving every person around me. I was starting to like the Ducks.

In my first year at Oregon in 1994, the Ducks football program had one of the most iconic plays in its history. It was against their rival, the Washington Huskies — one of the top teams in the nation at the time.

Late in the game, the Huskies were marching down the field and were just yards away from a game-winning touchdown. But right at the goal line, Washington quarterback Damon Huard threw an errant pass — right into the hands of Ducks defender Kenny Wheaton. Wheaton intercepted it and took it 99 yards the other way for a touchdown.

Many say that single play marked the turning point for Oregon football forever.

I wasn't at the stadium, but I was at the student union, watching the game with other students. And when that play happened, I went absolutely bonkers. I couldn't believe it. To this day, I don't think there's ever been a single sports moment that got me so fired up in the moment. It still gets me emotional whenever I think about it.

From that day on, I was an Oregon Duck. And nothing could ever change that.

That year, Oregon went on to win the Pac-10 Conference championship and earned a spot in the Rose Bowl against Penn State — something no one ever expected. Not long after, Oregon football began to rise in national prominence. The university's most celebrated alum — and the founder of

Nike — Phil Knight, started pouring millions of dollars into the program. His support transformed Oregon into one of the most successful and recognizable college football programs of the last 30 years.

Another wonderful memory I have of Oregon, and something I'm always grateful for, is the people.

At first, I didn't know anyone, so I joined the Korean Student Association to try to make some friends. Initially, it was mostly Korean international students who joined, hoping to connect with others who spoke their language. I was totally fine with that. At the time, I just wanted to meet people.

Somehow, I ended up organizing a pizza and bowling night, and that's when I first met some of the Korean-Americans on campus.

Even though Koreans and Korean-Americans might look alike, they're often worlds apart. One group are foreigners navigating an American world. The other are Americans who didn't think much about their Korean identity until college, when they realized that people tended to group by ethnicity. That's when many Korean-Americans started feeling the need to explore their roots and connect with others who looked like them.

You might think that because they share the same ethnicity, they'd naturally have a lot in common. But more often than not, they each feel more at home in their own worlds. So they don't tend to mix unless there's a reason. But if there's anything that can bring both sides together, it's pizza and bowling.

As part of the KSA, I also took part in the Korean Cultural Night festivities during my freshman year. I had no prior theater experience, but somehow, they tasked me with the challenge of putting together a play.

With the help of several friends I had met through a Christian fellowship group, we created a musical adaptation of an old Korean folk tale called *The Old Man and His Mole*. It's a quirky story about an old man who has a beautiful singing voice but also a hideous mole on his face. One day, some demons from the forest come out to devour him, but the old man cleverly tricks them by claiming that his ugly mole is the secret to his magical singing powers. He ends up selling the mole to the demons for a hefty sum of gold.

Not only did I produce the play, but I also starred as one of the demons. It was a lot of fun, and an experience I'll never forget.

Although KSA was fun, I didn't end up making many close friends there. Most of my best friendships were formed through the Korean-American Christian Fellowship, or KACF.

A guy named Nick, whom I knew from KSA, invited me to check it out. The first meeting was a bit of a culture shock. The room was full of Korean faces, but everyone was speaking fluent English. That alone felt strange to me.

Even in Canberra, most of the Koreans I met still felt more Korean than Australian. But at KACF, even though everyone looked Korean, it was obvious they were very Americanized. It was something I wasn't used to, and it caught me off guard.

They started the meeting with an icebreaker game to help people get to know one another. One of the leaders told half the room to take off one of their shoes and toss it into the middle, while the other half had to go pick a shoe, find its owner, and strike up a conversation.

I was in the group that had to throw in a shoe. Had I known about this in advance, I definitely wouldn't have worn one of my old, dirty, beat-up shoes from Korea. Unsurprisingly, no one picked it, and I was left standing there without a partner.

I still remember the guy leading the event picking up my shoe, inspecting it briefly, making a frowning face, and tossing it aside. It wasn't exactly the warmest welcome to a Christian fellowship group. I remember thinking, I'm never coming back. But for some reason... I did.

KACF was eye-opening for me because I had never seen young people worship God like this, especially in English.

As a kid, I had gone to the Camp Walker Chapel in Daegu, but back in middle and high school, most of us were there just because our parents made us go. It felt more like an obligation than something meaningful. But here, at KACF, it was different. These students *wanted* to be there. They wanted to worship God. And that desire was infectious. For the first time in my life, I found myself wanting to worship God too, not because my parents told me to, but because something in me was genuinely drawn to Him. At first, it was a great feeling.

However, it was at KACF that I also got my first taste of what it felt like to be punched in the gut by someone I trusted. Just as I was beginning to let my guard down and allow myself to be vulnerable, I got hurt badly by one of the older student leaders. And as a result, I turned away from God and faith for a very long time, well into my adult years after college.

At the aforementioned Korea Night performance, I had asked some of my friends from KACF to help out with the play, and they were happy to join. But one day, one of the upperclassman leaders pulled me aside and said, "Joe, what are you doing? Why are you leading our friends in a secular activity? Why are you leading them into sin?"

I was stunned. I didn't think I was leading anyone into sin. I was just trying to put on a fun play for Korea Night. How was that sinful?

I felt confused and deeply hurt. I had respected that person. But in that moment, I began to dislike him. He suddenly seemed so fake, and the whole KACF thing started to feel hypocritical to me.

I made up my mind: *If this is what it means to be a Christian, then I don't want anything to do with it.*

I still went to meetings for a while, mostly because some of my friends were there. But internally, I began pulling away. I started to not believe in God anymore. And slowly, the people around me at KACF began to feel two-faced and hollow.

Ironically, it was also during this time at KACF that I met some of the best friends of my life. I think a big part of it was because, for the first time,

I found myself in the company of people who were *like me*. They were Korean, but not quite Korean enough. They were American, and could function just fine in American society, but deep down, they sensed they weren't *fully* American either.

One of the first friends I made in Eugene was Nick. He was the older Korean guy who had first invited me out to KACF. Like me, he was from Daegu, but he had spent some time at a community college in Oklahoma before transferring to Oregon.

Nick was a big guy who spoke with a slight accent — a unique mix of the American South and southern Korea. Because we were from the same hometown, he took it upon himself to look out for Daniel and me. He'd treat us to meals, take us out to watch movies, and play basketball with us. I'll always be grateful for that.

One time, Nick invited us to the home of one of the Korean professors at the university. I wasn't exactly sure why we were going, but when we arrived, it turned out the professor and his wife wanted a night out. Without asking us, Nick had volunteered both himself and us to babysit their kids. Thankfully, the professor's wife had prepared a delicious home-cooked meal, so we weren't complaining.

After dinner, we were sitting in front of the TV watching a movie when there was a sudden knock at the door. Nick and I went to see who it was, and there stood a woman, visibly shaken.

"Please, you have to help me," she said. "There's a naked man in my apartment!"

We probably should've just called the police. But instead, Nick and I followed her back to her place to investigate. We walked through her apartment, checking each room and hallway. Everything seemed clear.

But as we stepped outside, we spotted him — a guy standing stark naked in the middle of the courtyard.

Without thinking, I took off after him. I caught up to him, leapt on his back, and locked in a full nelson wrestling hold, taking him to the ground. He fought back, flailing and trying to get free, but I cinched in tighter.

"Hold still or I'll break your arm!" I yelled.

That's when it hit me. I was lying on top of a completely naked guy. I was fully dressed, but still, being face down on the bare butt of a stranger was more than a little unsettling.

As it turned out, he was just a teenage boy, probably high on something.

"Murder, sex, death! Murder, sex, death!" he kept repeating over and over.

I held him down until the police showed up. They covered him with a blanket and took him into custody.

A few days later, I was at the local Korean church with Nick and Daniel, and I overheard some little kids talking about the incident.

"So the guy who caught him was huge! He was super strong," one said.

"Yeah, that guy was like a hero," another chimed in.

I stepped in casually. "You guys know who that was? That was me."

They just stared at me for a second, then shrugged and said, "Whatever," before turning back to their conversation.

Another good friend I had during that time was an upperclassman named Christian. He had come up from Southern California, where he was known as Steve, but he changed his name to Christian when he got to Eugene. I guess he needed a fresh start.

Like me, he was originally from Korea and still held a Korean passport. But unlike many other Korean international students, he didn't hang out much with that crowd. Instead, he mostly spent time with Korean-Americans. Still, every now and then, he gave off some serious FOBBY energy, especially with his silly Korean slapstick antics.

For example, one time we took a trip to Portland together and shared a motel room with twin beds. The next morning, he suddenly jumped into my bed, flashed a big, goofy grin at me, then jumped back into his bed and shouted, "Room 9!"

I didn't understand what he meant — until the awful smell hit me. That's when I realized "Room 9" was code for *banggu*, which means "fart" in Korean. He thought it was hilarious. I did not.

Christian and I did a lot together. Besides that trip to Portland, we also went skiing during the winters. The first time, he just showed up at my door one morning and said, "Come on. Let's go!"

I didn't even know where we were going, so I just threw on a jumper and a pair of blue jeans. Turns out, we were going to hit the slopes.

It was my first time, and I fell — a lot. By the end of the day, my clothes were completely soaked... and I had nothing to change into.

One time, we also did a road trip down to San Francisco, L.A., and Las Vegas with a couple of other guys. The group included Ben — the same guy who had tossed my shoe aside at that first KACF meeting — and another guy named Daesun. None of us were particularly close with Daesun, but somehow he ended up coming along.

We rented a tiny Ford Escort wagon, which we affectionately nicknamed "Betty."

None of us had much money, but we were hopeful. Our plan, if you could call it that, was to win big at the casinos in Las Vegas and use the winnings to fund the second half of the trip. (Never mind that, other than Christian, we were all underage.)

At Circus Circus, I hit a slot machine and quickly won about thirty dollars. But the celebration didn't last long. A security guard asked to see my ID, and I got kicked out immediately.

At another casino on the Strip, Daesun lost a couple hundred bucks at the blackjack table within the first hour. We had to pull him away, even as he insisted he was "just about to get hot."

After that, we decided to cut our losses and stick to enjoying the buffets.

On our drive back into California, we couldn't find an affordable hotel, so the four of us ended up sleeping in that cramped Ford Escort, parked somewhere in the California desert near Bakersfield.

Holidays were tough for Christian and me. When Thanksgiving came around, most of our friends went home, but Christian, my brother Daniel, and I had nowhere to go. So the three of us spent the holiday together, getting turkey and gravy sandwiches at the Denny's diner. It wasn't a traditional Thanksgiving dinner with all the trimmings, but for us, it was enough. It meant we didn't have to spend the holiday alone.

After college, Christian returned to Korea and found a graphic design job with a Japanese advertisement firm in Seoul. When I moved back to Korea in 1999, we reconnected and continued our friendship. Later, he moved to Hong Kong, where he landed a job with Nokia.

I tried to keep in touch and even had the honor of emceeing his wedding. But over time, we drifted apart. It wasn't because of anything either of us did — life just happened, as it does.

My best friend from Oregon was Jay Yeum. I still consider him one of my closest friends today, even though he lives in Portland and I live in Korea. We only see each other every three or four years, but when we do, we pick up right where we left off.

I first met Jay while playing basketball one day at the Esslinger Gym on campus. He and his roommate John walked in, both loud and obnoxious.

Well, more John than Jay. John loved to talk a big game, but he could never back it up on the court. And boy, did John talk. If basketball were won by words alone, he would be a national champion. Too bad his skills never matched his mouth.

At first, John's antics tainted my impression of Jay. But once I got to know him, I realized Jay was a really solid guy. He wasn't the best student, but he was hardworking and genuinely tried his best.

When I started feeling disillusioned with some of the hypocritical people at KACF, Jay felt the same way. Perhaps that's why we began hanging out more, just the two of us.

We did a lot of dumb stuff together.

One time, we went to Meier & Frank department store and bought linen sports coats so we could dress up like Boyz II Men. Then we drove out to the dunes on the Oregon coast in Florence, pretending we were in the music video for their song "Water Runs Dry."

Another time, we both shaved our heads. I did it because of a dumb dare from some of the guys. We were having one of those classic "boys' night" hangouts, and someone said, "Hey, let's all shave our heads!"

I went first. Then... no one else did. I guess the joke was on me.

Jay shaved his head for different reasons. He did it because he had really curly hair, and hoped that if he shaved it, his hair may grow out straighter. My brother helped him by putting shaving cream and a razor on his scalp. I still remember Jay screaming out, "Daniel, hurry up! It burns!" Unfortunately, Jay's hair never grew out any straighter after that.

Whenever McDonald's had their special 10-cent hamburger deals, Jay and I would make our way over and buy as many as we could. The limit was ten per person, so we'd each grab our ten, bring them back to his place or mine, and try to eat them all in one sitting. When you're a poor and hungry college student, you do stuff like that.

Then, we'd go back the next day, buy ten more each, and throw them in the freezer for later. There was a stretch of time when all we ate were microwaved McDonald's hamburgers.

On many Friday nights, we'd head to Blockbuster Video to rent a movie. And when there wasn't anything good to watch, we'd rent a Sega Genesis game console and spend the whole weekend playing *NBA Live*.

It may not sound like much, but those were the moments I miss the most. I guess I also miss the fact that there's no longer a Blockbuster Video.

There was a brief time when Jay moved in with me and Daniel. It didn't last long, though. Jay couldn't handle all the squabbling between us. But during that short time, he showed up for me in ways I'll never forget.

While he was living with us, I hurt my knee pretty badly playing basketball. I wouldn't have made it home that day without Jay's help. Another time, I tore my groin muscle playing flag football and could barely walk. My entire right leg turned black and blue. Once again, Jay was the one I leaned on, literally, to get home.

After that first Thanksgiving at Denny's with Christian, Jay made sure we never had to spend another holiday alone. From then on, he would invite Daniel and me back to his home in Portland for the holidays.

Jay's sister Susie became like a little sister to me, and his mom became like my mom. I still love them dearly, think about them from time to time, and continue to pray for them. Jay and his family were my family in the U.S., and in many ways, they still are. Jay is my boy, in every good sense of the word — and he always will be, for life.

There's one more thing I have to mention about my time in Eugene.

Up to that point in my life, I was pretty convinced that I was stupid and destined to fail. But Oregon became the place where I began to find a new kind of confidence.

When I first arrived in Eugene, I still carried the belief that I wasn't particularly smart. But instead of waving the white flag from the start, I told myself I'd at least give it a good shot.

I didn't have any strong aspirations or a dream career in mind. So I decided to go with something practical — Business Administration. I figured, at the very least, it was a degree that could help me get a job and make some money.

The first college exam I took was in a Business Calculus course. A few of my friends were in the same class, so we studied together for it. Jay was also in that class. Everyone seemed to be struggling with the calculus, and I just assumed I would too. Math had never really been my thing.

But after that first midterm, I walked out of the classroom thinking, *maybe that wasn't so bad*. I didn't think I had aced it, but I didn't feel like I had bombed it either. A week later, we got our results. Out of a class of about 100 students, I had scored in the top three. I was absolutely shocked.

In Daegu, I was used to getting 50s and 60s out of 100, sometimes even less than that. But I never imagined that I would score in the high 90s on a college exam, and a calculus exam at that. I started to think that maybe I wasn't so stupid after all.

After that first exam, I started to enjoy studying. Every free time I had, I would either be at the library or the student union with a book in hand going over my class material. Some of my favorite times in Eugene were pulling all-nighters at the local Shari's diner, with some waffles and several refills of coffee throughout the night with Jay and a couple of other guys. After a while, I started tutoring some of my friends taking the same classes.

Oregon used an A-plus grading system, which meant the highest possible GPA was 4.5. After two years there, I had a GPA above 4.3, meaning I had earned either an A or an A-plus in every course I'd taken.

I don't share this to brag, but because, for the first time in my life, I felt like my efforts actually mattered. I was finally a fish swimming in the right waters again. After all those years in Korea — grinding over textbooks, trying anything just to keep up, and still constantly feeling like a failure — I finally felt vindicated. I finally felt like I was where I belonged.

Sometimes I feel like those years in Korea, and even the time I spent in Australia, were a kind of wandering in the wilderness.

In the book of Exodus, after God freed the Israelites from slavery in Egypt, they wandered in the wilderness for forty years. But in the midst of their wandering, God gave them a place of rest called Elim.

Elim was a desert oasis with twelve wells of water and seventy date palms — more than enough food and water for everyone. It wasn't meant to be their final destination, but it was a refuge. A place to rest, reflect, and be renewed before they continued on their journey. God allowed them to stop there — not to settle, but to recover and rediscover hope.

Eugene was my Elim. It was never meant to be permanent. I was only there for two years. But those two years were exactly what I needed.

For the first time, I no longer felt like a loser or a failure. I had new hope that maybe I *could* succeed. Maybe I *could* become somebody.

I now had friends who truly understood me. People who were like me — caught between two cultures, but still figuring it out together.

In Eugene, I could finally be myself — free from the pressures and expectations that Korean society had tried to place on me.

I was free. I felt alive. I was finally in a good place.

I'll admit that at the time, I probably wasn't walking that closely with God. But looking back now, I can see so clearly that He was divinely orchestrating everything in my life. How else could you explain a country boy from Daegu, someone who couldn't even get into the lowest-tier colleges in Korea, ending up in Canberra of all places, and then somehow landing in Eugene, Oregon? And all because someone told my dad that Oregon had a lot of trees? It sounds like the craziest string of random events... or the unmistakable fingerprints of God. And I'm convinced it was the latter.

If it were up to me, I would've never left Oregon. But wouldn't you know it? After my second year, God had other plans. It was as if He was saying, "Your time of rest is over. It's time to move on." So I did.

In my junior year, I transferred to Seattle and began attending the Business School at the University of Washington, the same school that was considered Oregon's bitter football rival.

My time in Elim was over. But I no longer felt like a failure. I no longer felt lost. I was a new man. And yet, my journey in the wilderness — and my journey with God — was far from over.

Chapter 12

Another End, New Beginnings, and Amazing Grace

T he year was 1996. That summer, the Olympic Games were held in hot and humid Atlanta, while in the fall, Bill Clinton beat Bob Dole and Ross Perot for his second term as President of the United States. In pop culture, everyone around the world was singing and dancing to the Macarena. And over the Christmas season, every parent in America was pushing and shoving in the shopping aisles to avoid disappointing their child by grabbing an ever-elusive Tickle-Me-Elmo doll.

Meanwhile, back in Korea, Kim Young-sam was in his third year as the country's first democratically elected, non-military president. But despite his civilian background, he was suddenly forced to make high-stakes military decisions. In September of that year, a North Korean submarine was discovered off the coast of Gangneung. The mission wasn't just reconnaissance — it was espionage, and reportedly even included an attempt to assassinate the South Korean president.

Somehow, an all-out war was avoided. But what followed was a deadly 49-day manhunt that shook the nation. Of the 25 North Korean commandos, 24 were killed — eleven of them executed by their own comrades. Only one managed to escape back to the North. On the South Korean side, four civilians and twelve ROK soldiers lost their lives.

It was a dark and sobering reminder that the Korean peninsula was still technically at war, even though the ceasefire had held for nearly 45 years.

Yet, an even more ominous threat was lurking in the shadows — one that didn't come from the North or any foreign adversary, but from within South Korea's own borders.

In 1996, South Korea was officially recognized as an economically developed country when it was accepted into the OECD — the Organization for Economic Cooperation and Development. It was a moment of national pride. After decades of hard work and sacrifice, Korea had risen from poverty and was finally standing shoulder to shoulder with some of the world's most advanced economies.

But what happened the following year wiped away every optimistic smile and crushed the collective spirit of the nation. It was a sobering reminder that Korea still had a long way to go before it could truly consider itself "developed."

When President Park Chung-hee began pushing aggressive economic development in the 1960s, he did so by showing preferential support to a few hand-selected family-run businesses he could trust and, more importantly, control. This was the beginning of the Korean *chaebol* conglomerates.

Almost every major economic initiative was funneled through these few companies. From buildings to bridges, shipyards to ships, textiles to electronics, and eventually automobiles — anything that could drive economic growth was handed over to the *chaebols*.

Naturally, these privileged few thrived, often at the expense of smaller companies. And even when they struggled, there was no real concern. They operated with the quiet confidence that the government would bail them out with an endless stream of bank loans — loans that were rarely questioned and almost never audited. In return for this generosity, the *chaebols* regularly paid kickbacks to high-ranking government officials, ensuring continued support even when their businesses were drowning in debt, riddled with inefficiencies, or operating at a loss.

On the surface, Korea looked like one of the world's fastest-growing economies. But beneath that glittering exterior was a hollow and fragile foundation, built not on sustainable growth, but on corruption, unchecked power, and systemic debt.

All of this came to a head in 1997, when the truth could no longer be hidden. The collapse of this system brought the nation to its knees. It was one of the darkest and most painful periods in Korean history that I can remember in my lifetime.

The financial crisis of 1997 began in Thailand, when foreign investors started pulling out due to rampant corruption and instability. This triggered the collapse of the Thai Baht and sent shockwaves through the entire Thai economy. But the crisis didn't stop there. It quickly spread across Southeast and East Asia like wildfire.

In Korea, the early warning signs were largely ignored. Many people simply assumed that the government had deep enough pockets to weather any storm. They were wrong.

The first serious cracks in Korea's economic foundation appeared early in 1997, when the Hanbo Group collapsed under a mountain of debt tied to its corrupt connections with government officials. Then, in July, Kia Motors, the country's third-largest automaker, declared bankruptcy. These events shook investor confidence.

Sensing deeper rot in Korea's economic infrastructure, foreign investors began rapidly pulling their funds from the market. Korean companies, now without foreign capital, scrambled to cover their massive debts. But the scale of the liabilities was far beyond what even the Bank of Korea could manage.

Bankruptcies began piling up. One after another, companies fell. The biggest collapse came from the Daewoo Group, once considered one of Korea's top three *chaebols*, alongside Samsung and Hyundai.

The impact on the economy, and on ordinary people's lives, was devastating. Eventually, the Korean government had no choice but to turn to the International Monetary Fund (IMF) for a bailout. In December 1997, the IMF agreed to lend Korea $58.4 billion, but only under strict conditions, which included sweeping economic reforms and corporate restructuring.

Ironically, most of the IMF funds were used to bail out the *chaebols*, the very system that had helped create the crisis. Daewoo was allowed to collapse, likely as a cautionary example, but the rest of the conglomerates emerged from the crisis largely intact.

The real victims of the crisis were the small and mid-sized businesses. Like the *chaebols*, they had been operating under the same flawed, debt-heavy system. But unlike the conglomerates, they had no safety net. There were no bailouts coming for them.

Many couldn't pay their employees or suppliers and were forced to shut down. Millions of people suddenly found themselves bankrupt or unemployed. Desperate to cover their debts, some tried to sell everything they owned, including their homes, only to discover that their equity was now worth just 50–60% of what it had been. Many lost everything.

Some couldn't take the pressure. Suicide rates surged, becoming the highest ever recorded among all OECD nations during any specific period.

The stock exchange collapsed. Shares that once held promise became worthless, little more than the paper they were printed on.

The currency took its worst hit in history. In October 1997, the Korean won traded at around 800 to the U.S. dollar. By mid-November, it had crashed to nearly 1,700 to 1.

For Korean college students studying overseas, this was essentially a death sentence for their academic careers. As parents lost their jobs or businesses, there was simply no way to pay for tuition or living expenses abroad. And even for those whose incomes remained stable, the currency crash effectively doubled the cost of education overnight. Many students had no choice but to pack up and return to Korea. An entire generation of hope was quietly and painfully cut short.

In 1997, while all of this was unfolding, I was in the middle of my junior year at the University of Washington. My dad still had a secure job at his university in Korea, but the monthly wire transfers he sent to support Daniel — who had just started as a freshman at the University of Oregon — and me, no longer came close to what they once were. Given the circumstances, the logical thing would have been to wrap up college and return to Korea, just like so many others had to do.

But here's where I must boast, not in myself, but in my God. Our God is the One who makes the impossible possible. He provides in ways we can't foresee, often before we even know what we need.

I'm fully aware that many others who shared my faith in Jesus weren't as fortunate during the IMF crisis. I don't take that lightly. And yet, somehow, God's amazing grace allowed *me*, of all people, to continue my studies and graduate without ever having to worry too much about finances. During one of the darkest times in Korea's modern history, God's grace was more than enough for me.

Let me explain how.

Back in the spring of 1996, I was going strong in my sophomore year at Oregon. I was getting straight A's, had good friends, and was really enjoying my life. Then one day, my dad had a conversation with a friend in Daegu, and he heard about this scholarship offered by the International Rotary Club.

As far as I knew, most international undergraduate students in America were not allowed any financial aid or scholarships, so the education cost was quite high. Since Oregon was a state run university, it didn't cost as much as some of the private schools, and even compared to some other state schools, it was still relatively on the mid to lower end of the scale. But it wasn't cheap either.

Every month my parents would send Daniel and me at least $1,000 for rent, food, and other necessities. This was in addition to tuition payments. That probably amounted to more than half my dad's salary at that time. Even though he didn't let on that things were ever tough, I can imagine it wasn't the easiest for him.

So, when he asked me to look into applying for this Rotary Club scholarship, I knew that getting accepted would really help out. But I also knew that the competition was steep. Of all the applicants in Korea, only one or two were going to be accepted. Later that spring quarter, I learned I was one of them.

My parents were overjoyed. I was happy too. Not only was the scholarship a massive financial help, but it also felt like a kind of validation — that I wasn't the stupid kid I had once believed myself to be. All the hard work I had put into school was finally being recognized.

A major criterion for the scholarship was academic performance, and since I had a perfect GPA, that certainly helped my case. Add to that my involvement in the Korean Student Association, sprinkle in a few extracurriculars (some of which were probably a bit... embellished, as many are), and top it off with a well-written essay about how I wanted to change the world, and somehow, all of that came together in my favor. I beat out the competition and got the scholarship.

However, there was one stipulation that I didn't quite understand or appreciate. The Rotary Club scholarship was called the Ambassadorial Scholarship, which meant I had to become an "ambassador". This involved leaving the place you were at and going somewhere else because that's what an ambassador does.

I thought this was bizarre. I didn't understand how leaving my current university to go to another school would suddenly make me an "ambassador" for the Rotary Club. It didn't make practical sense. So I wrote to them inquiring about this.

Their response was simple. If I wanted the scholarship, I had to transfer to another school. There were no exceptions.

I was very torn inside. I liked being at Oregon. For perhaps the first time in my life, I felt like a fish in water. I loved my school, my classes, my Ducks, my friends, and my life. How could I leave all of that behind? How could I start over again after it had been so hard to get to where I was right now?

It wasn't just that I didn't want to leave Oregon. In my heart, there was something deeper going on. I started having flashbacks — memories of my childhood in Tennessee and New Jersey. I had such a good life in those places. I felt like I belonged. But then, in the name of progress or a "better life," we always had to move on.

The trauma of my childhood came rushing back all at once. I found myself feeling like that scared little boy all over again. I had vivid flashbacks — back to when I was ten years old and someone told me I had to leave Randolph, New Jersey, for a "better life" in Daegu.

But it wasn't better. It was harder. Full of trials, confusion, and years spent struggling to find my identity and a place in the world.

Back then, I had no voice. No say. And so I had made a vow to myself: if I ever had a choice, I would never let that happen again. So even if it meant walking away from the scholarship money, I was determined — I would not leave my life in Oregon.

I tried to convince my dad that I didn't want the scholarship anymore. I told him I didn't want to leave the University of Oregon. I was doing well there — getting straight A's. That had to count for something, right? It could land me a good job after graduation, or at least help me get into a reputable MBA program somewhere down the line.

I argued that it was already so late in the process. What school would even accept a transfer at this point? And would I have enough time to pull it off?

I framed it all as if I had serious, logical reservations. But deep down, I knew I was just trying to come up with any excuse I could.

Eventually, I applied for a transfer to the University of Washington in Seattle. It seemed like the natural choice. It was only five hours north of Eugene, so I wouldn't be too far from my brother. And it had a strong academic reputation.

Sure, Washington was Oregon's bitter rival, but to be honest, it had a far better academic national ranking. I always suspected that a lot of the Oregon hate toward Washington came from students who secretly wished they had gotten in, but hadn't, and used the rivalry to make themselves feel better.

My application was accepted.

I was still torn. But after giving it some thought, I gave in. I decided to give Seattle a chance.

That summer, I made my first trip to check out the campus and take care of paperwork at the administration office. I still remember driving into Seattle for the first time and seeing the skyline. The iconic Space Needle stood tall over the shimmering waters of the Puget Sound, welcoming me into the city.

As I drove in, I also passed the Kingdome, the old stadium where the Seahawks and Mariners used to play before it was torn down in 2000. And then there was the U-Dub campus itself, nestled right along the scenic shores of Lake Washington. As soon as I saw it, it took my breath away.

To this day, I still believe Seattle is one of the most beautiful cities I've ever been to.

When I arrived in the University District — or the U-District, as it's known — I headed to the admin building, picked up my student ID, and got my dorm assignment. Afterward, I walked around the campus... and was completely blown away.

The buildings were stunning. The Suzzallo Library, with its grand gothic architecture, made me want to sit down and read a book, even if I had nothing to study. The Quad Courtyard called out for a lazy afternoon nap on a warm blanket under the sun. And then there was the Drumheller Fountain on the south end of campus. Right behind the jet of water stood majestic Mount Rainier, perfectly framed as if it were just beyond the trees, even though it was nearly a hundred miles away. It was breathtaking.

It wasn't Oregon. But it wasn't that bad after all.

There was one thing, though, about Seattle on that first trip that wasn't so appealing. Before heading off on the five-hour drive back to Eugene, I got hungry and decided to stop by a Burger King to grab a 99-cent Whopper. I hadn't stopped at an ATM, and when I checked my pocket, I realized I had just a single dollar bill. Still, I figured that would be enough for a Whopper. I'd skip the fries and just ask for a cup of water.

But I had forgotten one major difference between Oregon and Washington: Oregon has no state sales tax. Washington does.

So when I pulled up to the drive-thru and ordered a Whopper, expecting it to be 99 cents, I was stunned when the guy at the window told me it was a dollar and seven cents.

I panicked. I started frantically searching the glove compartment, under the seats, in the ashtray, and anywhere else I thought I might find loose change. I found a penny here, a penny there, but could only scrounge up four cents.

I was nearly in tears. This Whopper — this glorious, much-needed Whopper — was going to be taken from me over just three cents.

The guy at the drive-thru must have seen my desperation. He looked at my Oregon license plates, gave me a half-smile, and tossed in the three cents himself. He then handed me the Whopper. It was the best Whopper I've ever had. I didn't dare ask for a cup of water.

That Whopper story is a pretty accurate picture of my financial situation while I was in Washington. I didn't have much, but somehow, I always had just enough.

I picked up some odd jobs on campus here and there, though they didn't pay much. Still, I managed to buy the books I needed and keep myself from going hungry. God never let me go without. Not once.

I had a rotation of go-to restaurants — places I knew would give you ridiculous amounts of food for a very affordable price. There was a teriyaki place called Tokyo Garden, run by a Korean family. They didn't serve a ton of chicken, but they did pile on the rice. So I'd drench the rice in teriyaki sauce and make a meal out of it. It wasn't fancy, but it was filling, and that's what mattered.

My favorite spot was a Vietnamese noodle shop on University Avenue. I spotted it on the first day I moved to Seattle, and for my first official meal as a U-Dub student, I ordered a bowl of beef brisket and tripe pho. To this day, it's still one of the best bowls of pho I've ever had. The cream puff they handed me afterward? A sweet little bonus. Pho from that place became my comfort food — warm, savory, and just what I needed after long days.

There was also this convenience store run by a couple of Middle Eastern guys who sold the best gyros. They were cheap and packed with flavor, and I probably ate there two or three times a week.

None of these places would ever earn a Michelin star, but when you're a poor and hungry college student, they might as well be five-star dining.

But no matter how frugally I tried to live, I knew deep down that eating rice drenched in teriyaki sauce every day wasn't going to be enough to carry me through to graduation. And when I think about everything that was going on in Korea at the time, it's quite remarkable how I made it through.

Like everyone else, I was completely blind to the dark truth of my country's financial situation, until it hit me in the face. I had about a year left before completing my undergraduate degree when the news from Korea started to grow more serious. I didn't even know what the IMF was, but whatever it was, it didn't sound good. I began hearing stories of more and more Korean students packing up and heading home, unable to afford finishing their studies abroad.

My parents never let on that things were difficult. They kept doing their best to support me financially, but I could sense that the pressure was building, especially now that Daniel was also in college down in Eugene. So I told them to focus more on him. I assured them I'd be okay.

In all of this, my saving grace turned out to be that Rotary scholarship, the very one I once considered turning down because it meant leaving my friends and the comfortable life I had built in Oregon. Honestly, I probably wouldn't have taken it if it had only been for a few hundred, or even a couple thousand dollars. But the total amount, paid out in periodic installments over two years, was no small sum. It was $20,000.

That may not sound like much by today's standards, given the astronomical cost of a U.S. education, but in 1997, it was a significant amount. It was enough to cover my tuition and some basic living expenses during those final two years at Washington.

I didn't fully understand it at the time, but looking back now, I'm convinced it was one of the greatest moments of God's grace in my life. As I mentioned earlier, many Christians were struggling deeply during that season. So I'm not going to pretend this happened because of some extraordinary faith on my part, because it didn't.

To be honest, during my time in Seattle, I wasn't exactly a model Christian. When people invited me to church, I usually declined and stayed home to watch football instead. And if someone asked whether I went to church, I'd casually respond, "Of course. I go to First Presbyterian, just down the street." That wasn't true. I just didn't want to be bothered.

But none of that stopped God. He saw through my excuses. He saw the real me — and still, in spite of all that, He provided. Not because of anything I had done, but purely because of His amazing grace.

And I use that phrase intentionally — "amazing grace" — because that's exactly what it is. Grace doesn't follow logic. It can't be earned, explained, or deserved. It's given freely by the one who chooses to give it. That's what makes it so remarkable. When it comes, it flows from a place of pure love and goodness, even if the person receiving it doesn't deserve it — like me.

Back in college, I liked to think I got the Rotary scholarship because my grades stood out — that I was the most deserving candidate. But the truth is, I have no idea why they chose me. Maybe there were others more qualified. But now, looking back, I see the quiet, gracious hand of God behind that decision.

Back then, I didn't grasp what grace truly meant. But now, as I sit at my dining room table, trying to finish this chapter, in a quiet suburb of Korea — my three beautiful, loud, and slightly annoying children running circles around me on a Saturday, protesting homework and begging for more screen time — I realize something: none of this would've been possible without that scholarship I once considered turning down. None of this would've happened without God's amazing grace giving me a second chance at life.

Chapter 13

Somewhere I Belong

I wanna heal, I wanna feel what I thought was never real
I wanna let go of the pain I've felt so long
(Erase all the pain 'til it's gone)
I wanna heal, I wanna feel like I'm close to something real
I wanna find something I've wanted all along
Somewhere I belong

One morning in the summer of 2017, I woke up to the sad and shocking news that Linkin Park's lead vocalist Chester Bennington, who famously sang these lyrics to the song *Somewhere I Belong*, had taken his own life.

I used to really love Linkin Park, and *Somewhere I Belong* was one of my favorite songs. I never paid too much attention to the meaning of the lyrics, but on that day, with so many questions around why someone so young, promising, and seemingly successful would suddenly take his own life, it occurred to me that perhaps Chester was not able to find a place in this world where he felt like he belonged, and because of that, perhaps he had lost all hope. I haven't listened to a lot of Linkin Park since that day.

Where do I belong? That's a question we all wrestle with at some point in our lives. Deep down, every one of us wants to know that we belong somewhere — a place that feels familiar and safe. A place we can return to, no matter how far we've gone.

The shops may change. Some signs may fade. But the streets and buildings remain. We know that place by its unique, comforting smells, like morning dew on the pavement or the scent of fresh bagels baking down the street. Most importantly, it's a place where we are known and loved, just as we are. Where people celebrate our joys with us, and carry our burdens as if they were their own. It's a place where everyone knows your name, and you know theirs.

We all long for a place like that. A place we can call *home*. A place where we truly *belong*.

Although I live in Korea, my vocation as a pastor at an international church constantly brings me into contact with people from all over the world, many of whom are far from the place they call home. So whenever people around here meet someone for the first time, one of the most common questions that's asked is, *"So, where are you from?"*

Sometimes we ask this question to gain a better understanding of who we're speaking with. While we don't want to stereotype, knowing someone's background can offer a bit of cultural, societal, or even political context. But more often than not, I think the question is just meant to be an icebreaker, something to fill the silence when we're not quite sure what else to say.

It's the kind of casual conversation that goes:
"So where are you from?... Oh! I've never been there before. I'd love to visit someday."
And just like that, the conversation moves on.

However, as for me, this question has always been a tough one. It's not that people really care that much. As I said, it's usually just a way to break the ice. But for me, it brings back a flood of memories, both good and bad.

There was a time when I wanted to say I was from New Jersey. I enjoyed my brief time there, and it holds a special place in my heart. But that was in the 1980s, and it only lasted a couple of years. It's been so long that saying I'm from New Jersey now just feels outdated.

I guess the most technically accurate answer would be that I'm from Daegu. But Daegu holds a lot of bitter memories for me, memories I'd rather not revisit. So, if I can avoid saying I'm from there, I usually do.

These days, when I ask the same question to someone who's a TCK (Third Culture Kid — someone raised in a culture different from their parents' nationality or ethnicity), I often hear them say, "*It's complicated.*" And when I hear that, I simply nod and reply, "*I get it.*" Because I do. I know that "*It's complicated*" often means, "*It's a long story, and honestly, I don't even know where home is anymore.*" Many TCKs are still on a journey to find where they belong.

There was a time when I used to say, "It's complicated," too. But I eventually stopped. I found that whenever I said that, it often led to more questions. People would say, "*Oh! What do you mean?*" And suddenly, I'd be giving a condensed version of my life story: "I was born in Korea, moved to New York at age three, lived in Tennessee, then New Jersey, then Korea again, then Oregon, then Washington, then Korea again, and... blah blah blah."

Now, when people ask where I'm from, I just say, "*Seattle.*"

It's the easiest answer. I *could* say Seoul, but that's where I live now, not where I'm *from*. And when I do say Seoul, the next question is often, "*Wow! How come your English is so good?*"

Which, again, opens a whole new can of explanations I'd rather not get into. So... Seattle it is.

Although I only spent three years of my life there, from 1996 to 1999, Seattle is the last place I lived in the U.S., and that's good enough for me. Besides, I still carry some fond memories of my time there.

Seattle is such a beautiful city. It's known as the Emerald City, not because of any connection to *The Wizard of Oz*, but because it's majestic and lush, surrounded by towering trees and nature in every direction.

I think another reason I call it my home city is because my favorite football team is the Seattle Seahawks. I never went to any Washington Huskies games while I lived there, but I did get to enjoy Seahawks games at the old Kingdome. The Kingdome itself wasn't much to look at. It was just a plain, ugly dome built to shield fans from the constant Seattle rain. I couldn't afford anything beyond the top-level nosebleed seats, but to me, it was magnificent. Every time I got to cheer on the Seahawks from that stadium, I felt like a wide-eyed kid all over again.

The Mariners baseball team also called the Kingdome home. The '90s were a golden era for the Mariners. They had stars like Randy Johnson, Alex Rodriguez, and of course, Ken Griffey Jr. I remember one game where I saw "The Kid" hit a home run, then follow it up with a triple in his next at-bat. Those were certainly the Mariners' glory days.

But at the time, more than any other sport, I loved basketball. Back in the '90s, the Seattle Supersonics were my team. I loved going to Key Arena to watch them play. The 1996 squad was legendary. Shawn Kemp and Gary Payton led the way to the NBA Finals. But they ultimately lost to Michael Jordan and the Bulls in six games. Then again, *everyone* lost to Michael Jordan back then.

It was a dark day in 2008 when the Sonics were sold and moved to Oklahoma City, becoming the Thunder. Even though they no longer exist as a franchise, the Supersonics are still my favorite team. And I still hold onto the hope that one day, they'll return to the NBA.

So yeah, even if it's just because of my love for sports, Seattle is still my favorite city. And whenever anyone asks me where I'm from, the simplest and most honest answer I can give is, *"I'm from Seattle."*

However, when I first moved there in the fall of 1996, I wasn't too excited about it. As I mentioned, I enjoyed being in Eugene, and so it was very painful for me to leave.

I wanted to commemorate my last night in Eugene, so I went out drinking with John, my friend Jay's old roommate. We ended up getting so drunk that it was nearly impossible to wake up the next morning. But I had already packed all my stuff into the U-Haul truck and needed to drive it up to Seattle that afternoon. Hungover and groggy, I grabbed a couple of Big Macs for the road, hoping they'd help me recover, and then hit the highway northbound on Interstate 5, leaving Eugene behind.

That afternoon I arrived at my dorm just off Lake Washington and moved all my stuff in. Not that I had a lot, but it was enough to have to rent a truck.

After settling into my dorm room, I realized how quiet it was. It was really quiet, except for some Canadian geese honking outside on the grass yard. I didn't like those geese. They were loud and mean. They would chase you if they didn't like you. And they would poop their green goose poop everywhere on the lawn, so it made it impossible to hang out on the grass outside the dorm.

I was assigned to a quiet dorm. And boy, was it quiet. It was a stark contrast to Eugene, where people would casually say "hey!" to each other in passing, even if they were complete strangers. But here, in this dorm, everyone seemed to keep entirely to themselves.

After a while, the silence started to wear on me. It got kind of depressing. Some days, I'd go without saying a single word to anyone. I'd go to class, sit silently through the lecture, come back to the dorm, eat a cup noodle for dinner, and spend the rest of the evening alone in my room. Then I'd wake up and do it all over again.

Sometimes, a whole week — or even two — would pass without me speaking a single word to another human being. I never realized how quickly silence and solitude could turn into something heavier. I didn't know how easy it was to slip into a kind of depression when you go that long without real human connection.

It hit me one day when I went to the convenience store to buy some milk. As I walked in, the guy at the counter looked up and said, "Hey, how's it going?"

I was so overjoyed! Someone had spoken to me. And so I replied, "Good. How 'bout you?"

It wasn't much of an interaction, but because it was the first words I had spoken to anyone for a very long time, it felt great! And then that was it. I returned to my dorm and went back to my very silent cave.

Unlike when I first got to Canberra or Eugene, I did not consider getting involved with the Korean Student Association at Washington. I think I was a little older and tired of having to start over again in such a way. Perhaps a part of me also wanted a new start without too many Korean people around. Korean people can be good, but they can also be tiresome and judgmental, and I wanted a fresh beginning with mostly American people. Also, deep down I think I still wanted to identify as American.

Since I didn't have a circle of friends in Seattle, I hoped to meet people through my business classes. But business school at U-Dub was a lot tougher than it had been at Oregon. On top of that, I was spending so much time alone that the depression I had quietly slipped into started to take a real toll. I felt unmotivated and disconnected during that first term.

Back at Oregon, I had left with a perfect GPA — over 4.0. But in my first quarter at Washington, I could only manage a 3.3. Not a bad grade by any means, but it felt painfully average compared to what I had grown used to. And more than just the number, it reflected how off-balance I felt in every other part of life.

On a side note, one of the biggest regrets from business school that I have was that I didn't invest in an upstart local company that I'd done a case study on during one of my classes. This new company sold books online and was planning an IPO. I didn't have any money to invest, so I passed. I also thought to myself, *This idea will never work. Why buy books online when you can go to Barnes and Noble?* I wasn't much of a visionary back then, and I don't think my failure to invest harmed the company, because Amazon did very well without my money.

Besides my average performance in the classroom and my poor investment judgment, what I remember most about business school at U-Dub were the people. There were some pretty confident — and honestly, pretty cutthroat — students there. I reckon they were the ones who truly belonged. I'm sure many of them went on to become ruthless and savvy business leaders.

I wasn't quite like them. I was more about studying hard and just trying to be a decent person. But you know what they say about nice guys in business: They don't finish last... they finish broke.

But I was a nice guy, and the people I ended up connecting with were often the quiet ones — the non-sharks and the introverts. They weren't exactly nerds or geeks, but there was a hint of insecurity in some of them, and somehow, they just seemed to gravitate toward me.

Tanya was in one of my first classes during my first term. She was a very awkward-looking white girl with unkempt curly brunette hair and thick glasses that she didn't clean often — there were visible grease smudges on her lenses. We were paired together for a class assignment, and we actually worked pretty well as a team. She was sweet, but it was clear she didn't have much confidence in herself or in her appearance.

I can't say we became good friends, but she liked talking to me. I think it was because I didn't judge her for how she looked.

After that class, we lost touch. But then, sometime the following year, I ran into her on campus — and she looked completely different. She was now trendy and put-together. Her glasses were gone, her hair was still curly but now looked stylish and intentional. She lit up when she saw me and invited me over later that week to catch up.

When I went to her place, she introduced me to her live-in boyfriend. She told me she had started taking swing dance lessons and that she and her boyfriend even performed on stage. She played some music and, right there in the living room, started showing me some of her moves.

It was random and unexpected, but I was genuinely happy for her. That awkward, unsure girl I had met a year earlier had clearly found her rhythm, and a place where she belonged.

There was another girl in one of my classes — I think her name was Keo, or maybe Kail or Gail. I honestly can't remember, but it was something like that. She was Laotian. When I first saw her in class, she seemed to hang around with a lot of the jocks, so I just assumed she was popular.

As with Tanya, we ended up being paired for a project. She invited me over to her place a few times to work on it, and over time, I got to know her story. Her parents were refugees who had come to the U.S. after the Vietnam War, and she told me how tough life had been growing up. As we talked more, I realized she wasn't nearly as outgoing or confident as I had first thought. In fact, she was very shy, and deeply insecure.

I tried to encourage her, and told her she was kind, intelligent, and appealing in ways she didn't seem to recognize. One day, when she was sick, I brought over some hot Vietnamese pho for her. She was grateful. We sat in her apartment for a while in awkward silence. I had a sense she wanted me to kiss her, but I didn't have feelings for her that way. Besides, she was clearly ill, with tissues everywhere and snot running from her nose. It just wasn't the moment. After that day, and once our class ended, we lost touch.

In another one of my classes, there was this guy who randomly asked me to hang out with him one day. For the life of me, I can't remember his name, but I remember he seemed really cool. He was tall, good-looking, with long curly blond hair, and he wore a leather jacket and rode around on a Harley Davidson. To me, he was like the U-Dub Marlboro Man, even though he didn't smoke. He just had that kind of aura.

He invited me to go rock climbing. I'd never done anything like that before, but I figured why not? He pulled up in front of my dorm on his motorcycle, tossed me a helmet, and told me to hop on. We rode out to a small climbing wall not far from campus. He handed me a pair of climbing shoes, showed me a few basic grips and holds, and told me to give it a go. It was challenging, but kind of fun.

Afterward, we grabbed some beers and he dropped me back at my dorm.

It was a pretty cool experience, but something about the whole thing felt a little strange. The vibe I got was that he expected us to become best friends right away. But we didn't really know each other. There was no history between us. And behind that confident, Marlboro Man exterior, I sensed someone who was kind of lonely — someone who was maybe just looking for a friend or his own place to belong.

We stayed cordial after that, but we didn't really hang out again.

These were just a few of the people I met in Seattle. One thing I sensed from them, and from others I haven't mentioned, was that there were a lot of lonely people in that city. It felt like they were all searching for something, or someone, or someplace where they truly belonged.

Back in the '90s, in a Seattle where it rained endlessly and grunge music like Nirvana and Pearl Jam ruled the airwaves, there seemed to be so many lost souls. I know I was one of them. Even though some of my classmates tried to befriend me, the feelings just weren't mutual. So I kept searching for a place where I felt I belonged. But the more I searched, the more I began to realize that maybe the place I felt most at ease... was being alone.

Eventually, I started withdrawing from people. At first, I didn't have a TV in my dorm room, so if I wanted to watch anything, I had to go to the common room. But that meant negotiating what to watch and making small talk with others. So I bought a small TV of my own. It was perfect. I could watch all the Sonics games and Simpsons reruns I wanted, from the comfort of my bed.

As for meals, I stocked up on cup noodles, which meant I no longer had to step into the shared kitchen and make more awkward small talk. I didn't care much for food anyway. I just ate to fill my stomach.

Over time, the isolation deepened, and so did the depression. I listened almost exclusively to alternative and grunge music. I only went outside for my classes and when I absolutely had to. I'd often walk through the rain without an umbrella, soaking wet, not caring if I caught pneumonia.

It got really bad. Even to the point where I thought, *If I don't get out and talk to someone soon, I could just die and rot away in this room, and no one would even know.*

That's when I decided to venture out. I told myself I just needed to get out of my dorm before I lost my mind.

I wandered around University Avenue, aimlessly. I stopped by Tower Records to see if there were any new CDs that interested me. Nothing. So I kept meandering up and down the cold, wet streets of the U-District, not sure what I was looking for.

It started to get cold, and I thought about heading back, but then I saw the sign for a pub. I didn't know what to expect, but it looked warm. So I walked in.

The College Inn was just up the street from my dorm. It was a very old-looking place. I'm not sure when it first opened, but it looked like it had been around since the 1800s. Some stairs led down to a pub in the basement of the building. I went down, and as soon as I walked in, I fell in love.

It was just a regular, old-fashioned beer pub. Nothing particularly special. The bar had several taps, pouring what soon became some of my favorite Pacific Northwest microbrews. I don't remember exactly what I ordered that first night. Maybe it was a Sierra Nevada Pale Ale or a Pike Place IPA, because those quickly became my go-to drinks. That first sip was majestic, like a divine oasis in the dry and desolate desert of my soul.

In the back corner of the pub stood two inviting pool tables. Back at my dorm, I avoided most common areas like the plague, but the one space I occasionally visited was the pool room. So when I saw the tables, I decided to try my hand. Anyone who wanted to play just wrote their name on the chalkboard and waited their turn. I scribbled "Joe" in sloppy handwriting, picked out a cue stick, and waited for the break. I think I won the first three games before losing. Then I wrote my name on the board again and ordered another beer.

That pub quickly became a second home to me. I'd go just to sip on a beer and shoot pool with strangers. It was a safe place, a place where I could enjoy relative anonymity, yet still be surrounded by people. It pulled me out of my spiral of isolation and depression.

I even had my first experience of getting a girl's phone number at a bar there.

One night, I was drinking an IPA and playing pool. After winning a couple of games and then losing to some guy with a ponytail, I went up to the bar to get another drink. That's when a girl came up to me and said, "Hey, see that girl over there by the pool table? She thinks you're cute."

Without a hint of subtlety or coolness, I looked over immediately. There was a petite, pretty Asian girl standing near the table. I couldn't tell if she was Filipina or Hawaiian. She had short hair that fell just below her ears, big expressive eyes, and a warm, dark complexion.

I'd never tried to hit on a girl at a bar before, so I wasn't exactly sure what to do. But I figured the least I could do was walk over and say, "Hi." Her name was Jade, and she was there with some friends. I don't remember much of what we talked about. I was mostly just amazed I was speaking to a pretty girl in a bar for the first time.

At the end of the night, she gave me her number and told me to call her. I did.

But the relationship didn't last long. As I got to know her, I found out her roommate was actually her ex-boyfriend. That made things complicated, to say the least. We went on a couple of dates, but it soon became clear that the ex didn't want to stay an ex. So I stopped calling her.

Going out and being social again helped pull me out of my depression, so I decided to make more of an effort back at the dorm. The first real friend I made was the guy in the room next to mine. His name was Mark. He was a short, stocky, and very hairy white guy from Everett, a town about an hour and a half north of Seattle.

One weekend I visited him at his home and met some of his buddies. We spent the entire afternoon out on a small motorboat sipping beer on a lake. I never knew how relaxing it could be to do absolutely nothing but float on the water with a drink in hand until then.

Every so often, Mark would get adventurous enough to join me on outings around the University District. We tried all kinds of ethnic food. One day we stumbled upon this little Mexican restaurant that served the spiciest salsa I'd ever tasted. I loved it, but Mark's face turned so red I thought he might choke or have a heart attack.

That same place turned out to host karaoke nights on Thursdays. They'd pull out a karaoke machine, and anyone could sign up and sing. Being Korean, I was no stranger to karaoke. I'd spent plenty of time in *noraebangs* back home, so I wasn't shy about getting up on stage. Mark, on the other hand, needed a bit of liquid courage — specifically, a few tequila shots.

When he finally got up there, I sort of wished he hadn't. It wasn't just that he couldn't sing (though, let's be honest, he couldn't). It was also the way he fully committed, head-banging and screaming along to Guns N' Roses' *Paradise City* like he was Axel Rose himself. The whole bar seemed to pause for a moment, wondering, *"Who is this guy?"*

But Mark didn't care. He wasn't there to win a talent contest. He was there to have fun. And honestly, I loved it. We had a blast that night.

In the room next to Mark lived this athletic black guy named Alex. He played defensive back on the Husky football team. I never told him I was an Oregon Ducks fan. We didn't hang out much, but we were cordial and exchanged small talk in the hallway.

Then one day, out of the blue, Alex and Mark came up to me and asked if I wanted to go to a club with them. It felt kind of random. Honestly, I never imagined the two of them would want to party together, let alone invite me along.

"Okay," I said.

When they said "club," I didn't realize they were talking about a strip club. We ended up at the Déjà Vu. It was well known for its cheeky slogan: *"Where there's always 50 beautiful girls and 3 ugly ones."*

If you stop and think about it, it was kind of hilarious. It felt like the start of a bad joke: *"A white guy, a black guy, and a Korean guy walk into a strip club..."* But in this case, there was no punchline. That *was* the punchline.

I'd never been to a place like that before, but it was clear that Mark and Alex had. They came prepared with stacks of $1 bills. One of them even paid ten bucks for a private dance for me from a heavily-tattooed girl named Cricket, though I seriously doubt that was her real name.

Now, I'm not here trying to endorse or glamorize strip clubs. I've seen places in the world where it's obvious women are being exploited, and there's nothing entertaining about that. A lot of those places need to be shut down. But I'd like to believe that the establishment we went to that night — naively and with youthful zeal — was a bit different.

For one, the dancers didn't bare everything. It wasn't some wild, anything-goes scene. There was no alcohol served, which helped keep things from getting out of hand. And they had a strict "look but don't touch" policy, enforced by a couple of intimidating, 250-pound bouncers.

In the end, it wasn't really about the club. It was about three young guys trying to escape the stress of school and life for a night — just trying to have a little fun and feel like we belonged somewhere, at least together, for that one night.

There were other people in the dorm I'd say "Hey" to in the hallways or common areas, but for the most part, everyone kept to themselves. Overall, it was a pretty quiet and uneventful place. Honestly, it was pretty boring.

But then, on the last day of the school year, someone came up with the idea of throwing a party on the front lawn — the same lawn where the Canadian geese usually roamed around terrorizing us. I figured it'd be a low-key gathering. Up to that point, I thought most of my dorm-mates were introverted or bookworms.

But as soon as people started showing up with booze, cigars, and other questionable things, I realized I'd completely misjudged them. Turns out everyone in the dorm loved to party. They just didn't do it at the dorm. And when they partied, they partied way harder than I ever could have imagined. I could barely keep up. By the end of the day, I was dizzy and green in the face.

Who were these people, and where had they been all year? They certainly didn't seem like the quiet, boring dorm-mates I thought I knew. I guess we weren't such a boring dorm after all.

After my junior year living in the dorm, I felt it was time to move out. I ended up finding a small room in a co-op apartment tucked behind University Avenue. In many ways, it wasn't all that different from the dorm. I had my own little room with a phone and a TV, and I shared the kitchen and living room with others. Most of the residents were Asian, but I didn't really get to know them. I mostly kept to myself, just like before.

It took a lot of effort for me to get to know new people. When people meet me today, they think I'm a natural extrovert. As a pastor, you kind of have to be.

The truth is, I've always had a deeply introverted side. I think a big part of that comes from moving around so much as a kid. I was constantly missing old friends and quickly grew tired of the effort it took to make new ones. I've always preferred the old and familiar to the new and unknown. That's probably why my closest friends in Seattle ended up being a couple of familiar faces from my time in Eugene — Stephanie and Micah.

Stephanie and Micah were fellow Ducks who moved up to Seattle after graduating from Oregon. They had been roommates back in Eugene. And in case you're wondering — yes, Micah is typically a guy's name, pronounced "My-kah," like the Old Testament prophet, but this Micah was a girl, and she pronounced her name "Mee-kah," sort of like the first part of Pikachu's name from Pokémon.

Stephanie was pursuing a Master's in Nursing at Seattle Pacific University. She'd often call me up to study together, and we spent countless hours either at the Suzzallo Library or the Barnes & Noble bookstore. Even though we were studying different subjects, she was my best study partner. During those stretches when I was feeling low or unmotivated, Stephanie was the one who'd pull me out of bed and kick my butt into gear. Thanks to her, I eventually found my academic rhythm again, and by the time I finished at the University of Washington, I graduated with honors as Magna Cum Laude.

Micah, on the other hand, was originally from Seattle. She was now back home trying to start her career. Her family was local, but that didn't necessarily make the transition easy. I remember she even worked for a time at her sister's deli in the business district of Bellevue. But Micah never complained or showed signs of struggle. She was one of the strongest people I knew.

If Stephanie was the engine behind my academic drive, Micah was the emotional anchor that held me down. There were still long stretches when I wouldn't talk to anyone, and whenever I was on the verge of slipping into another dark place, Micah would call. I don't know if she somehow sensed it, but her timing was always perfect. We'd talk for hours — about sports, the weather, current events, our old friends from Oregon, even the latest cartoons. It didn't matter what we talked about. It was the connection that mattered. And after every conversation with her, I felt okay again.

Micah was also the person I had the most fun with in Seattle. Ever since I first met her in Eugene, I knew she was ridiculously competitive when it came to games. She would even cheat during a friendly round of air hockey just to win. So when a new adult-themed video arcade called Gameworks opened up in downtown Seattle, we had to go check it out. More often than not, she got the better of me.

Sometimes we'd head over to this trendy pool hall called Jillian's. I really liked that place. The food and the pool were a bit pricey, but it was one of the few spots where I could throw on something nice and feel like an adult instead of just another broke college student. On certain nights, especially after a Supersonics game, I'd even spot my hero, Gary Payton, hanging out there, hosting players from the visiting team. And true to form, he talked just as much smack at the pool table as he did on the court. Micah and I always had a blast at Jillian's, even though, somehow, she ended up beating me most of the time.

Nowadays, when I share some of these stories about Seattle with my wife Juri, she finds them sad. She says college is supposed to be the best time of your life, but it didn't seem like that for me. Although it looks like I'm sharing a lot of sob stories, I don't remember a lot of the hard times unless I force myself to, and I feel that the good moments certainly outweighed the bad. A big reason for that is because I had Stephanie and Micah in my life.

As the summer of 1998 approached, I started to get stressed out. Graduation was right around the corner, but I had no job, no internship lined up, and honestly, no idea what I was going to do with my life.

On top of that, I was haunted by the looming possibility that not just my time in Seattle, but my entire life in the U.S., might be nearing its end. Being a Korean-born male, I knew military service was mandatory. I was afraid I'd be called back to Korea and that the life I'd worked so hard to build would come crashing down.

I began searching for job opportunities with whatever energy I had left. One in particular caught my eye: a marketing position with Nike International, based either in Portland or Hong Kong. The application asked for a creative sample, so I had an idea. I remembered passing a basketball hoop tucked in an alleyway somewhere in downtown Seattle. One night, I asked Micah to drive me there. The pavement was slick with rain, the alley was dark, and the only light came from the headlights of her old Honda Civic, reflecting off the puddles. I brought a basketball and just started shooting, jumping, defending — moving as if I were in the middle of a game. Micah stood back and took photo after photo.

We didn't have digital cameras back then, so I had to get the film developed at a local Kodak shop. Once the prints were ready, I took the best shots to Kinkos and had them scanned. With the help of my dorm buddy Mark, who was great with Photoshop, we turned them into two posters.

The first was of me mid-jump in that wet alley, superimposed next to Gary Payton, as if the two of us were locked in a one-on-one duel. The caption read: **"What Dreams Are Made Of."**

The second showed me in a defensive stance, the car's headlights casting a dramatic beam across the court. That one said: **"Who's Got Next?"**

The ideas were mine, but Mark did an incredible job bringing them to life.

I submitted the posters to Nike, and they must've liked them because they called me over the phone for an interview with one of their executives. The call went really well, until I made one of the dumbest mistakes of my life.

They asked me, "If you were accepted for the position, how soon could you start?"

I should've just said, "Right after graduation." And stopped there.

But I didn't. I told them I'd love to start right away... *but* that there was a chance I might have to go back to Korea for mandatory military service. I even asked if there was any way I could defer the offer if that happened.

I never heard from them again.

After that, I started frantically looking for other jobs in the United States. I went to every job fair I could and sent out applications to Andersen Consulting, McKinsey, Boston Consulting Group, and other major consulting firms. I really wanted to work in consulting. Some of my classmates were getting hired by these companies, even guys who had worse grades than I did. But this was the start of the dot-com boom, and those guys had all studied Business IT, while I had chosen Marketing. In hindsight, maybe I should've picked IT instead.

I didn't get a single call back.

I also applied to local companies like Microsoft, Starbucks, and Boeing. Still, nothing. No callbacks. No interviews.

I started to get anxious and scared. It wasn't that I didn't believe I could eventually find a job. It was more that I desperately needed to find a way to stay in America. I was hoping to land a job that would sponsor me for a work visa. That, I believed, would be my ticket to remain in the U.S. and avoid having to return to Korea.

At the time, the U.S. had a system that allowed foreign graduates from American universities to remain for one year on a temporary work permit. They called it "practical training," but for most international students, it was more like a one-year "get-out-of-jail" card — buying them time to find a way to stay, whether that meant landing a visa-sponsored job, marrying an American citizen, or, for some, simply hiding and overstaying their visa.

Out of those three options, I was hoping to find a job. Though, to be honest, if I somehow found an incredible wife, I wouldn't have minded that either. But I knew my chances of that were pretty slim.

After many rejections, I finally landed a job with a company called Diversified Financial Concepts. When you hear that name, it might sound somewhat impressive. But in reality, it was just a mutual funds and life insurance sales company. Nothing fancy. Just cold calls and commission.

Sales turned out to be one of the hardest things I've ever done.

The first month was all training and prepping to pass my Series 7 license exam, which would allow me to sell mutual funds. I didn't get paid during that time. In fact, I had to pay out of pocket for the training and the license exam myself. On top of that, I needed a car for the job, but I had no money in the bank. So, I did the only thing I could — I put it on my credit card and bought a used Geo Prism.

I should've checked the car more carefully. Once I brought it home, I realized the windows didn't close properly unless you guided them at a very specific angle. And in a city like Seattle, where it rains nine months out of the year, that's kind of a big oversight.

I got my first paycheck in the second month on the job. Since it was 100% commission-based, I had to hustle. Some people were natural-born salespeople. You could just tell from the way they spoke and carried themselves. They had that smooth confidence, or maybe even cockiness, that made people sign on the dotted line whether they were ready or not. Those were the ones pulling in multiple deals a week and making serious money.

I was not one of them.

I struggled a lot. My first paycheck? Just over $90. That month, I ate a lot of Top Ramen.

One of the toughest parts of the job was Monday nights. We were expected to stay in the office until 8 or 9 p.m., lining up meetings for the rest of the week. If you had a big network or were bold enough to constantly ask for referrals, it wasn't too bad. But I didn't know many people. So I'd sit at my desk and cold-call strangers out of the phone book during their dinner time.

Some people would curse me out and slam the phone. That was discouraging. But even worse were the ones who were very lonely and didn't want to hang up because they were just happy to talk to someone. I once spent over an hour on the phone with an older woman who just wanted to talk about her kids, who she never got to see. I kept hoping I could turn the conversation into a scheduled meeting, but in the end, I had to hang up on *her*. I still feel bad about that.

Despite how tough it was, I stuck with it, hoping the company might sponsor me for a work visa. Over time, I started to do a little better. They started calling me "Two-Piece Park," because I somehow managed to pull off two pieces of business a week, almost like clockwork.

The deals weren't huge, and I still wasn't raking in the money, but at least I could afford a bowl of pho every now and then in addition to my usual 10-cent ramen noodles. Progress.

One week, I actually made it onto the list of the top 10 salespeople in the nation. That was a proud moment. I still have a printout of that list tucked away in my collection of memorabilia. The way I got there is actually kind of funny. It all happened as something of a fluke.

I had been struggling to find quality leads, so I tried something a little different: I set up a small table in front of a Safeway grocery store and offered free financial consultations to passers-bys. That's where I met an Eastern European immigrant woman. I pitched her on the idea that, with the right financial tools, I could help her make her money work for her, so she wouldn't have to work quite so hard herself.

She liked the sound of that and told me she had $10,000 just lying around.

When I heard that, I put everything else aside and sat down with her for a full meeting right there on the spot. I came up with a plan that included a mix of mutual funds, and I recommended a Variable Universal Life (VUL) insurance policy. She didn't have any life insurance at the time, so it made sense. Plus, the VUL plans paid out the highest commissions, so I always made sure to offer them when appropriate.

She liked the plan and was ready to sign. But when I asked for a check, she said she couldn't write one, because she didn't have a bank account. Surprised, I asked her where she kept her money, and she told me: in a sock, in one of her drawers at home.

So I drove her to her place, and sure enough, there was the sock. Then I took her to a bank, helped her open a checking and savings account, and got her all set up.

When I realized that the $10,000 was all she had to her name, I couldn't bring myself to invest the full amount. I left most of it in her bank account so she'd have liquid funds for everyday needs. I used a portion for a modest investment in a capital gains mutual fund and put the rest into a small VUL plan. I still feel good about that decision. I wasn't just some greedy life insurance salesman chasing commission, I was able to genuinely help someone who needed it.

That story became legendary back at the office. More importantly, it's the moment I take the most pride in from my short stint in financial sales, not just because I got the deal done, but more so, because I did it with integrity.

A few months later, I finally sat down with my managers and told them about my situation. I asked if the company could sponsor me for a work visa so I could stay in the U.S. They checked with HQ and their legal team, but the answer came back: they couldn't.

In my disappointment, all the motivation I had left evaporated. Not long after, I quit.

My manager at DFC, Jeremy Oliver, remained a good friend even after I left the company. People called him "JO," and he called me "JP." We'd go out for beers and play pool together. I think he felt bad that there wasn't anything he could do to help my situation, but I never blamed him. It wasn't his fault.

In hindsight, leaving DFC was probably the best thing for our friendship. While I was still at the company, even though he was only a couple of years older than me, I couldn't shake the feeling that he was my boss. But once I left, that dynamic faded, and I felt much more relaxed around him. I think he felt the same, because we started hanging out most weekends.

One thing I hadn't realized until then was that JO was a huge Star Wars fan. When *Star Wars: Episode I – The Phantom Menace* came out, he asked me to go watch it with him. Looking back now, I realize that was actually quite an honor.

There was another colleague at DFC named Katie Jo. When she heard about my visa situation, she offered to marry me. I still laugh out loud when I think about it, but she was completely serious. I appreciated the gesture deeply, but I never even considered it for a moment. I had no intention of marrying someone just to get a green card.

After leaving DFC, I still had a few months left on my work permit, so I needed to find another job, something that offered a steady paycheck without the stress of commission-based sales. I also had credit card debt piling up, including the steep interest on that crappy old Geo Prism I'd bought. I wanted to take care of those obligations before I returned to Korea.

I worked a few odd jobs during the final stretch of my time in the U.S. First, I landed a position at Nordstrom in the Gateway Mall, selling young men's clothes in *The Rail* section. It wasn't a glamorous job, but it gave me something to do and helped me pay off some of my debt. After a few months there, I headed down to Vancouver, Washington, just across the Columbia River from Portland, where I briefly worked at a convenience store owned by the parents of my friend Ben Kang from the University of Oregon.

One day while working there, something wild happened. Jimmy "Superfly" Snuka, one of my childhood WWF wrestling heroes, walked in. He looked me right in the eye and said, "What's up, brotha! Give me a carton of Marlboro Lights!" I couldn't believe it. I grew up watching this man fly off the top ropes, and now here he was, just casually buying smokes in the same store I was working in. That moment was kind of amazing.

Before I knew it, the summer of 1999 rolled around, and my time in America had finally come to an end. I sold my car, though I got nowhere near what I had paid for it. My dad had to help cover the remaining debt.

As my departure date drew closer, I wanted to say goodbye the right way. So I had one last hoorah with some of my closest friends from Oregon. We went out to the coast and camped on the beach, spending the night under the stars with the sound of the waves crashing nearby. Among the group was Jay, my best friend from Oregon, and Micah, my best friend from

Seattle. It felt fitting. That night was one last beautiful moment I had in America.

On the day of my departure, Micah drove me to the airport. I'm so grateful she did, because honestly, I don't know if I could have made that trip to the airport on my own. She was the last friendly face I saw on U.S. soil.

Then, I boarded a plane, flew over Alaska and Siberia, and before I knew it... I was back in Korea.

Looking back now, I loved being in Seattle. The city will always have a special place in my heart. But at the same time, I know it's not my home. Oregon isn't my home either. Neither is New Jersey nor Tennessee. If any of those places were truly home, I'd either still be there today or have roots to return to. But I don't. I have no roots in those places, only some friends or fond memories.

That doesn't mean Korea is my home either. It's the country of my birth and my nationality, and today, most of my family — aside from my brother Daniel, his wife, and their son in America — live here. But that doesn't mean I feel at home. If Korea were truly my home, I probably would have written this entire memoir in *Hangul*. But my Korean language skills aren't strong enough for that. In fact, if I genuinely felt completely at home in Korea, perhaps I wouldn't have felt the need to write any of this in the first place.

And so the question remains: Where is home? Where is the place that I truly belong?

Christians are taught that our true home is in heaven, and that we're just passing through this world. I believe that, but I've often wrestled with what it really means. Is heaven somewhere beyond the stars? A separate realm? Another world entirely?

Maybe. But what I've come to believe is that heaven isn't just a far-off destination — it's also something we're meant to experience here and now.

Not fully, not perfectly. But enough to give us hope.

In Revelation 21, we're given this powerful image: the new Jerusalem coming *down* to earth. God makes His home *with* us. Heaven isn't about escape — it's about presence. God's presence. And where His presence is, that's where we find our true home.

For a long time, I didn't know where I belonged. Was it America? Korea? Somewhere in between? I felt like I was always on the outside, looking in. But slowly, I began to see that home isn't just about geography or nationality. It's about relationship — being known, being loved, and being at peace.

And that's what I've found in Christ.

That doesn't mean life has been easy. When I moved back to Korea in 1999, I struggled, a lot more than I expected. I missed my life in America. I felt out of place. I had to learn how to adjust, how to live in a culture I was born into but didn't fully understand. But more than anything, I had to learn that my identity isn't just about where I'm from — it's about who I belong to.

And I belong to Him.

Wherever He is, that's where I'm at home. Whether in a church in Seoul or a pub in Seattle — I've learned to look for Him, to walk with Him. Sometimes with tears. Sometimes with laughter. Sometimes with both.

One day, I'll walk and talk with Jesus face to face. And on that day, I know I'll finally be home in the fullest sense. But until then, I'll keep walking with Him here — learning, growing, and remembering that even now, even in this imperfect world, I already have a place where I belong.

Chapter 14

The Reconciliation of
Daehanminguk

T he year 1999 was wild and unforgettable for a lot of reasons. For starters, it marked the debut of one of the world's most beloved and bizarre cartoon characters — SpongeBob SquarePants. At the movies, while sci-fi fans were eagerly awaiting *The Phantom Menace*, the first *Star Wars* film in 16 years, it was an unexpected new trilogy that stole the show: *The Matrix*, starring Keanu Reeves.

On the music charts, Ricky Martin had everyone *"Livin' La Vida Loca,"* and in the tech world, a game-changer called Napster launched. Suddenly, people could freely share MP3s with anyone who had internet access. It shook the music industry and signaled the end of the cassette tape era. Everyone was downloading their favorite tracks and burning mix CDs, even if it meant leaving the computer running overnight just to get that one song that took six hours to finish.

But 1999 wasn't just about pop culture highs and tech innovation. It was also the year of the Columbine High School shooting, when two students carried out a massacre in their Colorado school. It may not have been the first mass shooting in American history, but it marked a turning point. Since then, school shootings and public gun violence have become disturbingly common.

And then there was Y2K. As the year came to a close, anxiety was in the air. People feared that when the clock struck midnight on January 1, 2000, computers would glitch, systems would crash, and chaos would unfold around the globe. Some religious groups even predicted the end of the world. But when the countdown ended and the new millennium began, nothing happened. No meltdowns. No disasters. No messiahs descending from the clouds. The next day came like any other, and life carried on.

For me personally, 1999 was also a whirlwind. The previous five years — spent in Canberra, Eugene, and Seattle — had felt like a dream I didn't want to wake up from. I'd had incredible experiences, made lasting memories, and grown in ways I couldn't have imagined. But like Dorothy waking up from the colorful world of Oz to find herself back in black-and-white Kansas, I opened my eyes one summer morning in my parents' apartment in Daegu and realized my time abroad was over. I was back in Korea, and everything suddenly felt flat and colorless.

The adjustment was anything but easy. The first thing I noticed was just how *Korean* everything looked. I know that sounds obvious, but the impression hit me hard, just as it had when I returned from Canberra years earlier. Everyone had black hair and dark eyes and wore the same muted styles. I'm not saying there was anything wrong with it, but Korean fashion in the late '90s and early 2000s wasn't as vibrant or diverse as it is today. It all just felt... gray.

And then there was the language. I was once again in a place where English wasn't the norm. Not only that, but I was in a region where the Korean dialect was choppier, louder, and more aggressive-sounding than what most people are used to. Conversations often sounded like arguments, even if they weren't. It made the transition even more jarring.

Personal space was another challenge. In Korea, you can be on a nearly empty subway car and still find someone standing uncomfortably close.

When people talk to you, they do it face-to-face — *literally*. Close enough to smell what they had for lunch.

I also had to readjust to the cultural norm of not holding doors open. It wasn't rudeness — it just wasn't a thing. Still, it meant I constantly had heavy doors swinging shut in my face.

Daegu was the city of my childhood and teenage years, but it never truly felt like home. And returning from the U.S. didn't change that.

I had lost touch with most of my high school friends, and honestly, I wasn't eager to reconnect. In the five years I'd been away, we had grown apart — not just physically, but in mindset and outlook. Whenever I did run into someone from the past, I felt the distance immediately. They were deeply rooted in Korean culture, and I had become Americanized again — in my clothes, my speech, and the way I thought. I wasn't ready to "become Korean" again. And because of that, I struggled to find common ground with my old friends.

And then there was the looming reality of military service. My student visa had expired, so returning to Korea wasn't exactly optional. But even if it had been, I still had an obligation waiting for me. Like all Korean men, I was required to serve in the military. Most do it in their early twenties, often right after their second year of college. Some even begin at eighteen. But I was nearly 25, which meant I'd be one of the older guys in basic training.

I mentally braced myself for the verbal and physical abuse I imagined would come from younger superiors determined to break me down. I knew that being older might make me a target. They'd see it as their mission to crush my spirit and put me in my place.

But then, to my shock — and relief — I was completely exempted from service.

Originally, I had been classified as a top-tier physical candidate. But after submitting an MRI showing a torn ACL in my right knee from college basketball, I was granted a full exemption. Some men with medical issues were given partial exemptions, meaning they still had to do public service while living at home. Not me. I was released from all obligation, 100%.

In Korea, there's a term for guys like that: *Shin-ui adeul*, or "son of the gods." The phrase came from a time when only the sons of elites — politicians, high-ranking officials, or *chaebol* executives — managed to avoid military duty. These privileged few were seen as the untouchables, the sons of Korea's "gods." These days, pulling strings like that doesn't fly. The only way out now is either divine intervention, or, in my case, a wrecked knee. Apparently, the army decided my ACL was so shot that I'd be more of a burden than an asset. Whatever their reasoning, I was incredibly grateful.

So, that summer, instead of boot camp, I found myself undergoing knee surgery in Daegu. I spent a week recovering in the hospital. With no friends around, and only family dropping by, I was bored out of my mind.

One of the most exciting things during my hospital stay was watching Michael Jackson's first, and only, concert in Korea on TV. Just the fact that the King of Pop was performing in Korea felt surreal. But what made it even more special for me was that the SBS announcer covering the event was someone I had known back in Oregon. Her name was Seungyeon.

She had always been pretty and stylish when we were in Eugene, but I had no idea she aspired to be a TV announcer. Seeing her on SBS somehow made perfect sense. She looked so polished and confident. It was really good to see her. In a strange way, it felt like I had a visitor in the hospital, even if it was only through a television screen.

After I was discharged, recovery was slow. My knee kept me inactive, so I spent long, uneventful days at home. I still didn't have many friends nearby, and honestly, I wasn't in the mood to reach out to anyone. Being on crutches for nearly a month didn't help either. Getting around was a hassle.

That's when I discovered that you could meet people and make friends without ever leaving your house — as long as you had a phone line and a decent internet connection. If, in the U.S., there was America Online, then in Korea, we had Chollian.

When I first logged on to chat online, I quickly realized just how introverted and shy I was, especially so, since everything was in Korean. Anytime a stranger messaged me with a simple "Hello," I froze, panicked, and immediately disconnected. It felt like I was that shy girl at the school dance — you know, the one with thick glasses and braces, who bolts to the bathroom the moment a guy walks up to say hi.

What made it even weirder was that no one could see me. I was anonymous. But still, I hesitated. Maybe it was the discomfort of chatting with strangers in Korean. So I tried searching for English-speaking chat rooms instead.

Eventually, I found MSN (Microsoft Network) free chat rooms. Even there, I was nervous and awkward, but I decided to push myself. I'd give myself little pep talks before logging on: "Come on, you can do this. No one knows who you are. Just don't be weird. You've got this."

People would pop in and start with the basics — "M/F?" or "Where are you from?" If it was a guy, they usually left after I answered. But after a while, I started to feel a bit more comfortable. I often found myself chatting with girls — apparently, they wanted to talk to guys too. I wasn't looking for a girlfriend or anything like that. Honestly, just talking to anyone felt nice.

Of course, I had no idea what any of these people looked like. But in cyberspace, you're free to imagine whatever you want. I pictured everyone with kind smiles, nice teeth, and genuinely sweet personalities. That probably wasn't true 99% of the time, but that's the magic of the internet: anything can be true if you want it to be.

Though I wasn't trying to start an online romance, I'll admit, there were occasional moments of casual flirting. Most of the people I chatted with were from far-off places, so I didn't worry about being caught in a white lie or two. It was just lighthearted fun.

At first, I was totally unfamiliar with online slang. I remember not knowing what "LOL" meant. But people kept using it, so I just copied them, leading to some pretty funny exchanges.

PrettyLady206: So, where are you from?
Me: Korea! LOL! And you?
PrettyLady206: I'm from Cali.
Me: LOL
PrettyLady206: Sex?
Me: Not today. LOL. Just kidding. I'm a guy. And you?
PrettyLady206: LOL. I'm female.
Me: LOL
PrettyLady206: What are you doing right now?
Me: Nothing. LOL.
PrettyLady206: You seem very happy.
Me: Why do you say that? LOL.
PrettyLady206: Because you seem to laugh a lot.
Me: LOL. I'm not laughing at all. LOL.
PrettyLady206: You kinda are. And you're kinda weird.
Me: LOL. lol lol lol
PrettyLady206 has left the chat room.

After a while, I realized I was chatting with tons of strangers but wasn't forming any real connections. It all felt shallow. I was about ready to give it up altogether — until one day, I stumbled into a Korean chat room where everyone was speaking English. That changed everything.

It was a revelation. I didn't know who these people were, what they looked like, or where they were exactly, but I quickly came to understand that they were real people living in Korea. People who were looking for a space to speak English and connect with others who understood their in-between world. They were like me. And for a brief time, this was my community.

The only problem was our dial-up internet at home. It wasn't fast enough to keep up with the flood of messages. And since it ran through the house phone line, we couldn't receive calls when I was online. Plus, the phone bills were starting to stack up. That's when I discovered the neighborhood *PC bang* — Korea's version of an internet café, filled with rows of high-speed computers.

About 90% of the people there were glued to *StarCraft*, the insanely popular online game that had become a cultural phenomenon. There were even TV channels dedicated to broadcasting matches, and some players went on to become international stars. I, however, could never figure out the game. It was way too complicated for me.

I wasn't there to play games, though. I was there for the MSN chat room. I'd spend hours talking with my new Korean, English-speaking cyber friends. I had no job, and I was still recovering from knee surgery, barely able to walk. I had nowhere else to be. And in that little digital corner of the world, I made some real friends.

None of us used our real names in the chat room. There was Ellis, an English teacher in Busan who chose her nickname from the education system her school used. Then there was a younger guy named Sanghyeok, who went by Jerome. That was the name he had used while living in the U.K. before returning to Korea. Another friend was Rene, who picked that name because people told her she looked like the actress Rene Russo. And then there was Kay from Seoul, whose real name was Kyeonghee. She worked at a company where English was essential, and she used the chat room as a way to practice.

As for me, I went by Duckdawg. It was a nod to my time as an Oregon Duck and a Washington Husky. A little quirky, but I liked it.

People would come and go in the chat room. If they were friendly, we welcomed them. But if someone came in just to hit on girls or stir up trouble, we kicked them out. We formed a tight-knit little digital tribe, and though it might sound strange today, that group kept me from feeling completely isolated during those months in Daegu. Living back at home with my parents, stuck inside recovering from surgery, that chat room became my lifeline.

We even tried to be friends offline, though geography made it tricky.

I never met Jerome in person. He lived in Seoul. But we spoke on the phone several times. He was younger than me, but his intense voice and crisp British accent made him sound a decade older, and far more sophisticated.

I did get to meet Ellis once. I took the high-speed KTX train down to Busan, and we hung out at Gwangalli Beach, sharing some excellent sashimi and washing it down with a DIY cocktail of *soju* and cola. By the time I boarded the train back home, I had a solid buzz going.

I also met Kay in person once. We linked up in Seoul at Tower Records. It was a brief meeting, but meaningful all the same.

After a few months, my knee grew stronger and I was finally able to walk again, which meant it was time to move on. In early 2000, I packed up and headed to Seoul to look for work. Until I could find a job and a place of my own, I crashed with my younger brother, Albert.

I still logged on occasionally to check in with my old chat room crew, to say "hi" and see how everyone was doing. But life started to speed up. Things got busier. And eventually, I lost touch with most of them. As they say, life goes on.

Albert was living in a tiny two-bedroom house with two roommates, so space was tight. But they were kind enough to let me crash there until I could find a place of my own. All three of them were aspiring rock musicians, each with their own band and dreams of making it big.

One of them had already tasted some success. He played drums for the indie rock band *Deli Spice*, which had a few hit songs under its belt. The oldest of the group was a producer and guitarist for a band called *Sweater*. I'm not sure if he ever made it big, but for him, that was never the point. He just wanted to make good music, whether the world noticed or not.

Then there was my brother, Albert. He was the bassist and leader of a band called *Super Stone Hero*. I saw him perform a few times at clubs in the underground rock scenes of Shinchon and Hongdae, and every time, he lit up the stage. Eventually, he realized he couldn't make a living from music and pivoted to a career in English-to-Korean interpretation. But still, it was a good run while it lasted.

I've always been proud of Albert. He had a dream, chased it, and gave it everything he had. Most people never even try. He did.

Living with aspiring rock stars meant nights that didn't end until 3 or 4 a.m., and days that didn't start until well past noon. It wasn't because they were partying all night. That was just the regular hours they kept.

It wasn't ideal for me. I needed sleep at night so I could job-hunt during the day, but I didn't mind too much. It was fun getting to know the guys and living the rock-and-roll life vicariously through them, even just for a little while.

I had applied to a range of companies and interviewed for positions at Procter & Gamble, the Financial Supervisory Service of Korea, the Bank of Korea, KOSDAQ, and even a couple of U.S. financial firms for analyst roles. None of them worked out.

Eventually, I landed a job with the foreign planning team at a company called K-BEST.

K-BEST was located in the KBS Annex Building, tucked into the southern edge of Yeouido's financial, political, and broadcasting district. For context, KBS — along with MBC and SBS — is one of Korea's three major terrestrial TV networks. K-BEST had once been the official production arm of KBS, known as the KBS Production Company, responsible for many of its in-house dramas and documentaries. But just before I joined, the company had been privatized and forced to rebrand. It still produced programs for KBS, but was no longer officially part of the network.

As a result of this, most of the employees, who were previously part of KBS, had lost their KBS benefits, and morale was low. There were more than a few disgruntled people around.

My role was to develop international business opportunities, including importing and exporting content to and from overseas partners. The reality, though, was that K-BEST wasn't exactly producing global hits. Its content didn't have much appeal outside Korea, or even beyond KBS, so there wasn't much for me to actually do.

We tried to branch out into other areas. One attempt was to launch a new cable channel, which eventually aired as the *World Event Network*. Unfortunately, we didn't have much content to offer, so it mostly ended up recycling episodes of *Jeonguk Norae Jarang* — a long-running provincial talent show that, while beloved in rural Korea, wasn't exactly international fare.

We also dabbled in tech, attempting to launch a data hosting center — a server-filled building that companies could rent space in. On paper, it sounded promising. Korea was on the verge of becoming one of the most wired countries in the world. But in practice, this was far outside the company's wheelhouse. It never got off the ground.

Eventually, K-BEST was acquired by an online education company called KONES, which hoped to pivot us into an educational content production house. That plan fizzled out too.

As for me, with no international work coming in, I found myself stuck doing tedious Korean office tasks, despite my limited Korean language skills. Some of the documents I was asked to draft made absolutely no sense, and honestly, a fifth grader probably could've done a better job. But even that kind of work was rare. Most days, I just sat at my desk, doing absolutely nothing, except reading *ESPN.com* and playing computer games.

This was the year 2000, long before Facebook or the other social media platforms we know today, so I couldn't waste time scrolling endlessly like people do now. But Korea had its own version of digital distraction. One popular site back then was *SayClub*. It was kind of like *Match.com*, or in today's terms, *Tinder*, though not quite as obvious. Originally designed as a profile-sharing platform to make new friends or network, most people used it to flirt, date, or have casual flings.

Naturally, I got into SayClub too in order to meet new people. And by "meet people," I mostly mean "try to meet girls." On a few occasions, I even agreed to meet someone offline. And wouldn't you know it? They looked *very* different from their profile pictures. I mean *very*. But hey, that was the risk you take in online dating.

Another site that blew up around that time was *I Love School*. It was a social network for reconnecting with old classmates — from elementary through high school. But since most middle and high schools in Korea were gender-segregated, the most popular searches were for coed elementary school classmates. The dream was that you'd find that one childhood crush — they'd still be attractive, still single, and when you saw each other at the reunion, sparks would fly and an old flame would reignite.

I'll admit, it was the same for me. I had no interest in reconnecting with anyone from Sim-in Middle or Keisung High, but I was curious about old friends from Keisung Elementary. I joined the online community for my Class of '86. It's not that I had a ton of friends back then, but I was curious to see how everyone had changed.

By then, my dad had moved from Keimyung University in Daegu to a new position at Soongsil University in Seoul, so I had no reason to visit Daegu — except for one or two weekends when I returned for *I Love School* reunions. There were a couple of girls I met who I thought were cute, but sadly the interest wasn't mutual. Things fizzled quickly, and I lost interest in the whole thing.

So yeah... those were some of the dumb ways I wasted time at K-BEST. The hours were long, the job was boring, and I was doing everything I could not to lose my mind.

You'd think that once the clock struck 6 p.m., I'd rush out of the office to reclaim my day and do something fun or productive. But that wasn't really an option. My boss was one of those middle-aged Korean men who didn't want to go home — probably because he didn't want to deal with chores or help the kids with homework. So he'd just sit at his desk, chain-smoking cigarettes and checking stock prices until 8 p.m. or later. And yes, if you were the boss, you got to smoke in the office right at your desk, even with others around.

Another thing was that in that kind of office culture, you couldn't leave before your boss. It just wasn't done. So I'd sit around, pretending to work, watching the clock tick by until well into the evening. On most days, I waited until he left, then gave him a five-minute head start just so I wouldn't run into him in the elevator. Some days, I spent 12 hours at the office doing absolutely nothing. There's almost nothing more soul-crushing than that.

But believe it or not, those were the *better* days. At least two or three nights a week, I'd be out having dinner and drinks with members of the production teams. As I mentioned earlier, many of them were disgruntled — frustrated that they were no longer officially part of KBS. Most nights, they drowned their sorrows over pork barbecue and endless rounds of *somaek*, that infamous Korean cocktail of *soju* and beer. It's a staple at Korean work dinners — and a surefire recipe for getting drunk fast and waking up with a brutal hangover.

The PDs liked having me around because I could hold my own. I didn't sip my drinks timidly. They knew I'd match them shot for shot. Whether it was *somaek*, straight soju, or even a full mug filled to the brim with nothing but *soju*, I was game.

And of course, the night rarely ended at the restaurant. We'd often continue the party at a *noraebang* karaoke room, belting out songs in our drunken glory, before wrapping things up with some late-night *chimaek* — fried chicken and beer.

Most nights, I managed to get home without incident. But now and then, as soon as I stepped through the front door and knew I was safe, I'd let my guard down and completely lose it. The next morning, I'd find myself still fully dressed, and passed out on my bed, if I was lucky. If not, I sometimes found myself on the cold bathroom floor.

On rare occasions, the night went sideways before I even made it home. I'd have to call Albert to come pick me up, and I'm embarrassed to say, he may have found me taking a nap on the sidewalk a few times... just a few.

You might wonder why I drank so much, or whether I even had a choice. Technically, I did. But for many young professionals in Korea at the time, saying no wasn't so simple. Refusing to join after-work dinners and drinking sessions could quickly make you an outsider — or worse, unemployed.

If you wanted job security, you had to fit into one of two categories: be so good at your job that they couldn't function without you, or be the kind of person who knew how to drink and have a good time. Since I wasn't the former, I had to be the latter.

In those days, calling in sick because of a hangover simply wasn't an option. So I got very good at dragging myself into the office with a pounding headache and a queasy stomach. Most mornings, I'd sneak out for a bowl of hot, spicy *ramyun*. I'm not sure if it was the broth, the starchy noodles, or the sweat it induced — but somehow, it worked. I'd sober up just enough to survive the day... and by 5 p.m., I'd feel ready to do it all over again.

But eventually, the lifestyle caught up with me. I was eating and drinking too much and barely exercising, especially with my bad knee. One day, I stepped on the scale and was horrified to see I'd gained nearly 50 pounds (23 kilograms). I had always taken pride in being lean and athletic, but now, my belly jiggled when I walked and I had — no exaggeration — a triple chin.

There's still a passport photo I keep hidden away somewhere. In it, I look like Porky Pig. Three chins. Puffy cheeks. Dead eyes. I keep it as a reminder to never let myself go like that again.

Deep down, I knew this lifestyle was going to break me — either mentally, from the mind-numbing boredom of my workdays, or physically, from the endless cycle of alcohol and greasy food at night. So I started looking for a way out. I began searching for another job.

I updated my resume, posted it online, and spent my days combing through job listings. Some might say that's stealing company time, but from my experience at K-BEST, I'd learned that many Korean men spent their workdays doing one or more of the following:

1. Take endless cigarette breaks, while waiting around to drink with colleagues after work

2. Check their stock portfolios

3. Play office politics to climb the ladder without doing much actual work

4. Browse job sites for their next opportunity

I didn't do much of 1, 2, or 3, so naturally, I leaned into number 4.

One day, I got a call from a headhunter. She said she'd seen my resume online and was recruiting on behalf of a global sports marketing company called IMG, which was looking to hire a new salesperson. As soon as I heard the word sales, I was out. I'd already done that grind once. My first job out of college had been selling life insurance at DFC, and it was one of the hardest, most demoralizing things I'd ever done. I had no interest in doing that again.

I thanked her politely and declined.

A week later, she called again. This time, she said the opening was for a player manager position. I wasn't exactly sure what that meant, but I told her I'd consider it, as long as it wasn't sales.

The following week, I went in for the interview... and got the job on the spot.

IMG needed someone who spoke fluent English and understood both Western and Korean cultures. Apparently, I was the best they could find. Ironically, they also filled the sales role with a Korean-Canadian, whose name just so happened to be Joseph Park. Since he was older than me, they dubbed him *Joe Park Senior*, and I became *Joe Park Junior*.

That unexpected turn launched a 14-year career in the sports industry, with 13 of those years spent at IMG. My first stint ran from 2001 to 2007.

After that, I did a brief stint — less than a year — with the NBA. They had opened an office in Korea, and hired me to take the lead. My role there was to sell marketing rights to Korean companies interested in using the NBA brand. I still loved basketball very much back then, but it turned out that Korean companies didn't. It often felt like I was banging my head against a brick wall day after day. I didn't enjoy it, so I left.

Next, I moved to a company called TEC, which provided premium executive office space in Seoul's top business hubs: the Seoul Finance Center and Gangnam Finance Center. I thought this might be my path out of the sports industry — maybe a new chapter. But I quickly realized something: no matter how far I tried to stray, I couldn't escape sports.

Sure enough, in 2008, IMG called me back. I rejoined the company and stayed until 2013, when I finally left to pursue a new calling — this time, into ministry.

IMG was originally known as International Management Group. Legend has it that the company began in the 1960s with a handshake between its founder, Mark H. McCormack, and Arnold Palmer, one of the most beloved golfers of all time. Since then, it has grown into one of the largest sports marketing companies in the world — starting with golf, and eventually expanding into nearly every major sport.

I worked for the Korea branch, located in a modest office in Yeoksam-dong, within Seoul's Gangnam district. I had pictured a large, bustling office, so I was surprised to find that it was quite small. There were only seven employees in total.

On my first day, I arrived at 8:50 a.m., ten minutes early. But the lights were off, the door was locked, and no one was there. At 9 a.m., I rang the bell and knocked again. Then I kept waiting and waiting. When still no one came along, I decided to go grab a cup of coffee and come back. And then I waited some more. I started to worry. Was this a real company? Had I fallen for a scam?

Finally, a little past 10 a.m., the receptionist arrived and let me in. I remember thinking, *"What the heck? This is a terrible way to welcome someone on their first day of work."*

To make matters worse, the headhunter who had connected me to the job called later that morning to check in. She'd heard that the country manager was being sued by a client for fraud and wanted to know if I'd been affected. At that point, I seriously considered whether I should try crawling back to K-BEST.

Thankfully, the lawsuit turned out to be baseless, and the office was indeed legitimate. As for the late start time, I later found out that the company had a flexible work culture, which, in hindsight, I came to appreciate.

Despite the rocky start, I ended up having a fantastic run with IMG. Although our team was small, we were Korea's only true international sports marketing agency, and we worked with some of the biggest names in sports.

To drop a few: I worked with golf legends like Jack Nicklaus, Tom Watson, and Annika Sörenstam. When Tiger Woods came to Korea in 2004, I was assigned to greet him as his private jet landed on the tarmac at Jeju International Airport. We grabbed burgers and watched NBA basketball together. I also had the privilege of working with other golf stars like Rory McIlroy, Sergio Garcia, Adam Scott, and Michelle Wie, among others. Over time, some of these athletes became personal friends.

Occasionally, I had the chance to work outside of golf as well. In tennis, I worked with Roger Federer, Rafael Nadal, and Maria Sharapova. I never got to meet Serena Williams, but I worked closely with her older sister, Venus. She liked me enough to invite me to Sean "P. Diddy" Combs' New Year's Eve party once, but that world felt way too out of my league, so I politely declined.

But of all the names I could drop, the one that gets the biggest reaction from Koreans is the Queen herself — Kim Yuna.

I was her first manager when she transitioned from junior to senior-level figure skating. When we first met, she was a quiet high school student who couldn't go anywhere without her mom. She didn't stay with IMG very long, and she may not even remember me anymore, but I like to think I was one of the first people who helped her take her first steps onto the global stage.

I'll always be grateful for the memories and opportunities I had during those years. In fact, during the late 2000s and early 2010s, people in the industry would call me the "Jerry Maguire of Korea," after the 1997 Tom Cruise movie. If you wanted to bring a top sports star to Korea, you needed to go through me.

Nowadays, when my teenage daughter, Joanna, asks if I know any famous people, I tell her stories about those days when I would rub shoulders with global sports legends. She usually just rolls her eyes.

"Daddy, stop being such an old fart," she says. "I don't even know who those people are. I meant cool people. Like, people from *today*."

And of course, I roll my eyes right back at her.

When I first started at IMG in 2001, I had no idea what I was getting myself into. My very first client was none other than Korea's national heroine, Pak Se-Ri.

At the height of the Asian financial crisis in 1998 — when businesses were collapsing, people were losing their jobs, and the entire nation was in despair — Se-Ri lifted our spirits and gave us hope by winning the U.S. Women's Open in dramatic fashion.

In the final hole of an 18-hole playoff, she pulled her tee shot so far left that it landed on the grassy slope beside a pond. Had the ball gone into the water, she would've been penalized and lost the tournament on the spot. But when she found her ball just outside the hazard, she famously removed her shoes and socks, stepped barefoot into the water, and struck a miraculous shot onto the green. She avoided disaster, and was able to extend the match. Two holes later, she sealed the win and brought home the most prestigious trophy in women's golf.

The whole country had gotten up at the crack of dawn to watch it live. For a nation starved of optimism, Se-Ri gave us not just a reason to cheer, but a sense of hope. At a time when everything felt lost, she reminded us that something could still be won.

Anyone from my generation or older remembers her for that moment. Today's younger generation, however, probably knows her better from the Korean variety show *Noneun Eonni* (known on Netflix as *Playing Sister*), where she leads a group of retired female athletes on adventures — camping, wakeboarding, even parachuting. It's about reclaiming the joy they missed during their competitive years, and Se-Ri is the gang's fearless leader.

Though she played most of her career on the U.S. LPGA Tour, Se-Ri would return to Korea once a year to compete in the Korea Women's Open. I began working with her during the 2001 tournament.

To be honest, there was no training, no orientation — nothing. I was thrown into the deep end. So I kept quiet, stayed alert, and made sure to stay nearby in case she needed anything. If she did, I'd get it as quickly as I could. I didn't know if that was exactly what I was supposed to do, but apparently, it worked.

That simple formula — *stay low, stay sharp, and stay useful* — became the approach I carried with me for the rest of my career.

Right after Se-Ri returned to the U.S., I started working with another rising star in Korean golf: Choi Kyoung-Ju, better known on the PGA Tour as K.J. Choi. He was the first Korean man to play on the U.S. Tour. While he didn't receive the same level of media attention as Se-Ri at the time, he was a true pioneer for men's golf in Korea.

Over his career, he won eight times on the PGA Tour, including a memorable victory at *The Players Championship* in 2011. He also served as a vice-captain for the International Team at the Presidents Cup, lending his experience and leadership to some of the game's biggest stages. These days, he's still going strong on the PGA Champions Tour, and by most accounts, he's the most accomplished male golfer in Korean history.

Over the years, I got to know K.J. and his family very well. When his son, Ho-Jun David, was just six years old, I'd take him around the course catching dragonflies while his dad was a few holes ahead, winning the tournament. His wife, Hyunjung Kim, took a real liking to me. She called me frequently from their home in Texas, asking for help with all kinds of domestic matters. I'd call the gas company when the heat wasn't working properly, or help their son with his phonics homework over the phone.

Most people assume that being a player manager is all about standing outside the ropes at a fancy golf tournament, arms folded, nodding in approval. But that's not where you earn trust or respect. Where you really earn your keep is in the unseen moments — like helping a first grader with his English homework over an international call at 11 p.m. on a Thursday night.

Besides managing players, one of IMG's biggest roles was organizing golf tournaments. In 2001, we were hired to run the first-ever official U.S. LPGA Tour event in Korea, held at the brand-new Club Nine Bridges in Jeju. The course took great pride in being named one of the top 100 golf courses in the world, and the tournament was being billed as the most prestigious golf event in Korean history. All the top LPGA stars were expected to play.

Our corporate client was a daily newspaper called *Sports Today*, and they had sky-high expectations. The LPGA also put enormous pressure on us. Since it was their first tournament in Korea, they wanted everything to be perfect for their players.

The problem? IMG Korea had never done anything of this scale before.

We were sorely under-resourced. Our golf director had little experience with event execution. We hired a golf implementation manager, but he was just as green. I was responsible for player relations, but I had never even attended a golf tournament in the U.S., let alone helped organize one. To be honest, we weren't ready. We didn't have the capability.

To make matters worse, I was constantly pushed to secure sponsorships. During my job interview, I had made it clear I didn't want anything to do with sales. But later, I was told that *everyone* at the company was expected to do sales. As the youngest on the team, I was tasked with making cold calls to marketing departments across Seoul. I hated it, and I wasn't good at it. But then again, no one was.

We couldn't sell anything to anyone. We couldn't sell candy to a fat baby, even if our lives depended on it.

Needless to say, I was nervous. The writing felt like it was on the wall. In my mind, I was certain we were going to crash and burn, and for most of the year leading up to the event, it seemed like that's exactly what was happening. Nothing was coming together, and my worst fears were beginning to materialize.

Then came September 11.

When the planes hit the World Trade Center, it was nighttime in Korea. By the next morning, the tragedy was all anyone could talk about.

As I got to the office, the phone started ringing nonstop. Korean journalists wanted updates: "Is Se-Ri okay? What about K.J. Choi? Where are they now? Are the LPGA players still coming to Korea? Is the Jeju tournament still happening?"

Thankfully, both Se-Ri and K.J., my main clients in the U.S., were nowhere near New York and were completely fine, as were the LPGA players slated to compete. For a brief moment, it seemed the tournament might still go on.

But as the days passed and the shock of the tragedy settled in, the LPGA made an official announcement: all international travel and tournaments would be suspended for the rest of the year for player safety.

Some saw this as a massive blow to our inaugural event. But frankly, I breathed a sigh of relief. We had just been given a second chance — a full year to regroup, plan properly, and get things right.

And we did.

In November 2002, the tournament finally took place. The only problem? It was freezing. Players scrambled to find parka jackets on the course. Many foreign players — lured by the idea of Jeju being Korea's "island paradise," like Hawaii — arrived completely unprepared. For them, it was less like paradise and more like hell frozen over.

Still, the event went on. And while it wasn't flawless, it was good. Se-Ri won the inaugural championship, which was a dream outcome for the Korean media and sponsors.

As for me, I was far more prepared the second time around. With a year under my belt, I finally felt like I knew what I was doing. After the tournament wrapped, I even took a few players to the hotel *noraebang* karaoke room to celebrate and blow off some steam. That night sealed it: I became one of the players' favorite hosts on the LPGA Tour.

Someone even told me that a few of the players were already looking forward to coming back the next year — not for the golf, but to party with me. Turns out, all those long nights of drinking and singing karaoke at K-BEST had actually prepared me for something.

In 2003, both the director of golf and the events manager left the company. That's when upper management approached me and asked if I would step into the events manager role — *on top of* my existing responsibilities as player manager. I didn't want to do it, but in reality, I didn't have much of a choice. So now, I was wearing two hats.

Then came the kicker: they also asked me to head up sales for the golf division. *Ugh!* I had made it crystal clear from the beginning — *no sales*. But at this point, there was no avoiding it.

Over the course of my career at IMG, I ended up managing ten LPGA tournaments in Korea, one PGA Champions Tour event, a special event featuring Tiger Woods, three tennis exhibitions, a couple of figure skating galas, and several smaller corporate outings that honestly blur together in my memory.

It was hard work — grueling at times. There were periods when I was living out of hotels for more than four weeks straight. Some stretches required me to stay awake for 72 hours without sleep just to keep things from falling apart. The stress was overwhelming. After certain events, my body would crash, and I'd be bedridden for days, completely drained.

And yet, looking back, I'm grateful. Because for the first time, I felt like I belonged in Korea. I had found a place where my work mattered, where my efforts were seen, and where I didn't feel stupid — like I had back in my school days in Daegu. I had finally found my place.

In 2002, something else happened that further reaffirmed my growing sense that I was finally finding my place in Korea. That summer, Korea and Japan co-hosted the FIFA World Cup. While I'm not sure how Japan celebrated, in Korea, it was nothing short of extraordinary.

For every Team Korea match, people gathered in public squares across the country, cheering on the team in front of massive outdoor screens. The most iconic location was Seoul City Hall, where hundreds of thousands of people came together, united by the now-famous chant: "*Dae-han-min-guk!*" — followed by five rhythmic claps, repeated over and over.

I had never seen an entire country come together like that. And every time Korea won, which they miraculously did often during that tournament, the streets exploded in pure joy. Beer houses gave out free pitchers. Strangers hugged, high-fived, and kissed one another. People jumped and danced in the streets well into the night.

And it wasn't just Koreans celebrating. Foreigners joined in, too. If you weren't Korean during that time, you *wanted* to be. The 2002 World Cup was a month-long, nationwide party that united people regardless of nationality, race, gender, age, politics, or class. Everyone was invited, and it truly felt like *everyone came*. Nobody wanted it to end.

On the pitch, the matches were electric, full of unforgettable moments. It felt as though the energy of the fans had breathed new life into the players. Korea played with fire, grit, and something deeper — like they were possessed. It was a team the world had never seen before.

In the final Group D match, Korea faced Portugal, led by Luis Figo and a very young Cristiano Ronaldo. Korea *had* to win to advance. That's when a relatively unknown young player at the time, Park Ji-Sung, scored an incredible goal to seal a 1–0 victory, and with that the improbable became real.

Next came Spain. The game ended in a 0–0 draw and went to penalties. With the final kick of the night, captain Hong Myeong-Bo calmly slotted the ball into the back of the net, sending Korea into the next round to face Italy.

Italy was a tournament favorite, and with just two minutes left in regulation, they led 1–0. It seemed Korea's fairytale run was finally over. But then, in a moment of magic, Seol Ki-Hyun scored an equalizer that shocked the world and sent the match into overtime.

And then came perhaps the most legendary goal in Korean soccer history.

In the 117th minute, Ahn Jung-Hwan connected with a perfect cross, heading the ball past the Italian goalkeeper for a golden goal. Korea had defeated the mighty Italians and made it to the World Cup semifinal for the first time ever. The nation went wild.

I lost my voice more than once during that tournament, just like everyone else. Those matches were unforgettable, each one more miraculous than the last.

But for me, one game stood out for a very personal reason. It's a match that doesn't get talked about as much as the others. This was Korea's second group-stage game — against the United States.

When I first arrived in Korea as a little kid in the 1980s, people would sometimes ask me, "If Korea and America played each other in the World Cup, which team would you cheer for?"

Without a second of hesitation, I'd proudly respond, "America, of course! America is the greatest country in the world!"

But in 2002, when Korea faced off against the U.S., something felt different. Something had changed inside me. I wasn't exactly sure when it happened — or how — but instead of rooting for the Americans, I found myself cheering for Team Korea.

That match was played during the day, and I watched it from a meeting room at the office with my Korean colleagues. Everyone gathered around the TV, naturally cheering for the Taegeuk Warriors, as Team Korea is often called.

But as for me, before the match began, I figured I'd be quietly pulling for the Red, White, and Blue. After all, it was only Korea's second match of the tournament, and the full wave of World Cup fever hadn't taken over yet. I didn't even know the names of the Korean players. I actually knew more about the American team from articles I'd read on ESPN.

But as soon as the match kicked off, something unexpected happened: I soon discovered that I wanted Korea to win.

Within minutes, I found myself clapping and shouting *"Dae-han-min-guk!"* along with everyone else. I was swept up in the moment, and I wasn't faking it. It was real.

The game ended in a 1–1 tie. Most Koreans don't remember it much, probably because it wasn't a win. But in my heart, Korea had won. Because that day, I realized I was more Korean than I had ever admitted to myself.

It was a turning point. For most of my life, I had hated being Korean. My childhood and youth in Daegu had left scars I didn't like to revisit. But somehow, in that moment, I began to embrace Korea. It didn't mean I was fully comfortable in it yet. I still had a long way to go. But something had shifted. I was no longer fighting it. Instead of trying to deny or escape my Koreanness, I began to look for ways to find my place in it.

I won't say I suddenly loved being Korean — not even now could I say that with complete certainty. But back then, I started to try. And that was something new.

Why, though? Why did it matter then when it never had before?

The only answer I could come up with was simple: the people. I didn't care before, because I hadn't connected. But now, I did.

When I look back on this chapter of my life, I realize that when I returned to Korea, I came back with virtually no relationships. Whatever ties I had from high school or earlier years, I had deliberately left behind, because those memories were painful, and I wanted nothing to do with them.

But the reason I slowly began to accept my Koreanness was because I began to accept the relationships in my life again.

Sometimes, I look back with a nostalgic, sideways smirk at those days spent trying to make connections on *MSN*, *SayClub*, and *I Love School*. Part of me thinks I was so naïve, maybe even a little foolish. But another part of me knows exactly why I did it — because we are not meant to be alone. Even if those *MSN* friendships existed only online, they mattered to me. I cared about those people. In that season of life, they were my friends.

When I think back to my time at K-BEST — going out for drinks with the producers night after night — I know no one truly forced me. It was my choice. I could've said "no." But I didn't. Even though it was exhausting, embarrassing at times, and certainly not good for my health, I did it because of the relationships. I'm not saying it was wise or healthy. I'm just saying that's why I did it.

At IMG, I hated sales because it always felt so impersonal. But the rest of the work — attending to Pak Se-Ri's every need when she came to Korea, helping K.J. Choi's son with his homework late at night, putting together events for LPGA players and singing karaoke with them afterward — all of that was meaningful. And it was meaningful because it was rooted in relationships. I wouldn't have worked so hard if I didn't care about the people.

Even when I cheered for Team Korea during the 2002 World Cup, it wasn't out of national pride, or a deep love for the culture or the history. I'd come to appreciate that stuff later, but in the moment, it was because, for the first time, I had started to feel connected. I had begun to love the people — and I wanted to be in relationship with them. And because of that, where there had once been a heart filled with resentment toward Korea, there now emerged a quiet but unmistakable desire for reconciliation.

As I close this chapter, I want to reflect on what has been the central theme of this memoir: identity. And I believe identity is inseparable from relationships.

So much of who we are — our values, our mannerisms, our interests, and even our sense of purpose — is shaped through the people we connect with. But in a broken world, relationships often come fractured, whether with family, friends, colleagues, or society at large. If we want to understand who we truly are, we have to be willing to look honestly at those broken places. And if we want to become whole, we must seek reconciliation.

But reconciliation with others begins with something deeper: our reconciliation with God.

In Genesis 3, Adam and Eve broke trust with God, and that rupture became the source of all brokenness — between humanity and God, and between one another. Blame, shame, and distance replaced intimacy, and that condition has been passed down to all of us. Ever since, in the deepest parts of our souls, we've longed to be restored — not just to each other, but even more so, to God.

Some say the ultimate purpose in life is to be happy. So we chase happiness through our careers, friendships, marriages, and even in the hobbies we pursue. But if we're honest, these pursuits aren't just about success or fulfillment — they're about something deeper. They are really about relationship. Through the paths we take in life, we long to be connected, to belong, to be seen and loved. Whether we realize it or not, our pursuit of happiness is actually a pursuit of restored relationships. Because what is happiness if it's experienced in isolation?

But at the foundation of all our relationships is our relationship with God. And unless that relationship is restored, none of our other relationships can be fully healed, no matter how hard we try. Reconciliation with God is the starting point — and that reconciliation only comes through faith in Jesus Christ.

As Paul writes in 2 Corinthians 5:17–21:

> *"Therefore, if anyone is in Christ, he is a new creation. The old has passed away; behold, the new has come. All this is from God, who through Christ reconciled us to himself and gave us the ministry of reconciliation...*
>
> *We implore you on behalf of Christ, be reconciled to God. For our sake, he made him to be sin who knew no sin, so that in him we might become the righteousness of God."*

When I began to embrace Korea — its people, its culture, even its pain — it wasn't just because of an MSN chat room, a job in sports marketing, or a World Cup soccer match. What I didn't realize at the time was that, at the core of all of that, Jesus' grace was already at work, reconciling me to Himself. And through that reconciliation, He was softening my heart to reconnect with others as well.

His ministry toward me was a ministry of reconciliation. And later, He would call me to live out that same ministry for the sake of others, and ultimately, unto Him.

I want to finish this chapter with this one last thought.

There are two words in the Korean language for "person" or "humankind." One is *saram*, which most people are familiar with. It literally just means "a person". The other — the one I prefer — is *ingan*.

It carries the same meaning, but its roots go deeper. *Ingan* comes from Chinese characters that mean "person" and "relationship." In other words, to be a person is, by definition, to be in relationship.

That ancient insight tells us something profound: we were never meant to exist alone. We are relational beings by design. Whoever first coined that term probably wasn't a Christian, but even in ancient Eastern philosophy, we see a glimpse of God's truth — that to be human is to be in relationship.

And this is why reconciliation with God makes us whole. When our relationship with Him is restored, it reshapes every other relationship in our lives. Our humanity comes alive again, and we're drawn toward healing and restoration with others.

It would still take me a few more years, and some painful experiences, to fully grasp the depth of God's love and grace. But if there's one truth I can carry with me from this chapter of my life, it's this: Whether we know God yet or not, we cannot truly know ourselves apart from the reconciliation of our relationships. But true reconciliation and relationship can only come from God.

Chapter 15

I Want it All

I started 2002 weighing nearly 220 pounds (100 kilograms), most of it fat and blubber from all the heavy drinking and greasy late-night meals during my early years at K-BEST. Once I joined IMG, I realized I needed a serious lifestyle change. If I didn't turn things around soon, my health could take a major hit, if it hadn't already.

For the first time in my life, I decided to pay for a gym membership. And not just any gym, I joined the fanciest, glitziest gym in Seoul: California Fitness Center. With branches in all the trendiest parts of town — Myeongdong, Apgujeong, and Gangnam — my membership gave me access to all three. I made the most of it when I could.

The Gangnam branch was closest to my office, so I'd sneak over during lunch breaks for a quick 30-minute cardio session. After work, I'd hit the Apgujeong location to lift weights, then meet up with friends nearby. I visited the Myeongdong branch every once in a while, mostly just to say I had.

California Fitness was where all the top stars and beautiful people came to work out, or at least be seen in their stylish Nike gear. If Instagram had existed back then, I'm sure half the city would've been posting mirror selfies from CFC. Working out there was a status symbol. It meant you were young, upwardly mobile, and cared about your body.

On any given day, I might have Cha Seung-Won, the famous Korean model and actor, doing bicep curls on one side of me, and Rain, the world-famous singer, doing squats on the other. Across the room on a cardio bike might be Lee Cheon-Soo from the Korean National Soccer Team. I may not have been in their class, *but gosh darn it*, I was in their gym.

I'll admit, part of my motivation was the sheer thrill of being in that atmosphere. Who wouldn't want to be surrounded by celebrities, models, and ridiculously good-looking people? A part of me even thought it made *me* cooler by association. But more than anything, the steep membership fee gave me the push I needed to take my workouts seriously.

I was at the gym almost every day, after work and even on weekends. I cleaned up my diet, cut way back on drinking, and started eating healthier — low carbs, high protein. After six months of intense discipline, I was down to 180 pounds (82 kilograms).

Now, you might think all that hard work would have made me more grounded — more humble and focused on what truly mattered in life. But honestly, it had the opposite effect. I got vain.

One day at the gym, I looked at myself in the mirror, admired my lean, athletic frame, and said out loud, "Dang, boy! You look good!"

Right at that moment, as I stood in front of the mirror admiring my new physique, a thought came to me. It was silly, immature — even a little ridiculous — but I meant it with all sincerity. I thought to myself, *I want it all. I want the body, the looks, the clothes, the fame, the money, the power, the fancy job title, the women, the nice cars, the nice house... I want it all.*

I genuinely believed that if I just worked hard enough, nothing could stop me. After all, look at what I had just accomplished. I had completely transformed my body through a few months of discipline. So why couldn't I do the same with the rest of my life?

From that point forward, I set out to "get it all" — or at least what I thought "it all" meant.

Part of that vision included having the *right* friends. I wanted to surround myself with people who were rich, successful, stylish, and impressive. People who lived the life I was aspiring to. And ideally, I wanted them to be English-speaking, because that was still the language I felt most at home in.

At the time, I didn't have many friends who fit that mold. But then I stumbled upon an online community called KyopoUnion.com.

For context, a *kyopo* (or *gyopo*, as it's often spelled) refers to Koreans who grew up outside of Korea — though more recently, the term *haewae dongpo* ("overseas compatriot") has become more common. Whether you were Korean-American, Korean-Canadian, Korean-Australian, Korean-Brazilian, Korean-Chinese, or even Korean-Russian — if you were Korean and raised abroad, you were a *gyopo*.

But in English-speaking circles, *gyopo* generally refers to those of us who grew up in the West. And KyopoUnion.com was a space designed exactly for people like us — mostly Korean-Americans and Korean-Canadians, with a sprinkling of others from around the globe.

It was a brilliant concept for its time. Long before Facebook existed, this site allowed *gyopos* from all over the world to connect, share, and build community. For someone like me, still trying to find my place in Korea while holding on to my western identity, it was exactly what I needed. I was instantly hooked.

One of my first *gyopo* friends via the site was Ross. I'm not using his real name because if he ever reads this, he will get really upset and may want to do something harmful to me.

I am calling him Ross because he resembled the character of that name from the TV sitcom Friends. Although he was a good friend, we didn't remain so because Ross had one of the worst anger-management issues of anyone I have ever known. Eight out of ten times when we went out for food and drinks, he would seem to get into a fight with some random Korean guy. I would go to the bathroom for a moment, and when I'd come back, he'd be throwing punches or pointing his chopsticks at someone like a weapon, and we'd suddenly have to run away or be asked to leave.

Back in the early 2000s, Korea was still highly homogenous. It remains so today to some extent, but not nearly like it was back then. These days, it's common to see foreigners walking the streets of Seoul, speaking English openly. But at that time, it was still a relatively rare sight.

Of course, if a Caucasian person spoke English in public, it was often understood to be normal, since English was seen as their native language. But if you were ethnically Korean and spoke English in public, people tended to frown upon it. It was seen as a rejection of your roots, like you were turning your back on Korean culture and language.

More than once, when I spoke English with a friend, I'd hear a random passerby mutter something rude in Korean — things like, "If you're in Korea, learn to speak Korean, you idiot."

That kind of judgment stung. But it also highlighted the identity tension I, and many other *gyopos*, constantly lived with.

Stuff like this happened often on the subway, in restaurants, or at bars. You had to learn to ignore it, or at least control your temper. Unfortunately, Ross never really learned how to do that. He would get into arguments all the time, and I'd end up having to drag him away before things escalated.

Anyway, Ross and I first met through KyopoUnion.com. After realizing we both lived in Seoul, we decided to meet offline over some pork belly and *soju*. We also discovered we went to the same gym, which only deepened the bond.

Ross was tall, good-looking, and built like an Olympic athlete. He worked out constantly and even did some modeling here and there.

One time, Ross, a model friend of mine visiting from the U.S., and I walked into a restaurant. As we were paying for our meal, the female owner came over and told us that the women working there were all giggling and nervous in the back, because, apparently, we looked *so good*.

Yes, this is a true story. I swear.

Now, I'd like to believe it wasn't *just* because of the other two guys. I'm pretty sure I contributed to the fuss at least a little. And since there's no way to verify or disprove this story, I'm sticking with it.

Ross and I hung out all the time. Every weekend, we'd hit the gym, feast on barbecue to refuel on protein, and then head to a *pojangmacha* tent bar in Apgujeong for *soju* and late-night bites. Back then, Apgujeong was full of these tent bars. By day, they were car washes or parking lots, but at night, they transformed into bustling food tents, with plastic tables and chairs, and the whole area covered in a huge tarp. It was quite a vibe, and the food was legit. On the nights we didn't get into a fight, it was actually a lot of fun.

Eventually, Ross introduced me to some of his other *gyopo* friends. For some reason, he had held off for quite a while. I later came to think it was because he was a little possessive and didn't want to "share" me as his friend.

Whatever the case, I didn't mind. I was just glad to meet more people who, like me, were working and living in Korea but spoke English. I quickly became enamored with the group.

This was still before the days of smartphones and group chats, so every Friday night, we'd all agree to meet at the Apgujeong McDonald's by 7 p.m. From there, we'd head to a barbecue restaurant and feast on endless beef and *soju*. We found one spot we especially liked and went so regularly that we became friends with the owner — so much so that she later attended many of our weddings.

After dinner, we'd walk over to a trendy bar nearby. We were there so often that we got to know all the bartenders. We usually had a few leftover bottles of whiskey, rum, and other liquor that we kept behind the bar, and we'd use them to make our own cocktails and share them with people around us. Over time, we became quite popular there.

Around midnight or 1 a.m., we'd leave the bar and walk a couple blocks to our regular karaoke bar. We became well-known there too, mostly because we spent a lot of money, not just on singing but on bottles of whiskey. It became part of the weekly routine.

Then, around 3 or 4 a.m., for those who were still up for it — and most of the time, that included me — we'd catch a taxi to the Noryangjin Fish Market. There, we'd finish the night with fresh sashimi, hot fish stew, and, of course, more *soju*. On lighter nights, instead of sashimi, we'd settle for some spicy hangover *kimchi* stew before finally calling it a night.

Ross, unfortunately, fell out of favor with the group over time. His angry and bitter disposition just didn't sit well with everyone. But I, on the other hand, had a blast. I found myself joining this crowd nearly every Friday. Honestly, during that season of my life, this was my community. In fact, I was more religious about meeting up on Friday nights with these guys than I was about going to church. There was something magnetic about this gang. Maybe it was the shared love of partying, or maybe it was just that there still weren't that many English-speaking people around, and we were all the friends we had. Maybe it was because, in these people, I saw something I aspired to be.

In the early to mid-2000s, there were generally two types of *gyopo* in Korea when it came to occupations.

The first was the English teacher. Now, I have nothing against English teachers. Some of them truly loved what they did and took great pride in their work, and I admire that. But at the time, many were in Korea temporarily, just trying to make a little money before moving on. Most had no intention of staying long-term, so I didn't invest much time in getting to know them.

The second group was the young professionals, and even within that group, there were two distinct subcategories.

First, there were the investment bankers. They worked long hours at demanding jobs, but were compensated handsomely. Many of them drove fancy cars, dated beautiful women, and lived a high-rolling lifestyle. Honestly, they were out of my league, so I didn't spend much time with them either.

The second subcategory was the group I found more relatable, and even a bit inspiring. These were the *gyopo* business pioneers: professionals and entrepreneurs working in industries outside of finance. If they stuck it out, many would go on to become respected leaders in their fields.

There weren't many *gyopo* leaders at the time. Back then, most CEOS and executives of foreign companies in Korea were still blonde-haired, blue-eyed Americans or Brits, because Korean companies seemed to respect them more than they did English-speaking Koreans, regardless of how little they actually understood Korean business. But there were a few *gyopos* who tried to make their mark. Those were the people I wanted to befriend and learn from. And to a certain degree, I saw myself as one of those pioneers.

Of course, among these young professionals, there were some who were the real deal, and others who were fake pretenders. Actually, there were a lot of pretenders. They shamelessly boasted about their escapades with Korean women, wearing flashy clothes and speaking what native Koreans jokingly called "shala shala" English — a mocking term used for smooth-sounding but superficial speech.

There was this one fake pretender I knew named John, who was introduced to me by my MSN chat friend Rene. From the moment I met him, I could tell he was a complete wannabe. He didn't have a job, but he tried hard to look and act important, dressing the part and talking big.

I still remember a conversation I had with him one evening.

"Joe," he said, "do you know what you need to be successful in Korea?"

I raised an eyebrow. "What?"

"You need to own an Armani suit. If you have just one good Armani suit, you'll *look* the part. And trust me — *all* the girls will fall for you."

For John, getting girls was the ultimate measure of success. That was his metric. Not purpose, not calling, not integrity — just appearance and attention.

Even though I knew John was pretty fake, I still figured it wouldn't hurt to own a nice suit, so I went out and bought an Armani. And I'll admit, when I hit the trendy bars on Friday nights, that suit made me feel good. Wearing Armani made me feel like someone special.

But beyond that? I'm not sure it really made that much of a difference in my life.

Then again, maybe it did, because after that, I went on to buy more suits from Hugo Boss and Brooks Brothers. I even got featured in a trendy men's fashion magazine as one of their "Style Guys" of the month.

Did any of that make me a better businessman or a better person? Probably not. But at the very least, I looked the part.

Whether my fashion had anything to do with it or not, my professional career quickly took off. I was starting to make a name for myself.

As I mentioned earlier, I had the privilege of bringing some of the biggest stars in global sports to Korea — Roger Federer, Rafael Nadal, Rory McIlroy. But the biggest name of them all was Tiger Woods.

In 2004, we brought Tiger to Korea for a special exhibition match in Jeju, alongside Colin Montgomerie, KJ Choi, and Pak Se-Ri. There's still a well-known photo floating around the internet of me walking down the fairway, deep in conversation with Tiger. Because of that picture, I became known as Tiger Woods's manager in Korea.

At one point, a man even tried to bribe me with a thick wad of cash. He wanted me to pass along some "health products" for Tiger to test and possibly endorse. As he shoved the money into my hands, he kept calling it *"kimchi"* — his not-so-subtle way of saying it was just a small "side dish," with more to come if I played along.

I turned it down. And I'm glad I did, because later, I found out the guy was connected to organized crime. A few years after that, I even heard rumors that he had been found dead under mysterious circumstances.

By this point in my career, I had learned not to be starstruck. One of the fastest ways to ruin a relationship with a player-client was to act like a fanboy. Athletes could sense it instantly, and once they did, you'd lose their respect. That's why I don't have many photos with the stars I worked with, and most of the autographed items I own were just leftovers from signing events.

But when I first met Tiger Woods, I have to admit, it was hard *not* to be a fan.

When Tiger and his manager, Mark Steinberg, who also happened to be my global boss at the time, landed in Jeju on Tiger's Gulfstream IV, the pilot stepped out, looked at me, and asked who I was. When I told him I was with IMG, he said, "Come aboard."

I had met Steinberg before, so he recognized me. He led me to the front of the plane, where I noticed a familiar figure sitting quietly, reading a book.

Then Steiny turned to him and said, "Hey, Tigger!" — yes, that's what he actually called him, like the Winnie the Pooh character — "I want you to meet Joe Park." Then he looked at me and said, "Hey Joe, say hi to Tiger Woods."

In that moment, my stomach flipped like a little schoolgirl meeting her favorite boy band. But I knew my entire reputation, maybe even my future with IMG, could be shaped by this one handshake and the first words out of my mouth.

So I pulled myself together, stretched out my hand, looked Tiger in the eye, and said with a calm smile, "Hey, how's it going, Tiger? It's good to meet you."

On the outside, I was as cool as a cucumber. But on the inside? I was screaming, *Man, I'm never washing this hand again!*

And that's how my first encounter with Tiger Woods went down.

If I could share just one more story about Tiger...

Later that evening, we checked him into one of the best hotels in Jeju. The hotel had prepared a grand welcome — photographers lined the lobby, staff bowed, and we took plenty of photos of Tiger walking through the main entrance.

That was the only time we used the front door. After that, we entered and exited through a hidden employee entrance to avoid the crowds.

Naturally, Tiger was given the presidential suite. He and Steiny shared it. It was more like a penthouse, so there was plenty of space for both of them. After checking in, Tiger went into his room to freshen up, while Steiny and I sat in the living room going over the itinerary for the week.

A few minutes later, Tiger emerged from his room and looked at me.

"Hey Joe, can you help me with something?" he asked.

"Sure, what's up, Tiger?"

He motioned for me to follow him... straight into his bathroom.

The moment I walked in, I noticed a slightly funky smell, and saw that the toilet lid was down. Then, with a sheepish look on his face, Tiger said, "How do you flush the stinkin' toilets around here?"

For a second, I was completely confused. I mean, sure, Tiger Woods is like royalty, but... he knew how to flush a toilet, right? It's not like he needed a caddie for *that* part of the day.

But then I saw the issue.

There was no flush lever on the toilet itself. Instead, mounted on the wall beside it were about thirty buttons. This wasn't just any regular toilet. It was the fanciest bidet system I'd ever seen, packed with features like seat warmers, pulsating massages, and options for spraying, drying, and probably even playing classical music if you pressed the right button.

But there was one problem. All the buttons were labeled in Japanese.

Neither of us could read them. But then I noticed a pair of familiar Chinese characters: "大" (large) and "小" (small).

I took a wild guess and pressed the "large" button. And sure enough, we heard the sweet, glorious sound of rushing water — a perfect flush.

Tiger looked relieved.

And in that moment, it hit me: of all the things I'd ever do in my career, my greatest act of service to Tiger Woods... was teaching him how to flush a toilet in Jeju.

After that event with Tiger, it felt like everything I had ever wanted in life was finally coming true — the success, the notoriety, the cool and influential friends, and the fun, glamorous lifestyle I had once only dreamed about. I often thought back to that moment at the gym, when I stood in front of the mirror and boldly declared, "I want it all." And by all outward appearances, I was well on my way to getting exactly that.

But then one day, a scary thought crept into my mind — one I had never dared to consider before: *What if the track I'm on is the wrong one? What if everything I've been working so hard for... isn't really what I want after all?*

And that's when it hit me.

In spite of everything, there was still a black hole in my heart — a deep, gnawing emptiness that no amount of success, praise, or popularity could fill. I was achieving everything I thought I had ever wanted, yet the void inside me kept growing, no matter how much more I added to my life.

What could this void be about? And what could possibly fill it? There could only be one true answer to that question.

Around this time, I may have gone to church... or maybe I didn't. Honestly, I can't remember for sure. If I did, it was probably because I wanted to please my parents by showing them that their son wasn't all that bad a person, and so on random Sundays I'd try to go to a megachurch where I could blend in anonymously, just one face in a sea of people.

On a few of those Sundays, since I was already there, I might have taken the opportunity to confess a few sins — mostly for whatever I did the night before while drunk, not that I always remembered the details. But I certainly wasn't committed to any church. I hadn't been for a long time. Church and God weren't part of my equation for success, so I had little interest in making them part of my life.

Truthfully, I had another kind of church — one I attended faithfully every week: Friday nights. That was my real sanctuary. A place of Korean barbecues, countless bottles of *soju*, trendy bars, and beautiful people. It was fun, it was loud, and for a moment, it made me feel alive. So when I began slipping into an existential crisis, I didn't slow down. I partied even harder.

But no matter how religiously I showed up to my Friday night church, and no matter how hard I partied, the next morning always brought with it the hangovers, along with a lot of loneliness and emptiness. The people left. The fun faded. Everyone returned to their own lives, and I was still there, alone, with that same hollow ache inside me.

So what now? I asked myself. *What could possibly fill this emptiness? What could light up the darkness in my soul?*

I started attending church again on my own around 2006. When I share this part of my story in a testimony, I usually say, "God called me back to church." And while that's true in a spiritual sense, the more honest version is that I had simply run out of other options. I had tried just about everything to find happiness and peace, and everything ended up being a big fat flop.

When I finally decided to give church another chance, the first step was picking one to attend regularly. I ended up at Sarang Church's English Ministry, known as New Harvest Ministry (NHM). Sarang was, and still is, one of the largest megachurches in Korea. Today, its massive campus towers over the affluent neighborhood of Seocho, near Gangnam, but back then, the English ministry was still relatively small and intimate, since there weren't that many expats in Korea yet.

I wasn't ready to join a small group or Bible study, but I wanted to at least commit to going every Sunday. I hadn't given up my other life — partying with friends was still very much part of my routine — so Sunday mornings weren't always easy. More than once, I was so exhausted that I'd pass out as soon as the sermon started and only wake up when I heard the congregation say, "Amen."

Still, no matter what, I made it to church. And honestly, that was no small thing for me.

After a few months, I started dozing off less and paid more attention. I began to enjoy the praise and worship, and even found myself raising my hands during the singing, as if I were signaling a touchdown at a football game. No one told me to do it — I just wanted to.

The sermons were... okay. I can't say there was any single message that turned my life around. But at least I stopped sleeping through them. I made an effort to walk away each Sunday with some kind of takeaway, even if it wasn't the main point the pastor was trying to make.

I was still very hesitant about making any further commitment besides regular attendance. No way could anyone force me to be part of a small group. I'm not sure why. Perhaps the previous hurts I experienced at my college KACF fellowship group in Oregon still lingered after all those years.

About a year passed. Things were good. I was doing better. I still met up with my friends but didn't party as hard as before. We were all a little older and it just wasn't as much fun.

Then a really strange thought came to my mind: *Maybe now, it was time for me to join a Bible study or a small group. Maybe it's time for more. Maybe I am meant to go deeper.*

I immediately tried to convince myself against that. I'd tell myself, "No way. I'm not ready for that. That's totally outside of my comfort zone."

I did everything I could to shake off those thoughts. I tried to distract myself, tried to convince myself they were silly or sentimental. But no matter how hard I tried, I just couldn't. They wouldn't go away. And it wasn't just mental. These longings were coming from a place deep within my soul. All I wanted to do — in mind, heart, and spirit — was to worship God, and get closer to Him.

It was even more intense when I was alone at home. I'd try to watch TV to get my mind off of it, but the thoughts kept creeping back in. Even in sleep, they wouldn't let me go. I would wake up in the middle of the night, and find myself singing in my head:

Here I am to worship,
Here I am to bow down,
Here I am to say that You're my God.
You're altogether lovely,
Altogether worthy,
Altogether wonderful to me.

What was happening to me? I couldn't explain it if I tried. It was like some kind of metamorphosis was taking place, and I was powerless to stop it. I didn't just want more of God. In the deepest part of my being, I needed Him. He had become as essential to me as air and water, if not more. And no matter how much I tried to deny it or resist it, I simply couldn't anymore.

In the summer of 2007, I was hanging out with some friends when the conversation turned to religion and faith. I was 33 years old and had been back in Korea for about eight years. Up to that point, I was known among my circle as one of the most faithful partygoers. But in that moment, I surprised even myself when I said, without hesitation, that I was a Christian and that I didn't enjoy partying all that much anymore.

Among the friends there was a guy named David, a little younger than me. At first glance, he didn't strike me as the churchgoing type. He'd often brag about how drunk he got on weekends or casually talk about sleeping with his girlfriend. He wasn't exactly the kind of person you'd expect to be offering spiritual advice.

But when I mentioned that I was searching for more commitment and community, David spoke up and told me about a church he had recently started attending.

My first thought was, *This guy goes to church?!?*

Then again, many people probably would've said the same thing about me, so who was I to judge?

He told me it was a new church in Gangnam, full of young people and good energy. It sounded fresh and different. And then he invited me to check it out the following week.

Even though I had been attending NHM for about a year by then, something in me felt a quiet nudge. Maybe I had grown too comfortable. Maybe it really was time for something new. A new step. A new challenge.

I first stepped into Jubilee Church in June 2007. It was held in a small basement café called Ecclesia. About 80 chairs were set up in front of a modest stage, and a small worship band was leading praise. Most of the people there were fairly young, mostly in their twenties or early thirties.

The whole atmosphere felt less like a traditional church and more like a college or youth group gathering.

When the pastor came up to preach, I was genuinely surprised. I recognized Pastor David Hwang immediately, but I had no idea he was a pastor.

The first place I remembered seeing him was at my trendy gym in Apgujeong. I used to spot him working out there, but we never spoke. Honestly, I never would've guessed he was a pastor.

I also remembered him from a time I was invited to be part of a quiz show on Arirang TV, an English-language channel. The show, *The Contenders*, was sort of like *Jeopardy*, but featured mostly Korean-Americans and expats as contestants. I was asked to appear on one episode as a guest to read a few sports-related questions, and they came to my office to film me. Pastor Dave was a regular host on that show, though at the time, no one ever mentioned he was a pastor.

We didn't cross paths on set, but I clearly remembered seeing him on screen when I watched the episode later. Back then, he had somewhat curly, frizzy hair that hung down nearly to his shoulders. But now, standing on that stage in the café, he looked completely different — clean-cut, with a short, fresh haircut, and holding a Bible.

As of this writing, I'm 49 years old, and it's wild to think that of all the people I've known and called a friend over the years, David Hwang is the one who has been consistently in my life the longest. It's been sixteen years now. In that time, he's been my pastor, my friend, my co-laborer in ministry, my boss, my golf buddy, and even my fantasy football league commissioner. Many people have come and gone, but over the past decade and a half, he's been there for some of my highest highs and lowest lows. He has truly been a dear brother that the Lord placed in my life, and I'm grateful for him.

That said, I'll be honest: the first time I heard him preach, I wasn't exactly impressed. That first sermon I sat through at Jubilee lasted nearly an hour and a half. Just the sermon, not the whole service.

He and a group of others had just returned from a mission trip to Cambodia, and he was clearly excited to share every last detail of the experience. And I mean every detail. I was not prepared for such a long message.

To be fair, at the end of it, he acknowledged that it hadn't been a typical sermon, and promised that his future messages wouldn't be that long. To his credit, I don't think I've heard him give another ninety-minute sermon since... although, to be honest, there have been times when he's come close.

I joined the newcomers orientation that same day and got to know Dave and the church a little better. Not long after, I heard there were small groups I could sign up for. At first, I wasn't sure I wanted to. In fact, I wasn't even sure I'd come back to Jubilee at all, especially after that marathon of a service. But something inside me kept nudging me forward.

That something — or rather, someone — was God.

And before I knew it, I was signing up for my very first church small group.

The leader of that group was Paulo Rhee, who would go on to become another great friend of mine over the years in Korea. Paulo was a Korean-Brazilian. I had never met anyone from Brazil before. Actually, I had never met anyone named Paulo either. I kept calling him Pablo until he finally corrected me.

In that first small group, I began to tangibly experience the love of Christ. For the first time, I understood what it meant to be part of something genuinely good. The people were a lot like me, just trying to figure out who they were in this world. But they were open, kind, and real. They didn't pretend to have it all together. They shared, they listened, they cared for one another. They found their peace and security not in who they were trying to become, but in Christ — and in each other.

That kind of love and community was completely new to me. But it was good. It was really, really good.

A few months after joining Jubilee, I attended my first church retreat. To my surprise, they asked me to be one of the retreat's small group leaders. I had never been a leader in a church setting before. It was all new — kind of scary, but also exciting. As the retreat unfolded, I realized how much I enjoyed bringing people together in that way. I even discovered that I had a bit of a gift for it. Our small group bonded well, and we remained close friends even after returning from the retreat.

The following year, they asked me to become a Bible study small group leader. I didn't think I was qualified. But again, something inside me nudged me forward. And again, that something was God. So I said yes. And once more, it was good.

The rest, as they say, is history. I was hooked on Christ, and I became more and more devoted to Him and to the church at Jubilee. I still made time to meet with my other friends outside of church. I didn't want to turn my back on them completely. I learned to pray for them and, when possible, tried to share the gospel. It wasn't always easy, but I tried. They were still my friends, I still cared about them, and I genuinely wanted them to know the joy I had found in Jesus Christ. None of them ever came to church with me, but I wasn't shy about my faith. Like I said — I tried.

If I had any spare time, most of it was spent at church. I went to morning prayer meetings, Wednesday night services, and pretty much any other event that was happening. Church had become my happy place. It was a much better use of my time and energy — doing something meaningful to love God and serve others — than wasting my money and my life chasing empty pleasures in the name of loving myself.

As for my friend David, the one who first invited me to Jubilee, I'm sad to say I don't know what became of him. He left the church not long after I started attending. He had other priorities at the time, and once he was gone, we quickly lost touch. I still hope he's doing well, and that he's part of a loving community of believers somewhere.

Looking back now, it's incredible to think that a simple conversation about faith one night among party-going friends led me to Jubilee Church.

And now, some sixteen years later, it's still surreal and a little funny to think that I get to serve as a pastor here. I'll share more later about how that happened, but for now I'll just say this: God certainly moves in mysterious, and sometimes downright humorous, ways.

With all that said, I'd like to wrap up this chapter by returning to the question of identity — something I've wrestled with throughout this book, and also my life.

Who or what truly defines who I am?

Am I American because I relate more closely to American language and culture? Am I Korean because of my ethnicity, heritage, family roots, and nationality?

Is my identity tied to the work I've done? Was I defined by my past as one of Korea's top sports marketing agents — the guy who once walked the fairway with Tiger Woods? Or has my identity completely shifted now that I serve as a pastor?

Maybe it's about relationships. Was my identity once rooted in being part of the cool and popular crowd? Is it now found in my community of church friends, or in my role as a husband and father?

In a way, I'd say yes to all of these. Every single piece contributes to my identity. I am, in many ways, an amalgamation — a coming together — of all of these experiences, roles, and connections. They've all shaped me. They're all part of my story.

At the same time, I also have to say no. Because while all of these things help explain parts of me, not one of them is the most defining aspect of who I am. None of them is the root or foundation of my identity.

I've always struggled to find my identity because I've always wanted a simple, straightforward answer. But the truth is, I'm not a simple person with a simple past, so it's impossible to find a single definition that completely satisfies me.

When it comes to identity, we often want to fit ourselves neatly into a category — nationality, culture, career, or something else. But no one is so simple that we can perfectly peg ourselves into one hole and be fine with it. Life isn't that tidy, and neither are people.

Even for Christians, there's a common misunderstanding — an oversimplification of identity — that can cause a great deal of confusion, hurt, and even spiritual stagnation. Many are taught that being a "child of God" is identity enough and that nothing more is needed. While that's foundationally true, the problem arises when we stop there. When we ignore the unique ways God has made us — our personalities, backgrounds, experiences, and gifts — we end up with a version of faith that flattens individuality. We become cookie-cutter Christians, stripped of personal value beyond the label of "just a believer." But that's not how God sees us, and it's certainly not who we were meant to be.

Finding our Christian identity is absolutely essential, but it's not the only thing that defines us. We are all unique, and our unique experiences and qualities are not to be erased, but embraced and redeemed. What makes each of us special is not just that we're made in the image of God, but more so, that we're each made *uniquely different* in that image. Each of us reflects a part of God's beauty in a way no one else does.

Ephesians 2:10 reminds us that we are God's workmanship — His masterpiece. Our lives are being drawn, painted, and shaped into something awe-inspiring and beautiful, crafted specifically and intentionally by Him. The challenge is that we often don't see ourselves that way.

The key to unlocking that uniqueness in a healthy, meaningful way is this: our identity must first be grounded in the solid and unchanging foundation of Christ, and then our unique qualities and experiences need to be allowed to flourish. Only when we begin there can our individuality come alive in ways that honor God and bring joy and clarity to who we are.

Let me offer an illustration that might help.

As I've shared throughout my story, I spent much of my life searching for answers about who I was — looking to culture, ethnicity, vocation, hometown, relationships, life experiences, and more. I asked a lot of questions in each area, but none of the answers I found ever truly satisfied me.

Each of those things, in isolation, felt like a single dot on a page from a child's connect-the-dots puzzle book. I knew they were part of me and that they mattered somehow, but on their own, they couldn't tell the whole story. At first glance, all you see on that kind of page are scattered dots — nothing that makes any real sense. And for a long time, that's exactly what my life felt like: a series of disconnected experiences and memories. I could see each one clearly, but I had no idea how they were meant to fit together.

To solve the puzzle, you need a guide — a key that shows you how to connect the dots in the right order. When you follow that guide, the scattered points begin to form a recognizable picture.

For me, that key was Jesus.

Without Him, none of my life made sense. But with Him, the picture began to take shape — a unique and beautiful story that had been unfolding all along.

I know that picture won't be complete in this lifetime. I may never fill in every detail or paint it in perfect color. And yes, I still have questions about who I am — and maybe I always will — until the day I meet Jesus face-to-face. But now, when I look back on the many moments of my life — some of which I've shared in this book — they're no longer just random dots. I can see that Jesus has been drawing something intentional all along. Something meaningful. Something uniquely mine. There may be parts of my story that resonate with others. But ultimately, this is a picture only Jesus and I get to draw together.

I know many people are still staring at a page full of unconnected dots. It's their life — but they have no idea what it's supposed to look like. At times, it just feels like a mess.

But what they need is the key. And that key is Christ.

Even with Christ, the picture might not become clear right away. It may take time, trust, and prayer. But without Him, life stays a confusing and lonely puzzle.

It's only when we find Christ and begin to follow Him that the dots begin to connect. And piece by piece, the image of who we were always meant to be — His workmanship, created for a purpose — finally starts to come into focus. A masterpiece in the making, drawn by the hand of God.

Chapter 16

How I Met Your Mother

There's a television series I used to enjoy from time to time called *How I Met Your Mother*. The premise revolves around a father telling his kids the long, winding story of how he eventually met their mother — after a string of failed relationships. Admittedly, it's probably not the most edifying show for a Christian to watch, so I wouldn't be quoting it from the Sunday pulpit anytime soon. But I'll be honest: from the privacy of my own home, it gave me a good chuckle every now and then.

I bring it up for a couple of reasons. First, the story of my search for identity wouldn't be complete without telling the story of how I met my wife, Juri. And second, if my kids ever read this, I know they'll be curious about how it all happened.

So with that, here it goes.

Ever since I can remember, I've always liked pretty girls. I mean, what guy doesn't, right? But I was never very confident around them, and I definitely wasn't smooth. As a teenager, I was that tall, skinny, awkward kid with pimples and crooked teeth — deeply insecure and unsure of myself.

Even in college, when I mustered the courage to ask a girl out, I usually got the classic, "I'm flattered, but..." response.

But after I started working at IMG, got myself back into shape, and started wearing expensive suits, I'll admit, I got a little full of myself. My confidence with women went up, maybe a bit too much. There was even a time (embarrassingly) when I thought I was good-looking enough to date just about anyone I wanted. That was my perception, anyway, but reality may have told a different story. Still, I looked decent, dressed well, and had a network of rich and impressive friends, so I often found myself going out and, as the kids say these days, "I'd shoot my shot."

During that time, I dated several women, but strangely, I can't even remember most of their names. That alone shows how unready I was for anything serious.

Honestly, part of the reason I dated was simply because I was bored and lonely. It gave me something to do. Another reason was ego. I thought that having a pretty girl on my arm gave me the illusion of status. "Hey, look at Joe Park. He must be doing something right." I know — it's silly.

But beneath all that, I was still trying to figure out who I was. I thought maybe, just maybe, if I found the right girl, I'd find the answer I'd been searching for.

A lot of people make that mistake. They believe a romantic relationship will fill the emptiness in their hearts, help them discover who they are, or give their lives meaning. But here's the truth I eventually learned: when two people with holes in their hearts get together, they don't fill each other — they just make bigger holes. That's what I came to realize through all my failed relationships.

In 2006 and 2007, after many years of wandering — chasing fame, money, career success, and dating — trying to find myself through superficial things that could never truly satisfy, I finally returned to a relationship with God. And in that return, I discovered something life-changing: only God could truly complete me.

As I devoted myself to Him, I found it was good. So good, in fact, that I no longer wanted anything else. Whatever emptiness I had once felt was gone. I began to feel whole and complete in a way I had never experienced before.

That's why I made a personal promise to God: for the entire year of 2007, I would devote myself fully to Him. I wouldn't date, I wouldn't pursue anyone, and I wouldn't even entertain the idea. No one told me to do this. It wasn't some vow forced upon me. It was simply something I wanted to do.

That year was amazing. I drew closer to God than I'd ever imagined possible. I fell in love with Him. I came to know that I truly needed nothing else. God was enough.

As 2008 rolled in, I realized I didn't need to put a timeframe on it anymore. I had no desire to date. I wasn't opposed to meeting someone, but I also didn't feel the need to seek it out. My focus remained on my relationship with Jesus.

During that time, I was working outside of sports for a change — at a company called The Executive Centre, which provided serviced office spaces. One of our clients was Moneygram, and their local representative was a Korean-Australian guy named Jae Kong. Coincidentally, Jae was also attending Jubilee Church, so we quickly became friends.

One day, Jae approached me with an idea: a double date. He had a younger friend from his Bible study group back in Sydney — someone he saw as a little sister — and he thought she and I might hit it off. The plan was simple: she'd bring a friend, he'd bring me, and the four of us would meet for dinner.

At first, I wasn't that interested. But before shutting down the idea completely, I did get a little curious, so I asked if he had a photo. When he pulled up her Facebook profile, I saw her picture — and she was beautiful. I quickly changed my mind.

I thought, *One dinner can't hurt, what's the worst that could happen?*

We agreed to meet at a Brazilian churrasco restaurant in Apgujeong. Jae and I arrived first and took a window table overlooking the parking lot. A few minutes later, I looked out, and there she was. Juri and her friend had just pulled in and were walking toward the restaurant.

It's funny to think back on that moment, but even now, I still get goosebumps on my arms and butterflies in my stomach. Juri was stunning. I don't know if it was the way the sunlight reflected off her silver shirt, or the calm confidence she carried, but she had this angelic aura about her. To me, she was the most beautiful girl I had ever seen. She still is.

Maybe it was because I was so struck by her, but I didn't have much to say during dinner. Our conversation didn't exactly sparkle. It was actually pretty awkward. And I wasn't nearly as smooth as I thought I was.

Later, I learned that she had pulled an all-nighter at work the night before and was completely exhausted. She didn't want to be there but came out as a favor to Jae. Whatever the case, we didn't hit it off. By the end of dinner, she looked more than ready to head home and crash.

But Jae was insistent we go somewhere for drinks. He had paid for dinner, which meant drinks were on me. I wasn't sure where to go, but I remembered a new fancy building nearby with trendy bars, and suggested we check it out.

We ended up at a sleek wine bar that was clearly out of my league. The ambiance was nice, but the prices on the menu made my stomach churn. Juri suggested we leave, but my pride kicked in. I didn't want to look cheap on our first meeting, so I insisted we stay.

We were seated in a private room, and I was handed the wine list. I scanned it quickly and settled on the third-cheapest bottle — still close to 60,000 won (about $50). We finished it in thirty minutes, and I ordered another. Gulp!

If dinner had been dull, this was worse. The conversation dried up, and at one point, Juri and her friend were talking to each other while Jae and I just stared into space. Eventually, they asked if they could invite a couple of their girlfriends to join us. I agreed. More wine was ordered, and by the time the night was over, I had spent nearly 300,000 won (about $250).

It was an expensive evening, and it was clear nothing was going to come of it. I had gone all out and fallen flat on my face.

But Jae wasn't done. He suggested the original four of us go to one more place for a nightcap. It was nearly midnight. We were exhausted and not thrilled with the idea, but once again, Jae persisted, and we gave in. We ended up at a small beer bar nearby. Jae made sure I sat next to Juri to talk more, not that we had anything particularly interesting left to say. After about thirty minutes, we were all ready to call it a night — for real this time.

Juri, who hadn't drunk much — she doesn't really like alcohol, even now — said she was going to drive herself home. She only lived a few blocks away and couldn't wait to get to bed.

That could've been the end of the story. She would've driven off, never looked back, and I'd go on searching for love elsewhere. But for some reason, I decided I had to get into that car — even just for those three blocks. I figured after dropping $250 on the evening, I should at least get her phone number.

"Why are you getting in?" she asked, clearly annoyed.

"I figured you could drop me off up the street. It's easier to catch a taxi from there."

She sighed — long and loud — too tired to argue. "Fine."

She stopped at the corner near her place and told me to get out. That's when I asked for her number. With visible frustration, she grabbed my phone, jabbed her number into it with a little too much force, and tossed it back at me. I stepped out, and she drove off without as much as a goodbye.

I'm pretty sure I saw tire marks.

A few days later, one of my old IMG colleagues offered me tickets to a skating show featuring Kim Yuna. I was curious to see how they were managing things now that I was no longer with the company, but I didn't want to go alone. So I sent Juri a text to see if she'd be interested in going with me. Without even a hint of hesitation, she turned me down.

A month went by. After a couple of stressful days at work, I found myself wanting to do something lighthearted that weekend. I couldn't think of anyone to call. Then, almost out of nowhere, the thought popped into my head: *What if I try calling Juri again? Maybe she'd be up for grabbing a meal.*

My expectations were low. I fully braced myself for another polite (or not-so-polite) rejection. But to my surprise, she said, "Yes."

What I didn't know at the time was that my timing couldn't have been better. If I had called earlier, she would've turned me down. And if I had waited even a day or two later, it probably would've been a no as well.

As it turned out, she had been casually seeing another guy when we first met. It wasn't serious — they were just dating. On the day I called, she actually had plans to see him that Friday. But just minutes before I dialed, he had called to cancel. And not just cancel — he basically ended whatever it was they had going.

He told her, "I'm sorry, I just don't think this is working. You're a little too direct for me, and honestly... you kind of scare me. I don't think I can see you anymore."

Most people might be hurt by that kind of abrupt honesty. But not Juri. That's one of the things I've always admired about her. She doesn't let stuff like that get to her. Her response was more like, *"What the heck is wrong with him? Good riddance."* Then she thought, *"Wait! That was my Friday night. What am I going to do now?"*

And just then, the phone rang.

Our first date was on a hot and humid July evening in the trendy neighborhood of Itaewon. I showed up in a full suit and tie. Back then, I was so used to wearing a monkey-suit for work that I didn't think twice about dressing that way, even in the sweltering summer heat. But that evening, the air felt especially oppressive. I was melting.

And then, of all the dinner options I could've suggested, I made the very foolish decision to go with spicy Thai food. Don't get me wrong — I love Thai food. It's one of my favorites. But on a night like that, dressed the way I was, it was a horrible idea.

We went to one of my go-to spots, Thai Garden. We ordered tom yum kung soup, green curry with rice, papaya salad with chili, and maybe some crispy fried chicken. Everything except the chicken was blazing hot. The restaurant's air conditioning was on full blast, but it did nothing for me. I walked in already sweating like crazy, and the spicy food only turned my pores into geysers.

Unaware of just how bad it was, I sat there grinning like an idiot, thrilled to be on a date with this beautiful woman. Meanwhile, Juri was quietly horrified. Sweat was pouring down my face, dripping from my forehead and chin straight into my food. She later told me she was completely grossed out. I, of course, had no clue. I was just happy to be there. In hindsight, I was probably the dinner date from hell.

After dinner, we headed to a café across the street. At a nearby table was an actor. I didn't recognize him, but Juri whispered that it was Uhm Tae-Woong. I had no clue who he was, but I had heard of his sister, Uhm Jung-Hwa, one of Korea's top singers and actresses.

When Juri quietly pointed him out, I immediately whipped my head around a full 180 degrees to get a look.

She winced. "You're supposed to glance *subtly*, not make it so obvious!"

I thought I *was* being subtle... clearly, I wasn't.

Over coffee, I began to get a deeper sense of who she was. I expected some light small talk — favorite movies, travel stories, maybe a "What's your favorite color?" thrown in. But Juri wasn't interested in surface-level conversation. Instead, she looked me straight in the eye and asked, "What's your vision for your life?"

I froze. No one had ever asked me that on a first date before.

As for her, she told me that she had little interest in getting married or having kids. She genuinely enjoyed being single and living freely. In fact, she confessed that among all her friends, everyone assumed she'd be the last to get married.

She also shared that since college, she had carried a deep conviction to live her life for God. Years earlier, at a Korean Students for All Nations conference, she had been scheduled to sing on stage. But as the music began, she was so overcome by the Holy Spirit that tears streamed down her face, and she couldn't sing a single word. It was then that she knew that whatever her life would look like, it had to be dedicated to living for God in some meaningful way.

As I listened to her, I could see how deeply she loved God and how earnestly she longed for intimacy with Him. She had clarity. She had purpose. She knew what she wanted in life.

That should have been my cue to be thoughtful, careful, and attentive. Instead, I did the one thing *no man should ever do* on a first date — *and I mean NEVER EVER.*

She had just opened up about her heart and asked me more about myself — what kind of girl I liked, what I was looking for in a relationship. Wanting to show that I, too, was serious about my faith, I launched into what I thought was a spiritually mature answer.

"I'm also trying to live a life following Jesus," I said.

(So far, so good.)

"So when it comes to relationships, I don't want to just play around. I want to be intentional."

(Still holding strong.)

"When a man dates a woman, he should be thinking about marriage. That's how you respect the relationship."

(A wise point... but be careful what you say next.)

And with a big, goofy grin, I added: "So don't be surprised if by the end of the night, I ask you to marry me."

Cue the face palm. I mean, *who says that*?! What an absolute dork!

After that disastrous first date, I honestly don't know why she ever agreed to see me again. Maybe she felt sorry for this clueless guy who clearly had no idea how to behave around women. Maybe she was trying to save the rest of womankind from future painful dates with me. Or maybe, just maybe, it was the grace of God working through her. Whatever the reason, she did agree to see me again, and soon after that, we started dating.

We held hands for the first time while watching a movie. It wasn't a romantic one, but rather a pretty forgettable film called *The Mummy* 2. I don't remember much about the plot, only that I got to hold her hand. That, by far, was the best part of the whole movie.

I genuinely really liked her a lot. Whenever I had free time, all I wanted to do was spend it with her. Things were going really well, and me being 34 at the time, I kind of wanted to move things along in our relationship.

Around this time, I received a call from my old boss at IMG in Singapore. He offered me a big promotion and a raise if I returned to the company. I accepted and returned as Vice President and Director of Golf for IMG Korea.

Juri was working for Callaway Golf, a major golf equipment company, doing PR for them, so every once in a while our paths would cross at work. No one knew about us, which made it much more fun and exciting when we saw each other on the golf course.

One time, Annika Sorenstam, one of IMG's biggest clients, as well as one of Callaway's most prominent ambassadors, came to Korea for a couple of promotional appearances. I was next to her as her representative, while Juri was there with her Callaway team. As far as everyone else knew, we didn't know each other and we were meeting for the first time, but I would secretly send her little signs of affection that only she and I would know. That was pretty fun.

We dated for about five months, and then I got to meet her father, who had come to Seoul from their home in Busan to attend a wedding. We picked him up at the wedding and drove him to the airport for his flight home. We had Korean beef barbecue near the airport, and I tried my best to act properly and deserving of his daughter.

A few weeks after that, I told my parents, "I think she's the one." Then, I went out and bought a diamond ring with the intention of proposing.

Some of my friends had taken their girlfriends to exotic destinations to propose to them. One even took his to Paris. I didn't have the means to do that, but I had been to Jeju Island many times over the years for different sporting events, and I remembered some beautiful spots there that I had always thought would be a picturesque place to propose to a girl. The plan was to take her there on Christmas Eve for a daytrip, and then surprise her with the ring.

Before setting things in motion, I wanted to show my respect to her father, so I called him one day to ask for his blessing. I was nervous, but still, I felt it was the right thing to do. He was very generous in agreeing, and then we hung up. Little did I know that as soon as we got off the phone, he immediately called her to say I would propose. She didn't believe him. We hadn't been dating that long and she had made it clear that she wasn't immediately interested in marriage. She was only 27 and enjoyed her life. Marriage was the furthest from her mind. She agreed to the trip but highly doubted I would proceed with the proposal.

When we arrived at the airport in Jeju on the morning of the 24th, I quickly got our rental car and threw in the mix CD of Christmas songs I had made for that day. The diamond ring was burning a hole in my pocket, but I had to be patient because I knew exactly where I wanted to go to pull it out and pop the question. I was headed straight for Jungmun Beach.

After about 45 minutes, we arrived at the beach. But to my disappointment, everything felt dark and gloomy. When I had visited before, it was summer — sunny, vibrant, and full of life. This time, it was winter. The sky was overcast, the beach was scattered with litter, and the ocean looked more gray than blue. It wasn't nearly as picturesque as I had remembered. So instead of pulling out the ring right then and there, I decided to wait. I figured there had to be a better spot ahead — something a little more beautiful, a little more fitting. I just needed to be patient.

We got back in the car, and though I didn't have a specific destination in mind, I kept driving, searching for the perfect spot. But no matter how far we went, I just couldn't find it. We drove for so long that Juri started to get visibly irritated. And to make matters worse, Mariah Carey's "All I Want for Christmas Is You" came on again from the mix CD for perhaps what seemed like the twentieth time. If we'd heard it one more time, one of us, or maybe both of us, might've ended up in an asylum.

With our return flight to Seoul approaching, Juri asked me to start driving back to the airport. I could see she wasn't very happy, but I couldn't get on that flight without proposing to her. It was now or never, and if I didn't do it, I knew I would regret it.

Suddenly, I remembered a really scenic bridge I had once seen near the airport, so I asked her if it was okay to stop by there really quickly. She didn't want to — she just wanted to get back to the airport — but I insisted.

Once we got there, we walked to the center of the bridge, and I thought, *It's now, man! You gotta do it now!*

So, in that moment, I pulled out the ring, got down on one knee, and looked up at her. With the greatest confidence I could ever muster, I said to her, "Juri, I love you and want to spend the rest of my life with you. Will you marry me?"

The conversation that followed is legendary, if not comical.

Her: Ummm... What are you doing?
Me: I'm asking you to marry me.
Her: Uhhhh... Someone is coming this way. Can you please stand up?
    It's embarrassing.
Me: (Slowly standing up, and not knowing what to do anymore)
Her: Did you pray about this?
Me: (Scratching my head) Yes...?
Her: And what did God say?
Me: Ummm... To marry you?
Her: Are you sure about that?
Me: I think so.
Her: I don't know. I think we need some time to pray about this.
Me: Uhhh... Really? Uhhh... Okay...

That was it. She didn't say "yes," nor did she say, "no." She just said, "Let's pray about it." She didn't take the ring, so I put it back in the box and stuffed it in my pocket.

Needless to say, the flight back was awkward. She tried to break the tension by asking to see the ring again. "It's really pretty," she said, giving it back to me. That didn't help break the tension.

In Seoul, I dropped her off at home, went to a convenience store, and got a bottle of *soju*. She immediately called to check on me. It's like she had a radar on me or something because she straight up asked, "Are you drinking *soju*?" After a little pause, I said, "Uhhh... no..."

She tried to assure me that she hadn't said no, but wanted us to be sure that this was God's will for us.

"We should both take time to pray about it," she said.

I didn't like it then, but I knew she was right.

We kept dating after that, and I didn't mention marriage again. I wasn't going to do so until I knew the time was right, and it turned out I didn't have to.

About a month later, I was over at her place, and we were watching TV. Out of the blue she turned and said, "So you wanna get married?"

"Yeah."

"Okay, let's get married."

Six months later, on June 26th of 2009, on a Friday evening, we tied the knot. Frankly, I don't recall anything about our wedding. It was all a blur. The only thing I remember is that my shoes were really uncomfortable, and my legs hurt so much that I tried not to pass out while the officiant was giving his message.

The after-party was a lot more fun. One of my good friends, Tony, brought his turntable and DJ'd for us, and everyone had a great time. I was immensely blessed by all my friends who came out to celebrate with us. I was especially blessed by my friends Jay and Micah, who flew in from the U.S. I guess they had to see it to believe it.

I would love to say that from then on it was all happily ever after, but that's only in fairy tales. We've had our ups and downs. One of the biggest came early on. Before we had any children, we wanted to do some traveling together, and planned a winter trip to Greece and Turkey. Neither of us had been there. We booked the flights well in advance.

However, about a month before we were supposed to go, Juri became very ill. At first, we thought it was food poisoning since she felt nauseous and couldn't eat anything. When we went to the doctor to check, we found out she was pregnant with our first child. Of course, we were very excited. At the same time, though, we knew we couldn't do that trip anymore. It was a great up, but honestly, a great down, too.

We never did make it to Europe. I'm still hoping that one day we can, but I don't know when that one day might come.

Besides not being able to go to Europe, we had some other big downs in our first couple of years, even to the point I wasn't sure if we'd make it. Sometimes it's not wise to bring up past mistakes, so I won't go into too many specifics. Still, I will admit that most of it was because of my immaturity and misunderstanding about what marriage is about.

It's ironic that I've become somewhat of an expert in marital relationships. These days, as a pastor, I'm often asked to do marriage counseling or pre-marital counseling, and I've become very familiar with many of the common obstacles that can hinder a healthy marriage, such as:

- Disagreements over how to manage finances
- Differences about whether or not to have children — and how to raise them if you do
- Misunderstandings about gender roles in marriage
- Unreasonable expectations from parents or in-laws
- Miscommunication about how each partner experiences intimacy and love
- Poor communication skills in general
- And plenty of other challenges

Part of what I know comes from my studies — both personal and from seminary — but honestly, a bigger reason is because I've made almost every one of these mistakes myself at one point or another.

Perhaps my biggest mistake was assuming that once we were married, my wife was supposed to forget about her own identity, and bend over backwards to cater to my needs — and even to meet the demands of my parents. I now realize that mindset was deeply rooted in traditional Korean Confucian values, and it's incredibly damaging to a wife and a marriage. I didn't even know I carried that kind of thinking. I had always assumed I was fully westernized. But I did carry it. And that unspoken assumption almost killed my marriage.

It wasn't until I realized how much our relationship was in jeopardy that I came to a humbling understanding that a true marriage isn't about clinging to who you were before and expecting your spouse to revolve around you. It's about stepping into a new, shared identity — a joint life where self-sacrifice builds the foundation of oneness between husband and wife. While each individual still matters, the "one" that forms through marriage is greater than the sum of its parts. That was a hard lesson to learn, which is probably why I'll never forget it.

As for the highs in our marriage, there have been so many that we've lost count. Juri and I have shared countless moments of joy and laughter together. And now, with three kids, we've had even more fun, as a party of five. We love our children deeply, but let's be honest: they make us grow older every day! Still, there's something beautiful about growing old together.

I often joke with Juri and the kids that one day, they'll all grow up, move out, and start families of their own. Eventually, it'll just be the two of us again — old and wrinkled, with all the youthful vibrancy long gone. I say it jokingly, but deep down, I look forward to that chapter too. I cherish these years with our kids and will do my best to hold on to them for as long as I can. But I also look forward to the quiet joy of sharing life with Juri, just the two of us, once again.

One of our favorite things to do, when life allows, is to go for a walk around our neighborhood, hand in hand. I imagine that even when I'm 90 and she's 83, we'll still be walking like that. And when we get tired, we'll find a bench, sit down, and keep holding each other's hand. I don't know exactly what eternity in heaven will look like, but as far as my time on earth goes, we're stuck together, and I wouldn't have it any other way. My earthly identity is now forever intertwined with hers.

When I look back on how I met Juri, there's no denying that it was a story of grace. I did nothing to deserve her. In fact, I did everything wrong. I gave her every reason to walk away. And yet, by God's grace, I get to spend the rest of my days with her. Grace, by its very nature, is never deserved. It is mercy poured out on those who are not only undeserving, but least deserving. And when it comes to Juri, I know — I am the least deserving.

I sometimes catch myself thinking foolish thoughts — like how Juri could have married some other rich and successful man and might be living a far more comfortable life right now. Whenever I say something like that, she shuts it down immediately. "That's a stupid thing to say," she tells me. "I'm happiest with you."

I'm always humbled by that. After all, when she married me, I wasn't a pastor. She didn't sign up for this life. But when God called me into ministry, she embraced that calling with me. She's always stood beside me. She's sacrificed so much for our family and for me. And when I tell her I wish I could do more for her, she gently reminds me: "Don't be silly. I have everything I could ever hope for." I'm grateful she says that. God is good — and she's pretty great, too.

To be clear, Juri doesn't complete me or make me whole. Some people think marriage is about completing each other — but it's not. Only God can do that. I don't let her define my identity either. My identity is still my own, and it doesn't belong to her, nor does she control it.

But there's no denying I've changed since I married her. I've become a better version of myself — sometimes through her encouragement, sometimes through her well-placed (and often creative) criticisms. And there have been a lot of those over the years, with more surely to come. But mostly, I've changed because I no longer live just for myself. I'm part of something greater now.

That doesn't mean I've lost my individuality. In fact, a good relationship draws the best out of your individuality, but now it exists for a greater purpose: to contribute to the oneness of a family. Her uniqueness and mine, and even our kids' identities, all serve this same purpose. Whatever identity I carry now, it will always be intertwined with hers. And together, we are called to be one.

So kids, if you ever end up reading this — and you were curious how I met your mother... well, now you know.

Chapter 17

Do Not Conform to the Patterns of the World

T he year 2013 was fairly ordinary in the grand sweep of history. Barack Obama was sworn in for his second term as President of the United States, while Park Geun-Hye, daughter of former president Park Chung-Hee, became Korea's first female president — only to be impeached and later arrested on corruption charges just four years later.

But perhaps the most colorful political figure that year — for both Americans and Koreans — was none other than Dennis Rodman, the flamboyant former basketball star. He famously made a trip to Pyongyang to hang out with his new friend, North Korean leader Kim Jong-Un, even gifting him a copy of *The Art of the Deal*, written by none other than real estate mogul and reality TV star Donald Trump.

In pop culture, 2013 was ruled by Elsa. Every kid, and their parents, had *Frozen's* "Let It Go" on repeat, whether on CD players or iPods, since the iPhone 5 still maxed out at only 16, 32, or 64 gigabytes. Facebook and Twitter were the dominant social media platforms, and even the Pope joined the digital age with his first holy tweet: "Dear friends, I am pleased to get in touch with you through Twitter. I bless you all from the bottom of my heart."

In sports, 2013 was probably the biggest year of all — for me, at least — because my beloved Seattle Seahawks finally won their first Super Bowl, demolishing the Denver Broncos 43–8. They could've repeated the next year too, if not for the worst play call in Super Bowl history. Instead of handing the ball off at the goal line to the unstoppable "Beastmode," Marshawn Lynch, they chose to pass. It was intercepted. And just like that, they handed another championship to Tom Brady and the New England Patriots. Years have passed, but some losses still sting.

All in all, 2013 might seem like a blip in the wider arc of world history. But for me, it turned out to be one of the most pivotal years of my life.

I was 39, just shy of 40, though in Korean age, you're already one when you're born, which in Korean terms meant I had technically already hit that milestone. I bring this up because the number 40 holds deep biblical significance.

For instance, it rained 40 days and 40 nights when Noah and his family, along with the animals, were saved from the flood in the ark. Moses was 40 when he fled Egypt and God called him into the wilderness of Midian. He stayed there another 40 years before God sent him back to Egypt to lead the Israelites out of slavery. And even after the exodus, it took the Israelites another 40 years to finally enter the Promised Land. Then there's Jesus, who fasted and prayed for 40 days and 40 nights in the wilderness before facing Satan's temptations and launching His public ministry.

Now, I'm not trying to put myself on the same level as Noah, Moses, and certainly not Jesus. But in the Bible, the number 40 often symbolizes a period of fullness — a season of preparation, testing, training, or refining that marks the end of one chapter and the beginning of another.

So when I look back on myself in 2013, at the Korean age of 40, I can't help but wonder if that year marked a kind of spiritual turning point. Maybe it represented the completion of a season of God's training in my life — some of it painful, some of it humbling — all of it necessary. And maybe, just maybe, it was His way of preparing me for what was to come.

In 2013, I was well into my career at IMG as Vice President and head of the golf division in the Korea branch office. Of all the departments at IMG, it all started with golf, and so it was not only the largest, but also the most influential. So even though there were other VPs in the branch on the same official footing as me, it was generally understood — though never spoken aloud — that I occupied a slightly higher position in the internal hierarchy.

There was, however, one man above me: the Senior VP and country manager of IMG Korea. He was an older gentleman who had originally hired me back in 2001. But over time, he had lost trust with upper management, both regionally and globally, due to ongoing disagreements over the direction and philosophy of the business in Korea. That loss of trust trickled down into our branch office too.

When I rejoined the company in 2009, I was told explicitly that I didn't have to report to him. Instead, I would report directly to the regional head of golf in Singapore. And privately, that regional head confided in me: "In due time, you'll take over Korea." It was never officially announced within the branch, but everyone suspected it. I'm sure the country manager did too. After all, he wasn't even consulted about my return. He was just told about it. I can only imagine what that felt like for him — and from that moment on, I think he did everything he could to fight for his job and prolong his stay. Honestly, I might have done the same.

We did our best to be respectful toward each other, but let's be real — when power dynamics shift behind the scenes, office politics become inevitable.

I hate office politics. I really do. There aren't many things in this world I'd say I hate, but that's one of them. It stresses me out, breeds inefficiency, and poisons the workplace environment.

A prime example came in 2010, not long after my return. The PGA Champions Tour, what most people know as the senior tour, held its first tournament in Korea at the Jack Nicklaus Golf Club in Songdo, Incheon. As the head of the golf division, I was tasked with overseeing IMG's role in organizing the tournament.

Under normal circumstances, a press conference for such an important event would feature the country manager at the head table. But this time, upper management didn't even invite him. Instead, I was seated at the table — right next to the sponsors and the legend himself, Jack Nicklaus — fielding questions from the press.

It was a major boost for my career, but also, without question, a dagger to the man who still technically held the title of country manager. And everyone noticed — sponsors, competitors, journalists, and especially people within our office.

Even during the tournament itself, there wasn't much for him to do. But he showed up anyway, trying to remind anyone who would pay attention that he was still the boss. He started giving orders to my staff without knowing what they were working on, which left them frustrated and unable to do their jobs. He hovered around the press room, eating their snacks, drinking their coffee, and unintentionally upsetting the very journalists he thought he had a good relationship with. One of them, the lead golf reporter at Yonhap News Agency, actually left the event after being offended by something the country manager had said. I had to personally call and beg him to come back.

Even the sponsors were confused. They pulled me aside and asked, "Who is this guy who keeps saying he's the head of IMG Korea? We've never met him, but he's walking around like he runs the place."

All of this made my job infinitely more difficult, not just because it complicated logistics, but because I also understood where he was coming from. I could feel for him. His role was slipping away, and I didn't want to humiliate him. I tried to show him respect. I gave him space to assert himself, even though it created tension and confusion. The truth is, whether anyone liked it or not, he was still the official country head of IMG Korea. Not me.

Early on after I returned to the company, I had hoped, maybe even pleaded in my heart, that someone above us would step in and clarify our roles. Either draw a clear boundary between the two of us, or even make a decision that one of us had to go. During a tournament in Shanghai, I even pulled the global head of golf aside and told him directly, "You need to make a call on this. Otherwise, everyone in the office is going to stay confused."

But nothing changed.

Looking back, I think the decision-makers overseas were too afraid of the consequences, no matter which way they went. If they let me go, they'd lose their top-performing employee and future leader of the Korea office. But if they let the country manager go, they feared losing certain long-standing deals that were keeping the branch afloat.

So they did what many people in power do when the decision is too hard: nothing. They turned a blind eye and hoped the problem would magically resolve itself. It didn't. And the awkward, toxic dynamic dragged on for five long years.

Those years were excruciating. I woke up many mornings with a knot in my stomach so tight it felt like I'd swallowed a stone. My shoulders always felt heavy, like I was carrying a sack of cement around my neck. I'd look in the mirror and barely recognize the person staring back. I had once been easy-going, fun-loving, full of life. But the man I saw in the mirror was gloomy, tired, and shrinking into someone I never meant to become.

Outwardly, I kept it together. Most people probably thought I was fine. But inwardly, I was dying a little more each day.

I truly believe that if I had kept living that way, I would've eventually developed a terminal illness. In fact, my left eye was diagnosed with advanced glaucoma in my mid-thirties — a rare condition for someone my age, and irreversible. I'm convinced it was caused by stress.

There were days when I hated my life. And yes, there were even moments when I wanted to die.

But I didn't. And this — this is where the story begins to shift. Because while all of that pain and pressure was building, something else was quietly taking root in my heart. Something very different in nature. It was subtle at first — barely noticeable — but it was there. A stirring. A quiet whisper. A seed that had likely been planted long ago, when I was still a child.

It was the seed of ministry.

If I were to trace the seed of ministry back to its beginning, I think it may have been planted the moment I was given my Korean name: Eun-Seuk.

I mentioned this in an earlier chapter — it means *rock of grace*, a name given to me by my grandmother. You might say that Peter was the rock, since Jesus famously said to him, "You are Peter, and on this rock I will build my church." But even more than Peter, it's Jesus Himself who is the true Rock — the cornerstone. It is on *His* foundation that we are saved. It is on *His* foundation that the church is ultimately built.

So maybe, just maybe, this name — Eun-Seuk — was a small clue from the very beginning. A divine hint that, one day, I'd be called to build something... not on my own merit, but on Christ.

When I was ten years old, someone asked my brothers and me in New Jersey, "Which one of you boys will follow in your father's footsteps and become a pastor?"

Without missing a beat, I thought, *No way. Not me.*

And yet, all these years later, I still remember that moment vividly. But why? Why does that memory live rent-free in my mind after all this time? Was something quietly ignited in me that I spent years trying to ignore?

More seeds were planted during my senior year at Keisung High School in Daegu. By then, I had come to the difficult realization that I probably wouldn't get into any of Korea's top universities. The only one I had a shot at was the Presbyterian Theological University. I didn't want to study theology though. I wasn't even walking closely with Christ at that point. But oddly enough, the idea never fully left me. It lingered, tucked away in some quiet corner of my mind.

Years later, after a long season of running from God, I finally returned to the church. And as I sat in the pews listening to sermons, something strange started to happen. I would find myself imagining what I might say if *I* were preaching from that passage. I'd think about the structure, the stories, the heart behind the message. I wasn't just listening — I was preparing in my mind.

And then, on the rare occasions when I was asked to share my testimony or speak a short word about God in front of others, something deep inside me came alive. It wasn't just excitement. It was something closer to... purpose.

Even during my hardest days at work, one of the greatest joys in my life came from leading small groups at church. It gave me a space to care for people intentionally, to listen, to guide, to shepherd — however imperfectly. And I loved it. I *thrived* in it.

Which makes me wonder: If I loved it that much, why did it take me so long to realize it? Why did I spend so many years running so hard and so far away from it?

I had known God my entire life. I always had a relationship with Him. Even during the years I tried to deny Him, and I tried to push Him away, it was because I had a relationship with Him. I just didn't like that relationship at the time. So I ran. I ran hard.

Growing up, I felt I had already endured my fair share of hardship, and somewhere along the way, I started blaming God for it. So when I entered adulthood and finally had the chance to enjoy some of the finer things in life, I grabbed hold of them, not as gifts from God, but as trophies I had earned in *spite* of Him.

Besides, I was a pastor's kid. I saw that lifestyle, and it didn't appeal to me. I didn't like it, and I certainly didn't want it for my wife and children. I wanted freedom. I wanted success. I wanted to do whatever I wanted, and make a lot of money while doing it. So I kept running.

The career, the recognition, the money, the cool people — they weren't just perks, they were my escape. They were my way of numbing the pull I felt in my heart... the quiet but constant tug of a calling I didn't want to face. But no matter how far I ran, I couldn't outrun God. He was coming after me. And when God comes for you, you can't hide. It's only a matter of time.

In those final days at IMG, I felt beat up. Worn out. Hollowed. But something else was happening beneath the surface — something I couldn't fully see at the time. The seeds that had been planted long ago had taken root. And slowly, quietly... they were ready to break through the soil.

Looking back, I can see it now. All the office politics, the stress, the physical toll, the emotional weight — it was all God nudging me. Gently but firmly saying, "It's time."

It was a Thursday night in June when I finally decided to talk to Juri about the idea of quitting my job, going to seminary, and preparing for ministry. I waited until Joanna, our only child at the time, and just three years old, was fast asleep. Then I asked Juri to sit with me in the living room for a chat.

Now, this wasn't the first time I'd brought up the idea. I had mentioned it before, but always in passing — never like this.

Sometimes during small group meetings at church, I'd say something surprisingly profound, even to myself. Afterward, Juri would tell me how insightful I'd been. I'd half-jokingly say, "What would you think if I actually started teaching or preaching?" She'd just give me that side glance and laugh it off, never really answering.

Truth is, I was afraid of what she might say if I ever asked seriously. But I also knew she knew, it wasn't *just* a joke. And I think we both understood that one day, a real conversation would come.

That evening, I wanted her to know: this was that conversation.

Being the over-prepared salesman I was, I even came with a SWOT analysis — yes, a real one. I laid out my strengths and weaknesses, and the opportunities and threats of leaving IMG to pursue seminary. Not that it actually made a difference in our decision, but I wanted her to see this wasn't a passing whim. I had thought it through. I had counted the cost. I'll forever be grateful that she didn't just laugh in my face when I presented that SWOT analysis.

She listened patiently. Carefully. But she wasn't convinced — not yet — that God was calling our family into ministry.

One thing, however, was clear to both of us: it was time for me to leave IMG. That chapter had run its course. I had poured years of my life into building a career in sports marketing, so whatever came next wouldn't be a small move. It would require faith. It would require clarity.

So we agreed we wouldn't rush. We'd take time. Whether it was a week, a month, or however long it took, we would pray. We would wait.

That evening, we held hands and prayed together, asking God to guide our next steps perfectly. We had no idea that God's answer was already on its way.

The next day was a Friday. I arrived at the office by 9 a.m., just like always. My only plan for the day was to get through it quietly, without any unexpected drama, so I could spend the weekend in deep prayer and reflection after the conversation I'd had with Juri the night before. But that Friday morning turned out to be anything but quiet.

I had barely settled into my desk when there was a knock at the door. One of my best employees poked his head in and asked if we could talk for a minute.

Him: Director, I need to speak to you about something.
Me: Okay, what is it?
Him: I've been really grateful for the opportunity to work here, but I've been wanting to move over to the client side for a while now.

I already knew where this was going — I'd heard it before.

Him: I received an offer to do just that, and I wanted to ask if that would be okay.
Me: Are you asking me, or are you informing me?
Him: I guess I'm informing you.
Me: Can I ask which company it is?
Him: It's (some large Korean company), in their sports marketing department.
Me: Is it a step up in pay and opportunity?
Him: Yes, I believe so.

During this conversation, I could clearly see that his mind was already made up. There wasn't anything I could say to change it. So I gave him my blessing and told him we'd need to discuss his exit plan after I reported the news to regional HQ in Singapore.

Technically, all he had to do was inform only me, and that should've been enough. But when the country manager came in later that morning, the employee stopped by his office as a courtesy to let him know as well.

I overheard the conversation from down the hall, and it sounded very different from the one we had. The country manager raised his voice several times. By the time the employee stepped out, his face looked tense and burdened, not relieved.

Not long after, the country manager summoned me into his office.

Country Manager: Did you hear?
Me: Yes.
CM: This is unacceptable.
Me: What can we do? It's his decision. We can't stop him.
CM: Well, as head of golf, you need to do something about this.
Me: What do you mean? It's his life. I'm not his parent. There's nothing I can do.
CM: So you're just going to sit around and do nothing?
Me: What is there to do?
CM: I don't know, but you better do something!

We kept going in circles. He blamed me for the employee's departure, as if I had orchestrated it myself. I calmly insisted that the decision had nothing to do with me, and there was nothing I could do to reverse it. But the longer we argued, the more hostile it became. He accused me of not doing my job properly. I felt my temper rising.

By the time I walked out of that office, it was already well past 11 a.m. Over two hours had passed since I first arrived, and any hope of a quiet, uneventful day had evaporated.

I was so frustrated, I could hardly think. I needed air. If I didn't get out of there soon, I felt like I might explode. In that moment, it wasn't just the events of that morning that were bothering me — it was the weight of the past five years crashing down all at once. And I couldn't take it anymore.

I told my staff I was stepping out for a lunch meeting and would be back later that afternoon. There was no meeting. Instead, I walked to the nearest convenience store and bought four cans of beer. I wasn't hungry, but I needed something, and right then, that something came in the form of a cold drink. Or four.

I carried the beers to a nearby office building where I knew there was an employee rest area tucked away from view. It was still before noon, and the usual lunch crowd hadn't come out for their smoke breaks yet. The space was empty. Quiet. Just what I needed.

I checked to make sure I was alone, then cracked open the first can. This wasn't a slow, reflective kind of drinking. I didn't sip like someone quietly drowning their sorrows. No, this was violent. Furious. It was like I was trying to punch a wall, except I was too afraid I'd break my hand, so I drank instead.

I downed the first beer in seconds. Cracked open the second can. Same thing.

By the time I opened the third, I was muttering curse words under my breath, seething with rage.

But oddly enough, I wasn't angry at the country manager. Sure, he had frustrated me, but that was nothing new. I'd endured his drama for five years. What was one more day?

No, my anger was aimed higher. I was angry at *God*.

Standing there, beer in one hand and a fist clenched in the other, I found myself praying, if you can even call it that. It was more like a scream. A howl from the depths of my soul.

"God! For the past five years... *five years*! I have been praying and crying out to You to help me. I've endured so much. I've felt like I was dying inside. And not once did You answer me. Do You not see how much I'm hurting? Do You even see me at all? Do You care? Are You even *there*? Are You even *real*?!"

I don't know how long I ranted like that. A few minutes? Maybe more.

I let it all out — years of bottled-up pain and disappointment pouring out in a flood.

By the end, my head had sunk so low it couldn't drop any further. Tears fell freely. Snot ran down my face. It was the ugliest of ugly cries. But in a strange way, it might've been the most honest prayer I had ever prayed.

You may wonder how I could speak to God in such a defiant way. But if there's anyone who can handle our full, unfiltered honesty, it's God. That moment in the hidden corner of that building was the most honest I'd ever been with Him in my life.

When I finally finished ranting, I put the can of beer down and just sat there in complete silence. No more yelling. No more tears. Just silence. And in that stillness, something stirred in me. A memory of a passage of Scripture I had read just a few days earlier. It was the story of Elijah in 1 Kings 19.

Elijah, weary and alone, had climbed Mount Horeb, the mountain of God, desperate for an encounter. Many scholars believe he was in the depths of depression. Earlier in the chapter, while in Beersheba, he had cried out, "I have had enough, Lord. Take my life."

But God didn't take his life. Instead, the Lord touched him. He fed him. And then Elijah journeyed 40 days and nights to Horeb to seek God's presence.

There on the mountain, a great wind tore through the cliffs. Surely, God was in the wind. But He wasn't.

Then came an earthquake. A powerful shaking. Surely *that* must be God.

But no.

Then came fire. But again, the Lord was not in the fire.

After all that — after the chaos, the fury, the spectacle — came the silence. And it was *in the silence* that Elijah heard the gentle whisper of God.

In that whisper, God told him He still had plans. That it wasn't over. That Elijah should get up and prepare for what was next.

That day, in that hidden space with no one else around, I had my own Mount Horeb moment. The beer, the anger, the shouting, the tears, and the snot — those were my versions of the wind, the earthquake, and the fire. And once all that passed, there was only silence. And in that silence, I heard a whisper.

Now, I'd never been one to focus much on the more charismatic gifts of the Holy Spirit. I had heard stories of people hearing God's voice, seeing visions, speaking in tongues, but I had never experienced any of that myself. I was skeptical, even dismissive. So I was completely unprepared for what came next.

As I sat there, still and quiet, I very clearly heard the voice of God speak to me.

No, it wasn't audible — Morgan Freeman didn't boom down from the clouds. It was more like how you may be reading this sentence right now in silence — no sound, but still crystal-clear words echoing in your mind and heart.

And this is what He said: "Joe, I am with you. And I see you, and I hear you. I've been with you the whole time. All those times you cried out to Me — even since you were a little child — I've always been there. And I always will be. But I needed you to go through everything you've gone through. I needed you to feel all that pain — because one day, I will use it all to minister to and comfort My people."

I didn't fully understand what was happening, but I knew it was God.

And it was amazing. And assuring.

Then, He said something that puzzled me: "As for your cries... as for your burden... I will now release you from your burden."

I didn't know what that meant. But I felt peace come over me. And I would soon find out what it meant — later that very day.

I didn't finish the rest of the beers. Instead, I sat there for a while longer, trying to reflect on what had just happened. Was I imagining it? Was it real? It certainly felt very real.

I wasn't sure what to make of it all, so I resolved to keep my head down for the rest of the day. No more confrontations. No more drama. I just needed to make it through and get to the weekend. And then — pray. I needed to pray.

After I gathered myself, I returned to the office, closed the door behind me, and locked it. I just wanted to disappear for the rest of the day. Six o'clock couldn't come soon enough.

But as much as I wanted to stay invisible, it wasn't meant to be.

Around 5:30 p.m., the country manager called for me again. Apparently, to him, our morning conversation was far from over.

He had spent the day stewing on the issue and now had a theory: the real reason our employee was leaving, he claimed, was because the regional office in Singapore hadn't offered him a pay raise. According to him, the blame lay squarely on their shoulders. And now, he wanted me to put that in writing. Specifically, he wanted me to send an email to the global heads of golf in the U.S. and U.K., stating that the employee's departure was due to *IMG Singapore's negligence*.

I didn't agree. Not with his theory, and definitely not with the idea of putting it in writing. And then, this exchange unfolded:

Country Manager: Joe, you will write that email.
Me: I'm sorry, but I don't agree with you, so I won't write it.
CM: Joe! I'm ordering you to write that email!
Me: I disagree. I won't do it. If you feel that strongly, you know those guys too. You can write it yourself.
CM: Director Park! Either you write that email, or you're fired!

And here's the part that still surprises me. You'd think a threat like that would shake me. But instead, a strange calm came over me. It was as if the burden I had been carrying for years had suddenly lifted. Without hesitation, without a flicker of fear, I looked him in the eye and said:

Me: Then fire me.
CM: *What?!* You're fired then! Get out!

I didn't flinch. I turned around, walked straight back to my office, grabbed my jacket, and began heading out the door.

The entire office was stunned. As I walked out, all eyes were on me, but no one knew what to say. But I did. As I passed my team I calmly told them, "Don't worry, guys. Everything will be okay."

The truth is, I didn't know how things would be okay. But I just knew.

A few minutes later, I was sitting in my car with no clue where to go. No plan. Just silence.

Frankly, I was still a little shocked at how fast everything had unfolded. But beneath it all, there was something else — a quiet certainty. I had been released.

After I collected myself, the first thing I did was call Juri. "Honey, guess what? I just got fired."

She paused briefly and then replied, "Well, we agreed that we would pray for God's timing for the right day to quit your work. I guess that day was today."

That made me laugh.

"I guess so," I said. "Look, I need to clear my head a little bit. I'm going to drive around, and maybe get something to eat by myself, if that's alright with you. I'll see you back home in a few hours."

I didn't even give her a proper explanation as to how and why I got fired. I think we both just knew that it didn't matter. There were greater things afoot that God had in the works, so in the moment, no explanation was needed.

During the call, Juri was in a kids' café with Joanna on a playdate with another mom and her son. Juri told her friend the news and they both started praying for me.

When I got home that night, the first thing she did was give me a big hug. Although we knew that my time at IMG was coming to a close, neither of us expected it to happen as quickly and dramatically as it just had. She also sensed that the whole ordeal was somewhat traumatizing for me. We never expected things to play out like that in a million years. She tried to assure me that perhaps this was indeed God's plan all along.

She also told me about a dream she'd had the night before. In it, she saw me dressed in old, raggedy clothes — an old green t-shirt and a pair of beat-up blue jeans. I stood there silently, then reached into one of my pockets and pulled out what looked like an old, weathered key. She didn't know what the key was for or what it meant. But she felt certain it wasn't just a dream. It felt like a vision — a message from God. We didn't understand it at the time, but in a few days, we would.

On Sunday, I was eager to be at church. I knew that God was omnipresent — that He could meet me anywhere — but I *wanted* to be in His house. I longed to pray in that sacred space, to meet Him there face-to-face, heart-to-heart.

As the service began, I stood in the aisle near one of the corner sections of the sanctuary. Juri and little Joanna stood beside me. I wanted to sing, to lift my voice and praise God with everything in me... but the words wouldn't come.

I was overwhelmed. Part of it was the sudden uncertainty of my future. But more than that, it was because I felt the real faithful presence of God in my life in all that I went through. So instead of songs from my lips, tears poured freely from my eyes.

And then something happened — something I never imagined I would experience. I began praying in tongues.

It caught me completely off guard. I didn't plan it. I didn't force it. I had never even pursued the gift before. To be honest, I'd always been somewhat skeptical of that kind of thing.

But in that moment, my heart was carrying too much for words. There was so much I needed to say to God, but there were no words that could fully express my heart. So maybe, just maybe, the Spirit interceded for me.

As I prayed and wept, I could hear my daughter whisper to Juri, "Mommy, why is Daddy crying?"

And Juri gently answered, "Daddy's not crying, he's praying to God."

I soon fell to my knees, tears still flowing, tongues still pouring out of my mouth. In the background, I could hear the church singing:

"Jesus Messiah, Name above all names,
Blessed Redeemer, Emmanuel.
The rescue for sinners, the ransom from heaven,
Jesus Messiah, Lord of all."

Though I wasn't singing with my voice, my heart echoed every line. Even as I prayed in tongues, I was crying out these truths deep within.

Some may think it was all just gibberish, but I can tell you, it wasn't. Though the words weren't understandable to others, *I* knew exactly what I was saying.

My soul was in anguish, crying out to God with everything I had. And the only words that could possibly express what I felt were the same words Jesus spoke on the cross: "My God, my God, why have You forsaken me?"

But at the same time, I was proclaiming: "Blessed be the name of the Lord."

These weren't cries of despair. They were cries of surrender and joy. I wasn't falling apart. I was being remade. I was saying goodbye to my old life, crucified with Christ — and I was joyfully stepping forward into whatever new life God had in store for me. It was, without question, one of the most powerful experiences of prayer I've ever had.

A few days later I got an email from my boss at the regional headquarters in Singapore. He wanted a conference call, and asked his secretary to set something up. We agreed to do it the following week on Tuesday, June 25th, the day Koreans remember as the outbreak of the Korean War. I didn't know what to expect, and I was very nervous.

Before the weekend came, I told Juri that I needed some time alone to get my head straight. So she decided to take Joanna down to Busan to her parents' home. With the apartment to myself, I prayed for wisdom and courage all weekend.

When our arranged time on Tuesday came, I got on the phone and dialed in. My boss was on the other line, waiting for me.

Boss: Joe, how are you?

Me: I'm okay.

Boss: I'll get straight to the chase. First, what the country manager did? He had no authority to fire you the way he did. That was a huge mistake. I've been on the phone with headquarters in New York, and we've all agreed — it's time for him to go.

(Pause)

Boss: But we need you to step in. You'll take his place as the new head of IMG Korea.

I sat in silence. Processing.

Boss: Joe, come on. We've been talking about this for years. He dug his own grave. He's out. You're in. What do you think?

Me: ...I don't know. This isn't how I imagined it would happen.

Boss: (*now sounding frustrated*) Joe, think about it for a moment before you say anything else. Don't mess this up.

And then he said something I'll never forget.

Boss: *Joe, don't you realize you're being handed the keys to the kingdom?*

It was at that moment when it all became clear to me. The regional boss was handing me the keys to the kingdom of IMG Korea, but IMG Korea was not the kingdom I desired. It was never meant to be my kingdom.

Instead, my kingdom was a much different kingdom that God had been preparing for me all along. My kingdom was more like what Juri saw in her dream of me in faded jeans and an old beat-up t-shirt, holding an old battered looking key. My kingdom was not one of Armani suits, fancy parties, flying in private jets, and bars of gold, but instead it was a humble kingdom, and yet, it was a far better and more beautiful one than IMG or anyone else in the world could ever offer me.

At that moment, the real offer on the table wasn't the kingdom of IMG Korea by this boss in Singapore. Instead, God was offering me the keys to His kingdom in heaven.

As we wrapped up the call, my boss told me to take a day or two to think it over and get back to him. I thanked him for the call and hung up. Then I sat there for a moment, took a deep breath, and felt something I hadn't felt in years. Peace.

The weight on my shoulders... gone. The burden I'd carried for so long... lifted. I was free.

I didn't need a day or two. The decision was already made. I would give formal notice a few days later. But for now, I just wanted to enjoy the moment. To breathe in the freedom. And to thank God for the old key in my hand, and the better Kingdom He was leading me into.

After the call, I missed my family immensely. I had to be with them. I had to celebrate together with them.

I immediately packed a small bag of clothes and threw it in my car. Then, I had the best five-hour drive to Busan, where I surprised Juri and Joanna by ringing the bell at her parents' apartment. Everyone was surprised to see me, especially Juri's parents, who had no idea what was happening. But when I walked through the door, everyone could see from the bright expression on my face and the extra hop in my step that everything was good. I was now free from my burden, just as God had said.

To be clear, although I wanted to go to seminary and pursue a life in ministry, I was still not sure at this point that this was God's plan for me. For that reason, I hadn't made any plans. I was very aware that something traumatic had happened, and I was careful not to choose ministry simply because I was fleeing from my job. After we returned from Busan, I decided to spend a good deal of time in prayer and fasting.

I had never fasted intensively before, but I also had nothing to lose. It's not like I had a job to go to or clients to meet up with anymore.

I wasn't confident enough to do a full water-only fast, so I decided I'd drink only juice during meal times for 21 days. I figured it would give me just enough nutrients to get by. But if I had to do it again, I think I'd go with only water. That small amount of juice each day didn't satisfy my hunger, but it actually made me feel hungrier.

I didn't know what to expect from the fast. I had known other people who had done extended fasts, and they always seemed to have a specific purpose. I started thinking my purpose was to hear from God whether I was supposed to go to seminary, but I soon realized God had other ideas.

The fast wasn't just about not eating. I was very intentional about using that time to pray — every single day, and multiple times a day. Especially during meal times. While my family sat down to eat, I would go off to pray. Every hunger pang became a reminder to seek God more deeply.

I felt especially hungry in the mornings, so I'd wake up before the crack of dawn and walk up a small mountain behind our home. I'd spend most of the morning in prayer. Doing this, I discovered that my time on the mountain was about more than just what to do with my life. It was more about my identity and relationship with God.

One morning I started praying, "God, I'm scared. I don't know what I will do, and I'm scared for my family. Please, Lord, whatever You decide to do to me, I don't care as much, but when it comes to my wife and daughter, please don't let them suffer in poverty because of me."

After I was done praying, I sat there in silence and heard the Lord whisper to my heart, "Don't worry, Joe. I love them more than you do, and I have them in My hands. They will be fine. But there's something you need to do to know how much I will take care of your family. As soon as you come down from this mountain and go home, I want you to give an offering to Me. Whatever severance pay you received from your company, don't hold onto it so tightly like your life depends on it. Instead, I want you to tithe that to Me. Only then will you learn to trust Me fully. And then, after you do that, I want you to go and celebrate this day with your family."

When I heard that, I went straight home and told Juri, and without hesitation, she agreed. We both knew we needed that money because we didn't know how long we'd be without income. However, the need to trust God was greater than the need for money.

We started praying and looking for missionaries and people around us who could use financial assistance. That morning, we wired lump sums to about 5 or 6 people and causes. The total came to nearly 10 million Won ($9,000), which was about 20% of the severance, and more than what most people typically think of when they consider a 10% tithe.

After that, we decided that instead of sending Joanna to preschool that day, we'd go out and celebrate at a kids' play park.

Before my fast, we'd gone to a nice pizzeria as a final feast. While we were there, some people were at a nearby table enjoying a very delicious looking combination pizza. One of them came up to us and introduced himself as the president of an event company, and that they were planning a special kids' park exhibition at the KINTEX Convention Center in Ilsan. He said our daughter was really cute, and wanted to give us some discount tickets so we could take her there. He handed us an envelope with various coupons. We gladly accepted and thanked him.

As we pondered what we should do that morning, we remembered that envelope. We looked up the event and found that admission would not be cheap. It would come to 60,000 won (about $50) for all three of us, but we had tickets for 50% off in the envelope. We quickly washed up and started getting Joanna ready for a fun family day together.

When we got to the ticket window, we pulled out the envelope. As we did, we discovered a couple of tickets we had not seen before which said "free admission". We were puzzled because these tickets were not in the envelope when we checked earlier. When we asked the person at the counter what these tickets were about, she told us that two people could get in free, the third person could use a 50% off ticket, and that our total would come to only 10,000 won ($9).

We immediately knew that this was God's favor for us. It was a small but significant sign that if we put our trust in Him, He will care for all our needs, even something as trivial as a kids' play park.

During my fasting period, I experienced more amazing miracles than I'd ever imagined.

One night, I woke up around 2 a.m. I'd had a dream in which God showed me the nation of Israel in slavery in Egypt. Then, God showed me how He delivered them with His mighty hand. He said to me, "Joe, you are Israel. Don't ever forget that I am the one who delivered you."

A couple of nights after that, God woke me up again in the middle of the night. In a vision He showed me two marbles in my hands and said, "One marble is life and the other is death. You choose which one you want." I chose life and went back to sleep.

The next night, God woke me again, asking, "Do you want to go deeper?"

"Yes Lord, I want to go deeper. I want to go so much deeper."

I was tired from all these late-night visits from God, and so I told him, "But I also want to sleep, Lord. Can I get a little sleep tonight, and we can do this in the morning?" With that, I went back to bed. But I knew God had more in store for me.

That morning, I was up early and went back up the mountain. I felt I needed to go a little higher that day than where I usually stopped. I kept climbing and finally reached a spot overlooking the Han River and part of southern Seoul. It was quite majestic.

It was there that God showed me the whole purpose of my fasting. It wasn't just to hear from God about whether I was meant to go to seminary and ministry.

He told me, "Joe, you don't need ministry. You don't need anything. The only thing you need is to be in an intimate relationship with me. That's all you will ever need."

In that moment, everything became very clear to me. It was true. I didn't need anything else but God. He was more than enough.

The whole purpose I needed to fast was so that I could learn to completely rely on Him and Him alone. No job, purpose, seminary studies, or even a vocation of ministry could ever fully define me or satisfy me, even if they were good. There was only one thing, and that was my relationship with Jesus.

But God still meets us where we are, so I was bold enough to ask, "Lord, I understand that now, but I would still like to know if it is truly Your will for me to become a pastor. Therefore, if You are willing, please give me three signs. Only when I receive these signs will I know that You are calling me into ministry."

These were the three signs I asked for:

1.   I asked God to clearly show me through Scripture that it was indeed His will for me to go into ministry. I wasn't quite sure what that would look like, but I wanted to know, without any doubt, that God was calling me through His Word.

2.   I knew I couldn't do this without my wife's support. So I asked God to show me that Juri was fully behind this decision.

3.   I also wanted my father-in-law's approval. My mother-in-law had been the first in her entire family to believe in Jesus, and through her, many others came to faith. But Juri's father was different. I believe he accepts that there is a God, and he respects that, but he has always had one foot firmly planted in the world. I also knew he never imagined marrying off his precious only daughter to a pastor. So even if he couldn't be fully supportive, I needed to know that he wouldn't oppose it.

A few days later, my 21-day fast came to an end.

I stopped fasting, but I kept praying. I also kept exploring the possibility of finding other work. I didn't want to just assume God was going to instruct me to go into ministry, so I tried to find other jobs, and if it were to happen, I was even ready to concede that perhaps I was not meant to become a pastor. I even had a few job interviews, but the work I had done for so long in sports marketing was so specialized that I never got any serious offers from other companies.

KJ Choi called me one day, asking if I wanted to join his foundation. I appreciated the offer, but the last thing I wanted to do at the time was go back to golf. It would have been too close to my previous job and the people there, and I just wasn't ready for that yet. I thanked him, and respectfully declined.

With that, I kept praying for a few more months for any sign God may give me.

It was mid-September, and the Korean holiday of Chuseok was fast approaching. We had planned to go to Busan to spend the weekend with Juri's parents.

On the morning of our departure, I woke up early, and as soon as I gained consciousness, the very first thought that came into my head was a Bible verse: Romans 12:2.

> *Do not conform to the pattern of this world, but be transformed by the renewing of your mind. Then you can test and approve what God's will is – his good, pleasing and perfect will.*

It was interesting that the first thought in my head that morning was that passage. I had prayed over it a lot during my fast.

It is a very important one in the book of Romans because it basically means that if you have true faith in your salvation in Jesus Christ, you are to now go and live it out in your life, not like you did before in the ways of the world, but as a living sacrifice toward others for God.

I went to the living room to pray about this and opened my Bible app on my phone.

Many Bible apps have a "verse of the day," but I usually don't pay much attention to them. But that morning, it was hard not to, because as soon as I opened the app, the first thing I saw was Romans 12:2.

I thought that was quite an interesting coincidence. The thing is, with God, there is no such thing as a coincidence. When I opened the Bible reading plan that I had been doing for several months, the assigned reading for that morning completely shocked me. My New Testament reading for that day was Romans chapter 12.

When Juri woke up later that morning, I was so excited to tell her what happened to me. Three times that same morning, God showed me the same Bible passage. Could this be the sign that I had been asking and praying for? Juri knew this was not nothing, so she said we should also pray more about this.

Later that day, we were on the KTX train going to Busan. We were sitting there uneventfully, looking down at our phones and hoping the time would go by fast. Suddenly, Juri looked up at me as if she had seen a ghost. She was just browsing through her Facebook feed, and then she saw something that made her mouth drop.

Among our friends from Jubilee Church was a sister named Ruth, who was very charismatic and had the spiritual gift of prophecy. She had already moved away from Seoul and had no idea what was happening with us, but that day, God used her in an incredible way. On her Facebook feed, where she normally posted words of praise or reflections from her daily life, she wrote only one thing that morning: a single Bible verse — Romans 12:2.

On the train to Busan that day, when we saw her post, both Juri and I were convinced — God had answered the first sign I had asked for.

Our second confirmation came later that same day. Before the Chuseok trip, Juri had suggested that we speak to her father about my desire to go into ministry. I agreed.

We waited for the right moment, and sometime after dinner, Juri asked her dad to sit down because we had something to share. We were both nervous, especially me. My voice trembled as I tried to speak. I didn't go into the full story, but I shared a few key highlights. Then I told him that I was feeling led to go into ministry.

Although Juri and I had braced ourselves for a potentially heated response, to our pleasant surprise, he received the news calmly. He told us to think carefully about it and said that, in the end, we should choose to live our lives as we feel called. It wasn't a glowing endorsement, but it seemed like he was okay with it.

Later that evening, I learned that Juri's father had a separate conversation with her, expressing how difficult it might be to become a pastor's wife. It wasn't easy for her to hear, but I didn't take it as opposition. Rather, it felt like the honest concern of a loving father for his precious little girl.

I never received a formal blessing from him before starting seminary, nor did I receive any disapproval. But now, ten years into ministry, I sometimes overhear him refer to me as *Pastor Park* when speaking with others. And I know that, in his own way, he's proud. For me, that's more than enough.

Despite Juri sticking up for me with her father, she was still not convinced herself. She had seen me go through some amazing experiences with God, and part of her was envious.

In our early years of marriage, whenever I was skeptical of spiritual gifts, she was the one who experienced them and encouraged me to keep an open mind. But now that I was seeing visions and hearing from God, she was wondering why she could not get that same kind of supernatural confirmation I was receiving. But hers was to come.

In October, we attended a Jubilee Church married couples retreat. The organizers had invited a couple from Seattle, Bob and Gracie Ekblad, to speak to us. As typical Seattlelites, they were very chill and laid back, yet they had a tremendous ability to bring out the supernatural gifts of the Holy Spirit in others in a very natural way. When most people imagine charismatic speakers, they typically may think of someone preaching with fire and brimstone, shouting out declarations for the Holy Spirit to do His thing. But the Ekblads were as calm and cool as the other side of the pillow, and they just gently spoke the things of God into reality.

Toward the end of the Saturday evening session, they held an altar call and invited anyone to come out and receive prayer from them. Juri and I thought it would be a good idea to do that, so we joined the line. We also grabbed Joanna from the children's ministry because we figured that whatever decision we made would be a family one, and we wanted her to be there to receive prayer with us.

We waited patiently as they prayed for a few couples ahead of us. When it came to our turn Gracie laid her hand on me and started praying for me, and Bob laid his hand on Juri to pray for her. We did not tell them anything about us, but we just allowed the Holy Spirit to speak to them.

When Gracie prayed, it was quite amazing. She didn't know anything about me, but she started to pray and say to me, "Whatever desires that are in your heart, they are not yours, but they have been placed there by God."

It was amazing to hear this, and I felt like it was a great affirmation.

But never in a million years would I have imagined what would happen next to Juri.

Something told me to open my eyes, and when I did, I found she was no longer standing next to me, like she had been a minute earlier. Instead, she was sprawled on the floor, shaking violently like she was being electrocuted by a thousand bolts of lightning. I had no idea what was going on.

Someone suggested I take Joanna out of the room, as it may shock her to see her mother like this. I took her outside into the hallway, and sat with her. And there we waited.

We waited ten minutes — no one came. We waited another ten — still, no one came. Thirty minutes passed. Then Chris, a brother I was mentoring at the time who had come to the retreat to help with childcare, came out to check on us and see how Joanna and I were doing.

"Chris, what's going on? Is Juri okay?"

"I don't know. She's still doing what she was doing, but she seems fine."

"How could she be fine?" I asked him, "She's been at this for over 30 minutes. Shouldn't someone try to stop this? Maybe we need to call an ambulance or something... Oh God, I hope she's okay."

The three of us sat there waiting.

Finally, someone came out and told me it was okay to come back in. Joanna and I hurried to her side.

We found Juri sitting on a chair. She seemed to be fine. She didn't appear to be hurt or startled, but rather calm and at peace. When she saw Joanna, she gave her a big hug. Joanna started crying tears of relief. Juri had tears, too, but they seemed more like joy.

"Are you alright?" I asked.

"I'm fine," she replied. "I'm doing great! Honey, you wouldn't believe it. It's like the Holy Spirit was throughout my entire body, and Jesus was right there with me the whole time. It was amazing!"

I couldn't make sense of any of it. All I knew was that my wife was violently shaking on the floor just over half an hour ago, but now she was fine, and that's all that mattered.

The next day we had Sunday worship service at the retreat. As Bob was giving his sermon, he asked if anyone had experienced the Holy Spirit in any unique way they'd like to share. I've always been the one who enjoyed public speaking, not Juri. But in this case, it almost seemed like she was being called out. How could she not share after everyone saw what happened to her the night before?

Without hesitation, she raised her hand and went to the front. She shared how I had been fired from my job and that I'd been praying about going into ministry. It seemed like God was answering all my prayers, but there were still many doubts for her. She wasn't so sure.

But then, when she received prayer the night before, she experienced God throughout her body, and she knew for certain that this was God's plan for our family. She was now ready to follow.

After she shared, Bob invited me to stand next to her, and then he asked everyone in attendance to come up front to lay their hands on us and pray for our family. It was a fantastic time.

Once the service was over, we packed up and left. In the car, I asked Juri again what had happened the night before.

"It was amazing. I felt the Holy Spirit everywhere inside of me. But also, I distinctly remember a couple of sisters holding my hand and praying for me. One of the sisters prayed, 'How beautiful on the mountains are the feet of those who bring good news. How beautiful on the mountains are the feet of those who bring good news.' And she kept repeating it over and over."

I was stunned when I heard that. How could she have possibly known what was going on? There was only one conclusion I could draw: it had to be the Holy Spirit working through her to speak affirmation to my wife.

The following morning, I woke up early to meditate on the words that had been prayed over my wife. They came from Isaiah 52:7:

"How beautiful on the mountains are the feet of those who bring good news,
who proclaim peace,
who bring good tidings,
who proclaim salvation,
who say to Zion, 'Your God reigns!'"

This verse appears just before Isaiah 53 — one of the most powerful prophecies in the entire Old Testament. It speaks of the one who would become the suffering servant, led like a lamb to the slaughter, taking upon Himself the punishment for the transgressions of all people. Through His wounds, we would be justified and healed. It is the great prophecy of salvation through the cross of Jesus Christ.

That morning, something remarkable happened — something similar to what I experienced on the morning of that Chuseok trip to Busan. When I opened the Bible app on my phone, the verse of the day was none other than Isaiah 52:7.

This time, I wasn't shocked. I smiled and praised the Lord in my heart.

Then I opened up my assigned Bible reading for that day, and my praise grew even deeper when I saw it was from Romans chapter 10. In verses 14 and 15, it says:

"How, then, can they call on the one they have not believed in?
And how can they believe in the one of whom they have not heard?
And how can they hear without someone preaching to them?
And how can anyone preach unless they are sent?
As it is written: 'How beautiful are the feet of those who bring good news!'"

I shared all of this with Juri that morning, and together, we praised God with thankful and joyful hearts.

The following spring, I began a three-year journey of seminary study at Torch Trinity Graduate University. It was a huge blessing to be able to study theology in English while staying in Korea, which was far more affordable than studying in the U.S. I'm truly thankful for that. During that time, God also provided through scholarships, which helped us tremendously.

Juri was also blessed with a temporary job opportunity. Someone from church approached her about filling in for a friend on maternity leave at an international insurance company, working in PR and marketing. She had stopped working after giving birth to Joanna, so this was a big step. She did such a great job that the company wanted to keep her on full-time.

But just as we began discussing that possibility, something unexpected happened — Juri started to feel very sick. We soon discovered that it wasn't just any kind of sickness — it was morning sickness. We had never imagined she would become pregnant at that time. When the job became too physically demanding, she had to step away from it.

Still, the Lord continued to provide. I was given the chance to do part-time translation work for a daily devotional, published by one of Korea's larger churches. It didn't pay much by my old standards, but at $600 a month, it made a big difference for us at the time. We still had some savings, and with careful budgeting, we made it work.

The entire second year of seminary, Juri was very sick from the pregnancy. Unlike many others, her pregnancy sickness didn't go away after the first trimester, but lingered the whole term. It was like that when she was pregnant with Joanna, and it was the same for our second child too.

It was hard for me to see her like that. I did my best to juggle being a good student, a caring husband, and a loving father. I also began a part-time ministry internship at Jubilee Church. None of it was easy, but it was all well worth it.

In October of 2015, Juri gave birth to our second daughter. We named her Juel.

One day in the spring of 2016, now in my third year of seminary, I was having lunch in the cafeteria when a few of my classmates told me how amazed they were that I had managed to keep up with my studies, especially with how tough things had been at home during Juri's pregnancy the previous year. I nodded and told them honestly — it was tough. And I added, half-jokingly but sincerely, "I really hope I never have to go through anything like that again."

Later that afternoon, I was going to chapel, and got what appeared to be a very urgent text message from Juri. "You need to come home RIGHT NOW!"

I was concerned and perplexed. What could be so wrong?

I immediately called. "Hey, is everything alright?"

She replied with three words that sent shivers down my spine, "I'm pregnant again."

How could this be? She had only given birth a little over four months ago. I didn't even know this was biologically possible.

That entire third year of seminary turned out to be even more challenging than the second, but I couldn't complain. As difficult as it was for me, it was exponentially harder for Juri. We had hoped that the sickness and nausea she experienced during her previous pregnancies wouldn't be as severe this time, but sadly, that wasn't the case. And on top of that, she was now caring for an infant while enduring it all. I knew then — and I still know now — that I would have to work hard for the rest of my life to make it up to her.

Our son, Juno, arrived a month earlier than expected, in mid-November — just 12 months and 16 days after his sister. His arrival came right around finals week. So whenever I had the option between taking an exam or writing a paper, I always chose the papers, so I could stay home and be as present as possible.

I graduated from seminary in 2017. Later in the Spring of that year, I was ordained as Reverend Park Eun-Seuk. It was pretty surreal. I never imagined I would ever end up being a reverend. I guess people don't use that title much anymore, but I worked hard for it, and considering where I came from and what it took to get me there, I have to say that I'm sort of proud of it. It's not that I'm so deserving, but rather that God had such grace and mercy for a wretch and a sinner like me that I get to wear that title. I think that's pretty cool.

I've been serving on staff at Jubilee Church as a full-time pastor now for the past seven years. I'm in the middle of my seventh year sabbatical as I take time to write down all these memories and reflections. I don't know where God will lead me next. All I know is where I've come from, and that I am happy to be where I am today. When I look back on the entirety of my life to this point, I can see God's fingerprints all over me. He certainly has been with me and molding me all the days of my life, and I know He will continue to do so.

When it comes to my memoir, I'm going to stop here. I'm currently 49 years old. If I'm lucky, I'll have another 30, 40, maybe even 50 years to go. And perhaps, when I've lived more life and experienced more of God's amazing grace, I'll have the opportunity to share those chapters too.

For now, this is where I'll end my story. It's not complete — God is still writing it. But if you ask me, it's been a pretty fun story so far. And I'm looking forward to the next chapter — wherever and whatever that may be.

Chapter 18

Who I Am

I am...

I am Park Eun-Seuk. I am Joseph Park. I am Joe Park. I am Joe Eun-Seuk Park.

I am Korean, but when people meet me they don't think I'm Korean. My kids even tell their friends their dad is not Korean, but American, but they still know I'm Korean, if that makes sense.

I am American, but not technically American, at least not by the color of my skin nor my passport.

I am Korean-American, but not *really* Korean-American. I am probably more accurately American-Korean. Yes, I think I'll go with that. When I asked Google to look that up, it only gave me results for Korean-Americans, so if there's no such thing as an American-Korean, then I'll claim it.

Who I Am

I am the son of Park Yongwoo and Kang Sookjung. I am the older brother of Park Eun-Wook and Park Eun-Sung, as well as Albert Park and Daniel Park.

I am the son of a pastor. I am the son of a professor.

I am also a pastor, called by God not because my father was a pastor, but because God called me to be uniquely me. I am a son of God.

I am a former sports agent. I was once known as the Jerry Maguire of Korea. But I am no longer that. I am now just a sports fan and I'm satisfied with that.

I was on the Top 10 sales list of Diversified Financial Concepts' national sales team for one week in the month of September in 1998. I was also one of the top sales reps at the Northgate Mall Nordstrom men's apparel section during the winter of that same year. In 1999, I was a convenience store clerk for a small family-owned business in Vancouver, Washington.

I am from Gyeongju. I am from Daegu. I am from Chattanooga, Tennessee. I am from Randolph, New Jersey. I am from Eugene, Oregon. I am from Seattle, Washington. But at the same time, I am not from any of those places. None of them can I truly call home, yet all those places have been, at one time or another, my home.

I am a Duck, a Husky, and a Duckdawg. I don't know what the University of Canberra's mascot is or if they even have stuff like that in Australia, but whatever that may be, I was that for one brief semester in 1993.

I am a Seahawks fan, which makes me a Twelve. I am also a Sonics fan, if the Sonics ever make it back to the NBA, that is.

I am the husband of an amazing woman named Juri Kim. It is by amazing grace that I can be known as that, as I know I don't deserve her, and every day with her is a miracle.

I am the father of Joanna Jueun. I am the father of Juel. I am also the father of a little boy named Juno, who always wants to beat me at sports and video games, which probably makes me his rival. If I am proud of anything in my life, I am proud of my family.

I am complicated, yet I am a simple man. I am simply a man with many complications in my past.

I am a man of God.

I am...

That expression "I am"... It's something that all of us say every day in one capacity or another. Sometimes it's a statement of identity, like "I am Joe" or "I am Korean." Sometimes it's merely a statement of our current condition, such as "I am hungry" or "I am tired." We don't think too much about it when we say it, yet those two words — "I am" — are two of the most powerful things we can say daily.

When we say "I am," it's more than just a statement about ourselves. It's a statement about God and how we relate to Him. Let me explain.

In Exodus 3, we see the story of when Moses first met God in the burning bush. God tells Moses to go back to Egypt and the Israelite people there, and tell them that their God has sent him to deliver them from Pharaoh's oppressive hand of slavery.

Moses is puzzled and asks God, "Are you sure you want *me* to go to them? Who am I but a lowly shepherd? And besides, what would I even say to them? Who would I even say sent me?"

And to this, God gave to Moses His personal name. He says, "Tell them I AM WHO I AM. I AM has sent me to you."

In most English Bibles, you will see that "I AM" is written in all capital letters. This is because "I AM" here is the name of God. In the original Hebrew it is spelled out without vowels, so when transliterated into alphabet letters it would look like "YHWH", but in English we've come to call Him "Yahweh". Over the years, this has become "Jehovah," and many of us know this as God's name.

However, for the Israelites, the name of God was so holy that they would not dare speak it out loud like we do today. Although it is spelled like "YHWH," they would call Him "Adonai," or in English translation, "THE LORD". And so, in most English versions of the Old Testament, whenever you see "THE LORD" spelled out in all capital letters, it is referring to the name of God as revealed to Moses at that burning bush.

There is another place in the Bible where we see someone else refer to himself as I AM. This is in John 8.

Here, we see Jesus in a dispute with some Jewish leaders who question his authority. They see this barely 30-year-old rabbi claiming to have great authority, and scoff that there's no reason to follow him because they are descendants of Abraham. Abraham has more authority than him, they say,

At this, Jesus says something that causes them to get angry. "You guys don't know what you're talking about. Abraham would have rejoiced to see me. And guess what? He did see me, and He was glad."

The Jewish leaders can't believe their ears, and at first, laugh this off as if Jesus is a crazy person. "How can you say Abraham saw you when he's been dead for thousands of years? You're out of your mind!"

Then, Jesus replies, "Truly, truly, I say to you, before Abraham was, I am."

And at this, the Jewish leaders become furious and want to kill Jesus for blasphemy.

What Jesus is saying here, and the reason the Jewish people were so angry, is that He is the I AM — the same I AM that was revealed to Moses at the burning bush and who was referred to as THE LORD throughout the Old Testament. This I AM is the holy name of God, and by saying this, Jesus is asserting that He, Himself, is God.

Jesus makes several I AM claims in the gospel of John.

I am the bread of life.
I am the light of the world.
I am the gate of the sheep.
I am the good shepherd.
I am the resurrection and the life.
I am the way, the truth, and the life.
I am the true vine.

These are all declarations by Jesus that, as God, He is the one who holds the keys to salvation and eternal life in His hands for all humanity. Anyone can have these things, as well as a personal relationship with Him, by faith in who He is and what He did when He sacrificed Himself on the cross and rose from the grave.

But what does any of this have to do with me and my search for identity? It has everything to do with it.

When it comes to our identity, there are four ways we can say "I am." Although there are similarities, they are each different in meaning and can strongly influence us and how we live our lives.

The first way that people say "I am" is not a statement at all, but rather a questioning of who they are. It's an expression of uncertainty. They say "I am," but don't fully believe in their heart the positive qualities and identity thereof. Although outwardly they may be saying "I am," in their heart they are actually asking, "Am I?" This was Moses at the burning bush when he said to God, "Who am I to go back to the Israelites? Who am I but only a lowly shepherd?"

To use myself as an example, for many years after I had returned to Korea as a kid and couldn't keep up with my studies in middle and high school, I would outwardly try to tell myself that "I am a smart kid." But after several years of what I perceived as horrible academic failures, I started to question myself and wonder, "Am I really a smart kid?"

As I kept asking myself that question repeatedly, I began to lose myself. And it wasn't just about academics, but I began to lose all sense of self-worth in every aspect of my life as a person. I also forgot who God was in my life. I felt the need to find myself all over again in other things, and so I tried to do so in sports, smoking, drinking, and other things of the world that eventually never answered any of my identity questions. These things also caused me to fall into a deeper hole of self-doubt.

The second way we say "I am" is closely related to the first in that the first often is a precursor that leads to the second, perhaps even a warning sign. When we question ourselves repeatedly, we can get to a point when we are resolved to see our own identities in a self-deprecating way. When people constantly say "I am" in this second way, they have already resigned to the idea that they are not worthy of a positive identity, and a purposeful life that goes with it. They walk around constantly with a dark cloud over their heads.

Again, when I look back on my life, and especially throughout my younger years, after I asked myself, "Am I a smart kid?" I would come to the conclusion, "No, I am not. I am a very stupid kid."

It wasn't a true statement, but I believed it, and because I did, it became my identity for a time.

It's quite sad how so many people believe these "I am" statements about themselves: *I am stupid. I am not worthy. I am pathetic. I am a victim. I am not lovable. I am a loser*. But the truth is, that's not who you are. These are lies the devil is trying to whisper in your ear. And if you keep repeating them, you'll start to believe them, and eventually, you'll become them. It's a very dark and lonely path, one I wish no one ever had to walk.

Just as the first and second ways we say "I am" are related, so are the third and fourth ways, but the pattern is different.

The first two ways are in somewhat of a cause and effect type of relationship – "Am I? No, I am not."

However, the third and fourth approaches are fundamentally opposed to each other. While they are similar in that both involve an origin and a manifestation of identity — such as the idea of "I am, therefore I will be" — the origins and outcomes of each are quite different.

What I mean is that most people don't realize that just as I AM is the name of God in the Bible, every time someone says "I am" in daily life, they're actually invoking the name of the divine to define their identity. The thing is, the "divine" they're calling upon can vary greatly — and that's why the way our "I am" statements shape our reality differs as well.

I know this sounds confusing, but stick with me for a minute, and hopefully you'll see what I mean.

Some people say "I am" and believe they're invoking something sacred, but the god they're referencing isn't the I AM of the Bible, THE LORD God. Instead, their "I am" points back to themselves. When they say "I am," what they really mean is that they alone are the masters of their destiny, trusting only in themselves to chase after their own heart's desires. In this way, they become their own god.

Again, to use myself as an example, this is exactly what I was doing about 20 years ago when I stood in the gym and declared that I wanted it all. What I was really saying was, "I am Joe Freakin' Park! I am the Jerry Maguire of Korea! I am Mr. Hot Shot — the guy in the fancy suit! I am that impressive, that smart, that powerful, and fully capable of achieving everything I want — the things I believed would make my life complete."

My belief in my own "I am" led me to think that I was my own god.

But I was no god. I was only a mere man, and a small, petty one at that. And no matter how much I wanted to speak the divine "I am" into reality it was impossible, because it wasn't true. It was a lie I was trying to believe. And because I was trying to live out a lie, I was left feeling very empty inside. I was not living life, but instead every day I was getting closer to death.

So I humbled myself and came before God as a very broken man, and God touched me, fed me with His living water and bread of life, and saved me.

That is why, now, every time I say "I am," I know I am calling on the name of the Lord Jesus Christ, the I AM whom Abraham rejoiced to see, and the same I AM of Moses. I am saying that Christ is in me, and everything about my identity is now deeply rooted in Christ, and Christ alone.

That is the fourth way we can say "I am." It is a declaration that in every aspect of my life — whether in my name, my job, my ethnicity, my culture, my history, my hometown, my family, or anything else — there is Christ. And because of Christ, there is abundant life.

I started this chapter with a whole bunch of "I am" statements about myself. But when I make these statements, I'm also saying that I am all of them because of the great I AM who lives in me and allows me to be part of Him.

I am Park Eun-Seuk, and I am also Joe Park... *in Christ*. I am a husband and a father... *in Christ*. I am an American-Korean because of all my unique cultural experiences... *in Christ*. I am now a pastor... *in Christ*. I am a Husky, a Duck, and a Seahawks fan... *in Christ*. I was the former vice president of IMG Korea — not because I was so good, but because God allowed me to go through all of that... *in Christ*.

As the old Christian praise song goes, "Christ in me is to live."

Every time we say "I am" it is a declaration that Christ lives in me, and my life is one with Him. It is a powerful statement and we say it all the time without considering it. But when we say "I am" with the proper heart, it allows us to live our lives not in resentfulness and regret, nor in sorrow and gloom, as so many are in the habit of doing, but rather in the fullness of life in which God wants us to live.

But there's more to it than that. It's not that Christ is only in me, but He is in everything in the world.

Throughout my life, there were many times when I questioned my own identity. At times, I even hated myself. It wasn't just that I didn't know who I was — it was more that I didn't know how I fit into the world around me. So much of it didn't make sense. So much of it felt unfair. I often found myself blaming the world — the era I lived in, the cultural context, my nationality and ethnicity, even the social status I was born into.

When writing this memoir, I not only looked back on my own life, but I also took time to read up on the modern histories of both the U.S. and Korea. I did this because I wanted to make sense of certain things I didn't understand at the time. Every person is a product of where and when they grew up, and I am no different.

Part of who I am was formed even before I was born, in post-war Korea of the 1950s and '60s, when my grandmother, a single mother, taught the Bible at a small church in Gyeongju. That was the only way she could provide a future for her only son.

After I was born in 1974, my identity began to take shape against the backdrop of a poverty-stricken nation where life was so harsh that, for many, the only hope was to escape to other countries.

Once in the U.S., I became a product of very American, mid-to-lower-income neighborhoods in Tennessee — where people chewed Big League Chew and chewing tobacco, drove beat-up pickup trucks, and casually carried shotguns.

From there, I grew up in New Jersey during the era of *Star Wars* — both the one starring Mark Hamill and Harrison Ford, and the other launched by Ronald Reagan against the USSR.

After returning to Korea, I experienced air-raid drills, community campaigns to rat out communist spies, and university campuses filled with teargas and protests for democracy. I witnessed the incredible rise of Korean *chaebols*, and later, the collapse of the economy because of them. I saw the explosion of karaoke rooms, the emergence of K-culture in the '90s with Seo Taiji and Boys and *Winter Sonata*, and the electric unity of Team Korea in the streets during the 2002 World Cup.

I've lived through thirteen Korean presidents, from Park Chung-hee to Yoon Seok-yeol. I remember U.S. presidents from Jimmy Carter to Joe Biden. I even recall the days when Kim Il-sung died, then his son Kim Jong-il, and how his grandson Kim Jong-un came to power.

Even now, as Korea faces low birth rates, high depression rates, and an influx of foreigners moving into the country, these current events continue to shape my ever-evolving identity.

I may have resented many of these things in the past, but now I embrace them all because they are all part of who I am today. And in control of all of this is the great I AM, Jesus. Nothing in this world that happens is an accident or a coincidence. Just as the I AM is part of all of us as individuals, He is also doing the same in the world. Jesus is the I AM of all history, all nations, all races, all cultures, and all societies.

I look back on all my years — every experience, every culture, every person I've encountered, and every place I've been — and I know that each one has played a role in shaping who I am today and who I might become tomorrow.

And it leads me to a very important conclusion: none of it was a mistake. Not the good times, and certainly not the bad. *I* was not a mistake. I am who I am today because the great I AM has always been with me and is in control of everything. I know that He has a plan and a purpose for it all. He has a purpose for me. And I will continue to rejoice in who I am — because of the I AM, Jesus Christ, who lives in me.

About the Author

Joe Eun-Seuk Park is a pastor, writer, and lifelong seeker of identity. Born in Daegu, South Korea, and raised across multiple cities in the United States and Korea, Joe's story reflects the tension and richness of living between cultures. A former sports agent turned minister, he now serves a diverse congregation in Seoul and is passionate about helping others discover their true identity in Christ. Joe lives with his wife Juri and their three children — Joanna, Juel, and Juno — and spends his free time cycling, writing, and cooking meals that (usually) turn out okay.

Who I Am is his debut memoir.